HATE CRIMES

A Reference Handbook,
Second Edition

Other Titles in ABC-CLIO's
CONTEMPORARY
WORLD ISSUES
Series

Books in the Contemporary World Issues series address vital issues in today's society such as genetic engineering, pollution, and biodiversity. Written by professional writers, scholars, and nonacademic experts, these books are authoritative, clearly written, up-to-date, and objective. They provide a good starting point for research by high-school and college students, scholars, and general readers as well as by legislators, businesspeople, activists, and others.

Each book, carefully organized and easy to use, contains an overview of the subject, a detailed chronology, biographical sketches, facts and data and/or documents and other primary-source material, a directory of organizations and agencies, annotated lists of print and nonprint resources, and an index.

Readers of books in the Contemporary World Issues series will find the information they need in order to have a better understanding of the social, political, environmental, and economic issues facing the world today.

HATE CRIMES

A Reference Handbook,
Second Edition

Donald Altschiller

**CONTEMPORARY
WORLD ISSUES**

A B C 🕮 C L I O

Santa Barbara, California
Denver, Colorado
Oxford, England

Library of Congress Cataloging-in-Publication Data
Altschiller, Donald.
  Hate crimes : a reference handbook / Donald Altschiller.—2nd ed.
    p. cm. — (ABC-CLIO's contemporary world issues series)
Includes bibliographical references and index.
    ISBN 1-85109-624-8 (hardback : alk. paper) — ISBN 1-85109-629-9
(ebook)   1. Hate crimes—United States.   I. Title.   II. Contemporary
world issues.
HV6773.52.A47 2005
364.15—dc22

                                                      2005007151

09   08   07   06   05   10   9   8   7   6   5   4   3   2   1

This book is also available on the World Wide Web as an e-book. Visit abc-clio.com for details.

ABC-CLIO, Inc.
130 Cremona Drive, P.O. Box 1911
Santa Barbara, California 93116-1911

This book is printed on acid-free paper ∞.
Manufactured in the United States of America

Contents

Preface

Since the publication of the first edition of this book in 1999, the United States suffered the worst terrorist attack in its history on September 11, 2001. In its tragic aftermath, a surge of hate crimes spread throughout the country. The worst incidents involved the murder of almost a half dozen individuals who were thought to look "Middle Eastern."

In fact, they were mostly Sikh men—members of a non-Muslim, non-Arab religious group—whose male adherents wear turbans. Arab Americans and Muslims were also targeted; some were physically assaulted and a few mosques were vandalized and destroyed. The FBI and human rights monitoring organizations—which have been issuing studies on bias-motivated crimes since the early 1990s—reported that the greatest nationwide statistical increase in hate crimes occurred during the first few months after the attack.

Yet there also was much good news. According to a Harris Poll conducted one week after the attack, the vast majority of Americans believe that American Muslims and Arab Americans are loyal to the United States. Soon after the September 11 attack, the president of the United States personally visited the largest mosque in the nation's capital. Later, Congress passed a joint resolution condemning the "bigotry and violence against Arab-Americans, Muslim-Americans, South Asian-Americans, and Sikh-Americans." National, state, and local law enforcement agencies frequently and forcefully declared zero tolerance for hate crime perpetrators. Especially gratifying were the grassroots activities of Americans in large cities and small towns: churches and synagogues sponsored interfaith services and organized dialogue groups, and school administrators convened special assemblies to increase ecumenical understanding among young people. Although it was a time of great religious tensions, large numbers of Americans demonstrated both concern for the safety of their more vulnerable fellow citizens and also respect for their beliefs. One Muslim minister in Massachusetts gratefully noted that he was "inundated" by offers of assistance from local rabbis.

So, then, is the glass half empty or half full when we assess the problem of hate crimes—both in the United States and around the world? Unfortunately, the 9/11 hate crimes were not the only such crimes in the past few years. In a few recent rampages, the perpetrators targeted, sometimes en masse: African Americans, Asian Americans, Jewish Americans, and gays and lesbians. They also murdered some of their victims. While these violent criminals generally fit into a well-established profile— white males seething with homicidal rage against religious, racial, and sexual minorities—these crimes are no longer the sole domain of angry Caucasian men. As the United States becomes an increasingly multicultural society, the perpetrators of hate crimes are also found among a variety of ethnic, racial, and religious groups. In the following recent incidents, a new type of perpetrator emerges: a black male student severely beats a fellow classmate at an African American college because he believes the victim is gay; a Bangladeshi immigrant is murdered by Hispanic men in a racially motivated attack; two Arab American adolescents burn down a local synagogue; and a Laotian immigrant is violently assaulted by African American teenagers, who later brag about what they did to the "Asian man."

This volume will provide further details about these disturbing incidents and many other hate crimes committed throughout the United States and around the world. A completely revised and updated version of the earlier edition, the present work provides significant new material in every chapter.

The first chapter surveys the history of hate crimes legislation and provides basic background information on the actions of the government—legislative, executive, and judicial—to combat bias-motivated crimes. The chapter also focuses on the most frequently victimized racial, religious, and other groups and describes the nature and type of incidents they suffer.

The following chapter is a new section on hate crimes around the world, a topic that previously has been covered in a wide variety of often hard-to-locate sources. The third chapter provides a detailed chronology of hate crimes since the advent of the modern civil rights movement in 1955. The fourth chapter includes brief biographies of notable individuals involved in the study and/or control and prevention of hate crimes. Primary source documents are published in the following chapter: the most recent FBI statistics on hate crimes; excerpts from a manual for police officers on how to respond to hate crimes; two excerpted reports on campus hate crime prevention; and an abridged study of hate crimes on the Internet. The sixth chapter provides a detailed directory of national and local organizations that monitor extremist groups and also try to promote tolerance and understanding in our pluralistic society. The last two chapters contain annotated bibliographies of print and nonprint sources, which, I believe, represent the most comprehensive listings currently available. The chapter covering print resources also includes annotated entries of U.S. congressional hearings on hate crimes, a unique and comprehensive feature appearing only in this work.

Although my research has convinced me personally about the importance of hate crimes legislation, I have included a great deal of material that raises legal, political, and philosophical objections to these laws. My aim is to acquaint students, researchers, law enforcement officials, and others with the complexities of this serious social problem.

As with the earlier edition, I have spent a considerable amount of time attempting to find the names of the victims and to provide this information whenever possible. Not only can hate crimes inflict physical damage to an individual but the perpetrators of these harmful incidents also can demean the victim as a faceless member of a social category. Although the FBI hate crimes statistics offer very important information on the prevalence of these crimes, it is always important to remember that the victims are more than mere statistics. By listing the names of these victims, I fervently hope that their humanity will be respected. I am heartened to note that Sen. Gordon Smith (R-OR) has inserted more than 500 hate crime incidents including the names of the victims in the *Congressional Record* since March 2001.

I am very grateful to Ron Boehm, the CEO of ABC-CLIO, for his gracious and kind assistance. Martha Whitt, the senior production editor, is a marvelous editor who has greatly improved the manuscript. I can't say that it is a pleasure writing a book on this topic, but the love of my wife, Ellen, and my mother-in-law and father-in-law, Ruth and Milton Birnbaum, has always helped me to focus on the precious aspects of life.

Donald Altschiller

1

Introduction

A lan Berg, Vincent Chin, Matthew Shepard, James F. Byrd Jr., Balbir Singh Sodhi. During the past two decades, these names—previously unknown to the public—were in the news. They were all mentioned in newspapers and magazines; a few were noted in books, television documentaries, and even a theatrical performance. Although these five individuals came from different regions of the country and had vastly different professional, ethnic, and family backgrounds, they all had one terrible experience in common: they were victims of deadly hate crimes.

On June 18, 1984, Alan Berg, a popular Denver radio talk show host, was murdered in a machine gun attack in the driveway of his home. His assailants—members of a neo-Nazi group—were convicted three years later of murder. According to trial testimony, the murderers stalked him for several days because they were enraged by his frequent on-air attacks against white supremacists and neo-Nazis. "They killed him because of his job, and they did it because he was a Jew," asserted Thomas O'Rourke, an assistant U.S. attorney. During the economic downturn of the early 1980s, two unemployed Detroit autoworkers bludgeoned Vincent Chin to death, blaming this Chinese American—who looked Japanese to them—for their lost jobs. More than fifteen years later, on October 6, 1998, Matthew Shepard, a University of Wyoming student, was beaten, tortured, tied to a fence, and left for dead by local teenagers because he was gay. Only a few months earlier, James F. Byrd Jr., an African American from Jasper, Texas, was found decapitated and dismembered on a road near his hometown. His assailants, who had connections with the Ku Klux Klan (KKK), had tied him up and dragged his body with their truck. Two days after

1

the Arab terrorist attacks on September 11, 2001, Balbir Singh Sodhi, a Sikh gas station owner in Arizona, was viciously murdered by an assailant who thought that because the victim wore a turban, he was a follower of Osama bin Laden.

Although these tragic incidents are relatively rare, they nevertheless represent a disturbing phenomenon—the occurrence of hate crimes in the United States.

What is a hate crime? How does it differ from other crimes directed at individuals or property? According to the Federal Bureau of Investigation (FBI), a hate crime is a "criminal offense committed against a person or property that is motivated in whole or in part by the offender's bias against a race, religion, ethnic/national origin group or sexual orientation group." In short, hate crimes are directed against members of a specific group largely because of their membership in that particular group.

Hate crimes occur in different forms and against a variety of particular groups: a swastika scrawled on a grave in a Jewish cemetery; racist and threatening telephone messages against African Americans; physical assaults against gay men and lesbians. In some instances, hate crimes result in the deadliest form of violence: murder.

Most people would agree that hate crimes are odious criminal actions. But should they be punished differently from other criminal activities? Advocates of hate crime legislation directly address the rationale for special punishment. "Harm caused by violence that is motivated by bias can be greater than the harm done by ordinary acts involving the same amount of violence," writes Columbia University law professor Kent Greenawalt in the 1992–1993 volume of the *Annual Survey of American Law*. He continues, "The victim may suffer special injury because he or she is aware that race is the basis for an attack. Such crimes can frighten and humiliate other members of the community; they can also reinforce social divisions and hatred. For our society at this time, crimes of bias present particular dangers. That is a sufficient justification in principle to warrant special treatment under the criminal law."

History of Hate Crimes Legislation

Although bias crimes have occurred throughout U.S. history, it is only in the past few decades that specific legislation has been enacted in response to violent bigotry directed at specific groups. (For clarification, bigotry is the state of mind of a bigot, a person holding intolerant opinions and prejudices, which are protected under the First Amendment as long as the views are not accompanied by violence.)

According to New York University law professor James B. Jacobs, the term *hate crime* was popularized by three members of the U.S. House of Representatives who cosponsored a bill in 1985—which was later passed in 1990—requiring the federal government to collect and publish statistics on the increasing number of violent crimes motivated by ethnic, religious, and racial hatred. Jacobs noted that only eleven articles on hate crimes appeared in national newspapers that year; a few years later, more than 1,000 stories were published.

A century ago, bias-related crimes were prosecuted under a variety of laws, including the Civil Rights Act of 1866, the Enforcement Act of 1870, the Ku Klux Klan Act of 1871, and the Civil Rights Act of 1875. These federal laws were specifically intended to stop both the violent rampages directed against southern African Americans and the curtailment of their rights during Reconstruction. (For a more detailed historical discussion of each of these laws, see *Punishing Hate: Bias Crimes under American Law* by Frederick M. Lawrence.) Almost 80 years later, the modern civil rights movement successfully lobbied for legislation to ensure the full civil rights of black Americans and to strengthen already existing statutes prohibiting racially based violence.

However, it wasn't until the early 1980s that the concept of bias-motivated crimes expanded to include other religious and racial minority groups. In 1981, the Anti-Defamation League (ADL), the most prominent Jewish civil rights organization in the United States, drafted model hate crimes legislation to cover not only anti-Jewish crimes but all types of hate crimes aimed at minority groups. As of 2004, forty-six states and the District of Columbia have enacted laws similar to or based on the ADL model. The majority of states have at least one or more hate crime laws (consult the ADL website at www.adl.org for detailed charts covering statutes in every state). These laws establish a number of rules:

- They penalize criminal vandalism against religious institutions, including synagogues, churches, mosques, and other houses of worship.

- They prohibit bias-motivated violence and intimidation against individuals.
- They require state governments to compile hate crime statistics.
- They enact "penalty-enhancement" statutes for crimes motivated by hate.
- They mandate special training for law enforcement personnel.

Although expressions of hate protected by the Bill of Rights are not criminalized, actions motivated by hate receive more stringent punishment than actions stemming from other motivations. A convicted criminal is subject to an enhanced penalty if the victim is chosen because of race, religion, national origin, sexual orientation, or gender. The ADL model statute includes criminal penalties for vandalism aimed at houses of worship, cemeteries, schools, and community centers. This legislation allows for victims to recover punitive damages and attorneys' fees and holds parents liable for the criminal actions of their children. In 1996 the ADL added the category of gender to its model hate crimes legislation, because gender-based crimes are similar in nature to race- or religion-based hate crimes. Only seven states included gender in their hate crimes statutes in 1990; as of 2003, the number had grown to twenty-seven states.

The federal government also has many civil rights statutes that cover a range of activities, including the exercise of rights provided by the laws and the U.S. Constitution, the exercise of religious freedom, housing-related rights, and federally protected activities such as voting or the right to use public accommodations. The following are descriptions of significant federal laws and pending legislation on hate crimes, partially adapted from the ADL publication *1998 Hate Crimes Laws*, the Partners against Hate Web site, and the Library of Congress's THOMAS Web site.

Hate Crimes Statistics Act

Enacted in April 1990, this law requires the U.S. Department of Justice to acquire data from law enforcement agencies throughout the United States on crimes that "manifest prejudice based on race, religion, sexual orientation, or ethnicity" (U.S. Public

Law 101-275) and to publish an annual summary of these findings (issued by the FBI in January). Congress expanded coverage of the law in the Violent Crime Control and Law Enforcement Act of 1994, which requires reporting on crimes based on disability. This requirement was effective as of January 1, 1997.

The first report published under this act appeared in 1993 and covered the calendar year 1991. According to the ADL, many law enforcement agencies are gratified by this legislation. It offers them the ability to chart the national distribution of these crimes and thus discern patterns and forecast possible racial and ethnic tensions in different localities. Ideally, the act helps foster better police-community relations. Police demonstrate their concern for the welfare of citizens victimized by hate crimes in vigorously pursuing the criminal activities of violent bigots. This special reporting system also encourages victims to file charges.

Hate Crimes Sentencing Enhancement Act

A section of the Violent Crime Control and Law Enforcement Act of 1994 (Public Law 103-322), this provision requires the U.S. Sentencing Commission to provide a sentencing enhancement "for offenses that the finders of fact at trial determine, beyond a reasonable doubt, are hate crimes."

According to this provision, a hate crime is a "crime in which the defendant intentionally selects a victim, or in the case of a property crime, the property that is the object of the crime, because of the actual or perceived race, color, religion, national origin, ethnicity, gender, disability, or sexual orientation of any person." This statute also applies to attacks and vandalism that occur in U.S. national parks or on any other federal property. The amendment took effect on November 1, 1995.

Violence against Women Act of 1994 (VAWA)

Enacted as Title IV of the Violent Crime Control and Law Enforcement Act of 1994, this act covers the increasing problem of violent crime against women. Under this law, "persons within the United States shall have the right to be free from crimes of violence motivated by gender." Passed in September 1994, the law includes the following provisions: (1) education and training programs for police and prosecutors, (2) support for domestic violence and rape crisis centers, and (3) a "Civil Rights Remedy" for victims of gender-based violent crimes, including punitive and compensatory damage awards.

The provision for a Civil Rights Remedy has been challenged in several state court cases. On May 15, 2000, the U.S. Supreme Court, in *United States v. Morrison*, ruled that Congress had no legal authority to provide victims of gender-motivated violence access to federal courts. In a 5–4 ruling the Court decided that the VAWA's Civil Rights Remedy was unconstitutional and that Congress could not regulate intrastate criminal conduct under the commerce clause. Rather, this matter must be left to the states to decide. The Court declared that the Civil Rights Remedy strayed beyond Congress's authority to enforce the Fourteenth Amendment because it was directed against private individuals, not state jurisdictions. Some legal scholars and feminist organizations have charged that the *United States v. Morrison* case was a serious setback for women's rights.

In 2003, Rep. John Conyers Jr. (D-MI) introduced the Violence against Women Civil Rights Restoration Act. The bill responds to the Supreme Court's decision in *United States v. Morrison* and restores the ability of victims of gender-motivated violence to sue their attackers in federal court, where there is a connection to interstate commerce. As of the winter 2005, no congressional vote or further action has been taken on this legislation.

Church Arson Prevention Act (18 U.S. Code 247)

The series of publicized attacks against churches from 1995 through 1997 created a great deal of alarm among law enforcement agencies and the general public. Despite the widespread nature of these incidents, neither the government nor human rights organizations were able to document a national conspiracy of domestic terrorism orchestrated by violent extremists. The large number of these incidents—committed by individuals in different parts of the country acting independently—was nevertheless a worrisome phenomenon.

Sponsored by Sen. Edward Kennedy (D-MA), Sen. Lauch Faircloth (R-NC), Rep. Henry Hyde (R-IL), and Rep. John Conyers

(D-MI), the Church Arson Prevention Act was introduced to facilitate federal investigation and prosecution of crimes against houses of worship and to amend an earlier statute enacted by Congress in 1988 that mandated federal prosecution for religious vandalism incidents exceeding $10,000 in property damage.

In an unusual bipartisan effort, both the U.S. House of Representatives and the U.S. Senate unanimously approved legislation broadening criminal prosecutions for attacks against houses of worship and establishing a loan guarantee for rebuilding them. The legislation also authorized additional personnel for several agencies. The law was enacted on July 3, 1996.

Local Law Enforcement Enhancement Act

On June 15, 2004, the U.S. Senate approved legislation by a 65-33 vote that would expand federal hate crime protection to include sexual orientation, gender, and disability. Offered as an amendment to a Department of Defense authorization bill, this legislation, which would also increase federal assistance to local and state officials in the investigation and prosecution of hate crimes, was introduced by Sen. Edward Kennedy (D-MA) and Sen. Gordon Smith (R-OR) and was identical to provisions approved by the Senate in June 2000 and by the U.S. House of Representatives in September 2000. In both pieces of legislation, however, the hate crimes provisions were not inserted in the final version of the bill. Senators Kennedy and Smith plan again to submit revised versions of this hate crimes legislation in the late spring 2005.

Executive Branch

As a result of the above-mentioned legislation, the executive branch of the U.S. government has been involved in the following initiatives and other ongoing activities (check the Partners against Hate Web site at http://www.partnersagainsthate.org for more detailed information).

Some programs sponsored by the U.S. Department of Justice include the following:

- The Community Relations Service, the only U.S. government agency primarily mandated to assist localities in dealing with intergroup conflicts, has helped implement the Hate Crime Statistics Act by training police and other law enforcement officials.
- The Office for Victims of Crime has provided a grant for developing a training curriculum to improve the response of professionals to hate crime victims.
- The Office of Juvenile Justice and Delinquency Prevention (OJJDP) provided $100,000 for a study to identify the characteristics and types of juveniles who commit hate crimes (*Report to Congress on Juvenile Hate Crime,* July 1996). The OJJDP also provided funding for a "Healing the Hate" curriculum to assist the prevention and treatment of hate crimes committed by young people.
- Under funding provided by the Bureau of Justice Assistance, the National Criminal Justice Association issued a "Policymaker's Guide to Hate Crimes," which included a survey of legal cases and law enforcement hate crime practices.

In addition, the U.S. Department of Justice, the U.S. Department of the Treasury, and the U.S. Office of Education have been involved in hate crime enforcement, education, and prevention.

The ADL and other human rights organizations and professionals have assisted in a model hate-crime training curriculum for use by the federal Law Enforcement Training Centers, a program of the U.S. Department of the Treasury.

The Department of Housing and Urban Development (HUD) has organized seminars to discuss a $10 million loan guarantee rebuilding fund for houses of worship devastated in hate-motivated arson attacks. Under the National Rebuilding Initiative program of HUD, more than 100 institutions have received assistance.

U.S. Supreme Court Decisions

Although most legislation on hate crimes was enacted during the early to mid-1990s, many court cases have challenged the constitutional and legal grounds of these statutes. Three of the most important cases were eventually argued in the U.S. Supreme Court.

The first case involved a group of white skinheads who burned a cross in the yard of a black family in St. Paul, Minnesota, on June 21, 1990. Soon after, seventeen-year-old Robert A. Viktora was charged and later convicted of violating the local bias-motivated crime ordinance, which banned cross burning and displaying the swastika. The statute stipulated that these actions "arouse anger, alarm, or resentment in others on the basis of race, color, creed, religion or gender." Appealing the conviction to a Minnesota district court, the lawyer for Viktora claimed the law violated his client's First Amendment right of free speech. The district court ruled in favor of the defendant, overturning the conviction and declaring the law unconstitutional. The court claimed that the St. Paul ordinance was too broad in its application and violated First Amendment rights of freedom of expression.

In a counterappeal brought by the City of St. Paul, the Minnesota Supreme Court ruled that the local ordinance was valid because cross burning was similar to "fighting words"—a phrase used in a 1942 landmark U.S. Supreme Court decision—that incited violence and hence was not protected by the First Amendment of the Constitution.

R. A. V. v. City of St. Paul was finally brought before the U.S. Supreme Court on June 22, 1992. In a unanimous decision, the justices agreed that the St. Paul ordinance violated the First Amendment. Although offering separate legal arguments, the justices struck down the ordinance because it was unconstitutionally broad: The law had not criminalized all fighting words but only certain words based on their content or viewpoint. The decision declared that pure or symbolic bias-motivated speech, no matter how damaging to the intended target, cannot be outlawed solely on the basis of its effect on the victim.

A subsequent decision of the U.S. Supreme Court, however, did establish the legality of other types of hate crime legislation. The *Wisconsin v. Mitchell* case began on October 7, 1989, when a group of young African Americans gathered at an apartment complex in Kenosha, Wisconsin. After discussing a scene from the film *Mississippi Burning* in which a white man beat a young black person, the group went outside and saw a young white boy on the opposite side of the street. Todd Mitchell, a nineteen-year-old African American, shouted, "There goes a white boy, go get him." The group severely beat the boy, who was rendered unconscious and remained in a coma for four days.

After a jury trial in the Kenosha County Circuit Court, Mitchell was convicted of aggravated battery. Although the offense generally carries a maximum sentence of two years' imprisonment, the jury found that the defendant intentionally selected his victim because of the boy's race and increased his sentence to seven years based on the Wisconsin hate penalty enhancement statute. (The Wisconsin statute, modeled after the ADL's proposed hate-crime law, mandates increased penalties for a crime when the victim is targeted because of "race, religion, color, disability, sexual orientation, national origin or ancestry of that person.")

Mitchell's attorney claimed that the additional punishment violated his client's right to free speech, and the Wisconsin Supreme Court concurred by reversing the judgment. The state supreme court held that the penalty enhancement statute "violates the First Amendment directly by punishing what the legislature has deemed to be offensive thought." The decision also stated that "the Wisconsin legislature cannot criminalize bigoted thought with which it disagrees."

The State of Wisconsin appealed the decision of the Wisconsin Supreme Court. On June 11, 1993, the U.S. Supreme Court, in *Wisconsin v. Mitchell,* reversed the Wisconsin court ruling. In a unanimous decision, the justices agreed that the hate penalty enhancement ordinance does not violate the First Amendment. The Court held that the enhanced penalty is appropriate "because this conduct is thought to inflict greater individual and societal harm." Furthermore, the justices argued that the statute would not stifle free speech because the bias motivation would have to be connected with a specific act; the law focused on a person's actions, not on an individual's bigoted ideas.

The ADL, among other human rights organizations, promptly praised the U.S. Supreme Court decision. "Hate crime laws are necessary because the failure to recognize and effectively address this type of crime can cause an isolated incident to fester and explode into widespread community tensions," asserts an ADL publication.

Finally, on May 15, 2000; the U.S. Supreme Court ruled in *United States v. Morrison* that certain provisions of the Violence against Women Act were unconstitutional.

Hate Crimes Legislation at the State Level

In response to the support of human and civil rights organizations, many states have upheld local and municipal penalty enhancement statutes for bias-motivated crimes. According to the ADL publication *1998 Hate Crimes Laws,* the courts of four states—Ohio, Oregon, Washington, and Wisconsin—have upheld the constitutionality of these laws. The Georgia State Supreme Court, however, struck down that state's hate crime law on October 25, 2004.

The actions of the states where hate crimes statutes have been declared constitutional are especially significant because most prosecutions of bias-motivated violence occur at the state level.

The state government in Washington made the following statement, echoing concerns held by some other state legislatures:

> The legislature finds that crimes and threats against persons because of their race, color, religion, ancestry, national origin, gender, sexual orientation or mental, physical or sensory handicaps are serious and increasing. The legislature also finds that crimes and threats are often directed against interracial couples and their children or couples of mixed religions, colors, ancestries or national origins because of bias and bigotry. . . .The legislature finds that protection of those citizens from threats of harm due to bias and bigotry is a compelling state interest. (*Washington Rev. Code Ann.*)

Almost all states have some type of law that criminalizes hate crimes. In addition to broad-based protections against religious, racial, and other types of hate crimes, these statutes cover specific types of bias-motivated crimes and advocate prevention and education initiatives. Measures include the following:

- Prohibiting particular acts that have traditionally been associated with racial hatred, such as burning crosses or wearing masks or hoods. In 1951, for example, the state of Georgia passed an antimask law because of the violence and intimidation carried out by mask-wearing

members of the KKK. (These laws, however, exempt holiday costume masks or other "innocent activities.")
- Enacting statutes that provide compensation to the victims of hate crimes. These laws specify monetary damages (including damages for emotional distress and punitive damages), attorneys' fees, and other costs of litigation.
- Providing funding to school districts to implement programs designed to reduce and prevent hate-motivated incidents.

Like federal legislation, almost all state laws include race, color, religion, and national origin among the protected characteristics. Many state laws also protect sex or gender, disability, and sexual orientation. A few statutes include other protected characteristics such as age (California, District of Columbia, Florida, Hawaii, Iowa, Kansas, Louisiana, Maine, Minnesota, Nebraska, New Mexico, New York, and Vermont) and political affiliation (California, District of Columbia, Iowa, Louisiana, and West Virginia). The District of Columbia law covers the widest range of categories, including prejudice based on "actual or perceived race, color, religion, national origin, sex, age, marital status, personal appearance, sexual orientation, family responsibility, physical handicap, matriculation or political affiliation."

Critics of Hate Crime Laws

In the past few years, several legal scholars have raised serious legal, constitutional, and political questions about the need for hate crime legislation. In the December 1991 *UCLA Law Review*, scholar Susan Gellman summarizes the stance of many critics:

Those who oppose ethnic intimidation laws, or at least who question them most vigorously, do not disagree that bigotry (and certainly bigotry-related crime) is a serious problem. On the contrary, they are also from the ranks of the most civil rights–conscious thinkers and activists. These critics focus on threats to constitutional liberties under the First and Fourteenth Amendments. Their concerns are that these laws tread dangerously close to criminalization of speech and thought, that they impermissibly distinguish among people based on their beliefs, and that they are often too vaguely drafted to provide adequate notice of prohibited conduct. (Gellman 1991, 334)

In addition, these critics question the wisdom of enacting such laws; even if they can be drafted in a way that does not offend the Constitution, they may ultimately undercut their own goals more than they serve them. James B. Jacobs and Kimberly A. Potter, writing in volume 22 of *Crime and Justice: A Review of Research,* raise questions about the sociological and criminological consequences of hate crime legislation:

> The concept of hate crime is easy to grasp as an ideal type, but it is difficult to effectuate in a workaday criminal justice system. Most putative hate crimes are not ideologically motivated murders, although some of those do occur. . . . Whether it aids understanding of their conduct and of our society to brand them as bigots as well as criminals is not an easy question to answer. . . .
>
> Beyond the problem of definition, labeling particular incidents as hate crimes bristles with subjectivity and potential for bias. Nevertheless, the very existence of the term, the attempt to measure the incidence of hate crime, and the prosecution and sentencing of some offenders under different types of hate crime statutes have already changed how Americans think about the crime problem. At a minimum, the new hate crime laws have contributed further to politicizing the crime problem. . . .
>
> Rather than Americans pulling together and affirming their common ground by condemning criminal conduct, they may now increasingly see crime as a polarizing issue that pits one social group against another, thereby further dividing an already fractured society. (Jacobs, 1997, 41–42)

Conclusions

Few proponents of hate crime legislation believe that these statutes will eradicate the growing problem of hate-motivated violence in the United States. The festering problem of racism, anti-Semitism, and other forms of bigotry offers no easy legal solution. However, hate crime laws and severe criminal sentencing have certainly helped many victims and have presumably aided the safety and welfare of many communities. When a youth involved in an anti-Jewish crime is sentenced to serve time in prison, or the inciters of skinhead violence against African Americans are forced to pay restitution to the families of victims, or antigay felons are fully prosecuted for their crimes, violent bigots and their ilk are made aware that their hate-motivated criminal actions will have punitive consequences. This type of legislation is only about a decade old, so it is still too soon to assess its impact or success on U.S. society. Nevertheless, many human rights professionals agree with law enforcement officials that these federal and state laws are a useful interim measure in the long-term battle against hate crimes.

Recent Hate Crimes

Since the terrorist attack on the United States on September 11, 2001, Americans have become understandably fearful for their personal safety and security, and some groups have been especially blamed for this fear. Unfortunately, during other stressful times in U.S. history, some Americans were scapegoated or discriminated against because of their national, religious, or ethnic background. The internment of Japanese Americans during World War II is probably the most egregious example. Yet few Americans know that German Americans were subjected to discrimination during World War I or that American Jews were accused of dragging the United States into World War II and were subjected to economic and social prejudice during that war.

Some Major Targeted Groups

Even during peacetime, many U.S. citizens have been subjected to harassment, discrimination, and occasionally physical violence because of their religion, race, skin color, ethnic origin, economic class, or sexual orientation. The targets of this hatred have included Spanish and other non-English speakers; Italian, Jewish, and other European immigrants; and peoples from Asia,

Africa, and the Middle East. Sadly, the list of such groups is too large to enumerate.

This section surveys the recent history of hatred and violence directed against the four major groups that—according to FBI annual crime statistics—are most frequently targeted: African Americans, Asian Americans, gay men and lesbians, and Jewish Americans. As a result of the September 11 attacks, this section will also include a survey of hate crimes committed against Muslim Americans and Arab Americans.

African Americans

On May 5, 2002, Alonzo Bailey was found chained to a fence in an Oklahoma City industrial park. The body of this thirty-three-year-old African American had been set on fire and covered with wooden pallets. The suspected murderer, Anthony Lee Tedford, had KKK tattoos on his body. Although the FBI planned to investigate whether the murder was a hate crime, the crime was not prosecuted as a bias-motivated incident.

The grisly murder—regardless of whether it was racially motivated—recalled the tragic history of violence directed against African Americans throughout U.S. history. From 1882 to 1968, 4,743 people were reportedly lynched; of those, the vast majority were black. Black Americans have been the most frequent victims of hate violence in the United States.

While such violent incidents were generally ignored by the public during the nineteenth and twentieth centuries, antiblack violence is now met with outrage and shame. When James Byrd Jr., a forty-nine-year-old black man in Jasper, Texas, was dragged along an asphalt road for almost two miles by white supremacist attackers on June 7, 1998, this barbaric murder was condemned by President Bill Clinton. The accused perpetrators were later found guilty of the crime and executed by the state of Texas. The incident was reported and analyzed in three books, and it received widespread media coverage.

The most recent FBI hate crime statistics, covering the year 2003, reported that racial bias incidents represented the largest percentage of all bias-motivated incidents (51.4 percent of all reported hate crimes). The total number of reported racial bias offenses in 2003 was 4,574. The percentage of incidents that involved antiblack bias was 66.3 percent.

In recent years, the most publicized incidents have been the burning of African American churches in the southern United States. In June 1996, President Clinton established the National Church Arson Task Force (NCATF) to better coordinate the efforts of federal, state, and local law enforcement to combat such crime. The NCATF opened investigations into 945 arsons, bombings, and attempted bombings that occurred at houses of worship between January 1, 1995, and August 15, 2000. Since January 1995, federal, state, and local authorities have arrested 431 suspects and 305 defendants have been convicted. An NCATF report asserted that the arsons at both African American and other houses of worship "were motivated by a wide array of factors, including not only blatant racism or religious hatred but also financial profit, burglary, and personal revenge." The latest NCATF report was issued in 2002 and is available at http://www.atf.gov/pub/gen_pub/report2000/, the direct link for the e-book reader.

Although the NCATF report findings do not indicate a national conspiracy against black churches, this widespread criminal violence warranted the concern of law enforcement officials and the public. "If it is not a conspiracy," warned an ADL publication, *Hate Crimes Laws 1998,* "it only means that individuals in different parts of the country at different times, often inspired by hate, are acting independently to commit these crimes."

Although newspapers and other media extensively covered the rash of church bombings, it wasn't until *USA Today* published a three-day series of twelve articles June 28–30, 1996, that the exact nature of these crimes was examined in detail. However, investigative journalist Michael Fumento, writing in the *Wall Street Journal* (July 8, 1996), argued that *USA Today* was partially responsible for wrongly charging, in his view, that African American church arsons constituted an epidemic.

Epidemic or not, attacks against black churches have a long and tragic history. According to historian C. Eric Lincoln, the first recorded arson against a black church occurred in South Carolina in 1822. After the Civil War, the KKK targeted African American churches; almost a century later, four black children were killed in the Sixteenth Street Baptist Church bombing in Birmingham, Alabama, in 1963. It is worth noting that Secretary of State Condoleezza Rice was the kindergarten classmate of Denise McNair, who was killed in the bombing.

Other significant recent hate crimes committed against African Americans include the following:

- James Langenbach, a white man, deliberately drove over two black teenagers in Kenosha, Wisconsin, in a racially motivated hate crime on May 16, 1999. He was convicted of running over fourteen-year-old cousins Austin Hansen-Tyler and Dontrell Langston while they were bicycling on a sidewalk in Kenosha. Langenbach was sentenced to 176 years in prison. The boys survived serious injuries. It is noteworthy that the landmark U.S. Supreme Court decision *Wisconsin v. Mitchell* involved a racial incident also in Kenosha, Wisconsin.
- Ricky Birdsong, a black Northwestern University coach, was shot and killed a block from his Skokie, Illinois, home by Benjamin Smith, a twenty-one-year-old white supremacist. Starting on July 2, 1999, Smith engaged in a murderous three-day rampage in Illinois and Indiana. He shot ten other people—including African Americans, Jews, and Asians—before killing himself.
- Lawrence Lombardi, forty-one, an unemployed embalmer, was convicted of setting off bombs on August 31 and September 22, 1999, at Florida A&M University, which is predominantly black. He was sentenced to life imprisonment plus thirty-nine years in federal prison. Although no injuries were reported at the 12,000-student campus, the blasts caused minor damage to administration and classroom buildings. Lombardi was also sentenced for a hate crime—igniting bombs in an effort to injure, intimidate, and disrupt students because of their race. After the bombing, many students reportedly withdrew from the school out of fear for their personal safety.

Asian Americans

Following the September 11 terrorist attacks, some Asian Americans were victims of the most violent and deadly hate crime incidents. These incidents were ostensibly aimed at "Muslim-looking" individuals but were actually perpetrated against recent Asian non-Muslim U.S. citizens or recent immigrants. The National Asian Pacific American Legal Consortium (NAPALC), a nonpartisan organization to advance and safeguard civil rights, issues an annual audit of violence committed against Asian-

Americans. It is reportedly the most comprehensive, nongovernmental compilation of violent incidents directed at Asian and Pacific Americans.

The *2002 Audit of Violence Against Asian Pacific Americans: Tenth Annual Report* (the most recently available report before this book went to press) noted some of the following information:

- NAPALC recorded 275 bias-motivated hate crimes against Asian-Americans in 2002, a 48 percent decrease from the 507 incidents reported in 2001. Since this organization began compiling this audit in 1993, NAPALC noted the largest number of hate crimes were committed during 2001.
- The sharp rise is attributable in part to the backlash following the September 11 terrorist attacks; in the three months following the September terrorism, three people were murdered and 250 bias-related incidents were recorded. (Important note: Although some organizations have claimed that several other Asian Americans were hate crime murder victims, the police reports could not provide conclusive evidence indicating they were indeed backlash victims. To ensure the credibility of hate crimes statistics, it is important that only verifiable bias-motivated incidents should be included.)
- An estimated 80 percent of the incidents occurred in the several weeks after the September 11, 2001, attacks and these incidents included murders. Balbir Singh Sodhi, a forty-nine-year-old Sikh, was murdered at his Chevron gas station in Mesa, Arizona on September 15, 2001. Frank Silva Roque, a machinist, was convicted of this first-degree murder and sentenced to death on October 9, 2003. During his twenty-five-minute rampage, Roque also fired on the home of an Afghan family and shot multiple times at a Lebanese-American clerk without injuring him.
- Waqar Hasan, a forty-six-year-old Pakistani-American grocery storeowner in Mesquite, Texas, was cooking hamburgers in his store when he was murdered by Mark Anthony Stroman, a local stonecutter. After this September 15, 2001 killing, Stroman reportedly said, "We're at war. I did what I had to do. I did it to retaliate against those who retaliated against us." In a subsequent murder, Stroman shot to death Vasudev Patel, a forty-

nine-year-old naturalized U.S. citizen from India, at his gas station in the Dallas suburb of Mesquite. This October 4, 2001, murder was caught on a store surveillance tape. Stroman was also involved in a third shooting that wounded Raisuddin Bhuiyan, a Bangladeshi immigrant who was shot at a gas station. In April 2002, a Texas jury sentenced Stroman to death for these crimes.

- A majority of the hate-crime incidents occurred at schools or in the workplace. Some students were physically attacked or harassed, as were Asian-Americans at their place of work.
- A majority of the victims were of South Asian ancestry—Indian or Pakistani. Sikh men who wear turbans and long beards were specially-targeted.
- NAPALC claims that there is underreporting of hate crimes because many recent immigrants fear notifying police. In addition, the organization states that federal guidelines are not comprehensive enough to cover all incidents.
- On September 17, 2001, the fires of hatred were further stoked when U.S. Congressman, John Cooksey (R-LA) referred to Arab Americans and South Asians as "towel heads" and suggested racial profiling of these groups. The Louisiana representative said, "If I see someone [who] comes in that's got a diaper on his head and a fan belt wrapped around the diaper on his head, that guy needs to be pulled over." ([New Orleans] *Times Picayune*, September 21, 2001)

Despite these disturbing incidents, many Americans were heartened that President George W. Bush issued a strong statement on September 17, 2001, condemning violent incidents against U.S. immigrants and citizens. The U.S. Department of Transportation employees who had been subjecting Sikhs to rigorous searches at airports because of their turbans and other garb were issued formal guidelines, "Carrying Out Transportation Inspection and Safety Responsibilities in a Nondiscriminatory Manner," which prohibited inspection of an individual based on his manner of dress.

Another encouraging development was the congressional resolution to condemn "bigotry and violence against Arab-Americans, Muslim-Americans, South Asian-Americans, and

Sikh-Americans." This resolution urged federal and local officials to fully prosecute hate crime perpetrators in their respective
jurisdictions. The U.S. Senate unanimously agreed to the resolution on May 22, 2003 (S. Res. 133) and the U.S. House of Representatives agreed to its version of the resolution on October 7,
2003 (H. Res. 234).

Other notable crimes in the past few years include:

- Thung Phetakoune, a sixty-two-year-old U.S. citizen
  of Laotian ancestry, murdered by Richard Labbe in
  Newmarket, New Hampshire, on July 14, 2001.
  Witnesses overheard Labbe uttering anti-Asian racial
  comments before the attack, and Labbe reportedly told
  the arresting police officer, "Those Asians killed my
  brother and uncle in Vietnam. Call it payback." ("Hate
  Crime Charged in the Death of Thung Phetakoune" 2001)
  Although the defendant was originally charged with a
  hate crime, the state later dropped the charge, and Labbe
  pleaded guilty only to manslaughter. The dropping of
  the hate crime indictment evoked outrage among Asian
  American organizations.
- On April 28, 2000, Anil Thakur, thirty-one, a customer at
  the India Grocers store in Pittsburgh, Pennsylvania, was
  murdered and Sandip Patel, the store manager, was
  paralyzed from the neck down. The assailant was
  Richard Baumhammers, a white immigration attorney
  who professed hatred of minorities. He began his
  murderous rampage by killing Anita Gordon, his sixty-
  three-year-old Jewish neighbor. Later, he went to a
  Chinese restaurant and killed Thao Q. Pham, twenty-
  seven, a Vietnamese American, and Ji-Ye Sun, thirty-four,
  a Korean American. His final victim was Garry Lee, a
  twenty-five-year-old African American man. Although
  Baumhammers was initially sent to a psychiatric facility,
  a jury found him guilty of five murders and he was
  sentenced to death.
- Somahn Thamavong, a Laotian American man, was
  beaten unconscious with a broomstick after leaving his
  Baltimore home on August 12, 2000. His assailants beat
  him so badly that he suffered severe brain trauma and is
  now disabled. According to NAPALC, the African
  American teenagers who beat him allegedly bragged

about "what they did to the Asian man." (National Asian
Pacific American Legal Consortium [NAPALC] 2000)

- Mizanor Rahman, a Bangladeshi immigrant, was beaten
  to death in Brooklyn, New York, in a racially motivated
  mob attack on August 10, 2002. The thirty-seven-year-old
  journalist was attacked by a local Hispanic gang when he
  stumbled into a violent confrontation between local
  Dominican and Bangladeshi youths over a stolen bicycle.
- While working at a part-time job delivering pizzas in
  New Bedford, Massachusetts, Saurabh Bhalerao, twenty-
  four, was robbed, beaten, burned with cigarettes, stuffed
  in a trunk, and stabbed twice on June 23, 2003. He was
  later dumped along a road. His assailants shouted anti-
  Muslim slurs at Bhalerao, even though he is Hindu.
  Police and community leaders describe the attack as a
  hate crime.
- Buford O. Furrow, a professed white supremacist, went
  on a violent rampage in Los Angeles on August 10, 1999,
  and killed Joseph Ileto, a Filipino American postal
  worker. Earlier, Furrow had shot at the North Valley
  Jewish Community Center and wounded five people.
  Furrow pleaded guilty to the crimes, and on March 26,
  2001, the court sentenced him to two life sentences, in
  addition to a 110-year life sentence.
- During a murderous rampage from July 2–4, 1999,
  Benjamin Smith murdered Won-Joon Yoon, a Korean
  graduate student at Indiana University.

Jewish Americans

Hatred of Jews—commonly known by the semantically mislead-
ing term *anti-Semitism*—has a very long and bitter history. In
1991, British television aired a documentary series on the subject,
aptly titled *The Longest Hatred*. In the United States too, anti-Jewish hatred and violence has flared periodically. One of the most
notorious anti-Jewish incidents in the United States during the
twentieth century occurred in Atlanta, Georgia. Leo Frank, a Jew
who was part owner of a pencil factory, was wrongfully accused
of murdering a fourteen-year-old employee, Mary Phagan. In
July 1915, encouraged by widespread community anger and the
anti-Jewish invective of Tom Watson, a southern populist politi-

cian, a mob lynched Frank. This murder stirred immense fear among southern Jews and precipitated a massive exodus of Jews from the region.

Despite this incident and the rise of anti-Jewish hatemongers like Father Coughlin, Gerald L. K. Smith, and pro-Nazi groups during World War II, the virus of anti-Semitism has fortunately never exhibited a major strain in U.S. life. "No decisive event, no deep crisis, no powerful social movement, no great individual is associated primarily . . . with anti-Semitism (in America)," once wrote historian John Higham.

Nevertheless, anti-Jewish incidents continue to occur, ranging from swastikas being spray-painted at synagogues and Jewish cemeteries to harassment, intimidation, and violent assaults. In recent years, the most serious anti-Jewish incident occurred in the Crown Heights neighborhood of Brooklyn, New York, following a traffic accident. On August 19, 1991, the driver of a car that was part of a motorcade for Rabbi Menachem M. Schneerson (the spiritual leader of the Lubavitcher Hasidic movement) accidentally hit Gavin Cato, a seven-year-old African American boy, and his cousin, resulting in his death and the injury of his cousin. A riot ensued over the following three days, during which crowds roamed the streets yelling, "Get the Jews." Jewish homes, cars, and property were attacked.

On the night of the accident, twenty black youths assaulted Yankel Rosenbaum, an Australian Jewish scholar, stabbing him and leaving him bleeding on the hood of an automobile. He later died. Lemrick Nelson, age sixteen, was charged with the murder. On October 29, 1992, Nelson was found not guilty of the murder because the prosecution did not prove that the attack had caused Rosenbaum's death. Defense lawyers did not deny that Nelson had stabbed the twenty-nine-year-old Jewish scholar. His attorneys contended the slaying had nothing to do with the fact that the victim was Jewish—a crucial element needed for a hate crimes conviction.

Amidst angry protests by the public and the media about an unfair verdict, the U.S. government subsequently charged the defendant with violating Rosenbaum's civil rights. In 1997, Nelson was convicted of these charges and was sentenced to twenty-one years in prison. The U.S. Second Circuit Court of Appeals, however, overturned the verdict on the grounds of an improper race-based jury selection. Nelson was then sentenced to a maximum of ten years in prison and was released on June 2, 2004. Charles Price, fifty-one, who has served more than a dozen years for violating Rosenbaum's rights by urging the crowd to attack him, is scheduled for release in 2006.

On March 1, 1994, Rashid Baz, a Lebanese immigrant, shot at a van carrying fifteen Hasidic Jewish students over the Brooklyn Bridge. One student, sixteen-year-old Aaron Halberstam, died in the attack. Three other students were wounded; one of them, eighteen-year-old Nachum Sasonkin, fell into a coma and had few prospects for a normal life. Although he still has a bullet lodged in his brain, Sasonkin has had a miraculous recovery. He later married, became a father, and was ordained as a rabbi. The murderer once vowed to "kill all Jews." (*New York Times*, April 7, 1994, B3)

In another violent incident, a Jewish store owner in Harlem wanted to expand his clothing store, Freddy's Fashion Mart, to a space occupied by a black-owned record store. The owner of the record store didn't want to move, and some community activists supported his decision. For several weeks, they picketed Freddy's Fashion Mart, occasionally shouting anti-Jewish slurs and rhetoric, including the term "bloodsuckers"—a phrase that Nation of Islam leader Louis Farrakhan had used only a few weeks earlier in a widely publicized interview to describe Jews. On December 8, 1995, Roland Smith, one of the protesters, entered Freddy's brandishing a revolver and shot four people. He then doused the store with lighter fluid. Eight people—including Smith—died in the blaze. Although none of the victims were Jewish, anti-Jewish hatred was nevertheless an underlying factor of the crime.

According to the FBI's *2003 Hate Crime Statistics* tabulations, the overwhelming majority of religious-based attacks upon individuals or institutions—approximately 69 percent—are directed against Jews or Jewish institutions.

Since 1979, the ADL has published an annual survey of anti-Jewish hate incidents throughout the United States. The 2003 *Audit of Anti-Semitic Incidents* recounted some of the following information:

- In 2003, 1,557 anti-Jewish incidents were reported; 1,559 such incidents were reported in 2002. At the same time, anti-Jewish incidents reported on campus—which had been progressively increasing from 2000 through 2002—

declined from 106 incidents in 2002, to sixty-eight in 2003. (See ADL Web site at http://www.adl.org/PresRele/ ASUS_12/4243_12.asp)

- On November 13, 2003, a Holocaust museum in Terre Haute, Indiana, was destroyed by arson. This museum memorialized children who were victims of Nazi medical experimentation.
- On June 18, 1999, Congregation B'nai Israel and Knesset Israel Torah Center in Sacramento and Congregation Beth Shalom in Carmichael, California, were set ablaze, causing an estimated $3 million in damage. The arsonists also killed a gay couple a few weeks later.
- During the July 4, 1999, weekend, Benjamin Nathaniel Smith, a twenty-one-year-old white supremacist involved with the World Church of the Creator, went on a murderous rampage in Illinois and Indiana and shot at Orthodox Jews in a Chicago neighborhood. He targeted minorities, killing Ricky Birdsong, a black coach at Northwestern University, and Won-Joon Yoon, a graduate student at Indiana University. He left nine people injured before he killed himself after a police chase.
- On August 10, 1999, Buford O. Furrow Jr., a member of the Aryan Nations, entered the North Valley Jewish Community Center in Los Angeles and wounded several people, including a small child. Furrow later claimed that his action was a "wake-up call to white America to start killing Jews." Furrow also killed Joseph Ileto, a Filipino American postal worker.
- On October 8, 2000—the eve of Yom Kippur—two firebombs were thrown at Congregation Adath Israel in Riverdale, a Bronx neighborhood in New York City. The perpetrators, Mohammed Alfakih and Mazin Assi, were convicted of attempted arson and weapons possession. They were the first defendants to be charged under New York state's new hate crime statute, which went into effect that same day, just hours before they committed the crime. (*Jerusalem Post*, December 15, 2002, 3)
- Leo V. Felton and Erica Chase, members of a white supremacist group, were indicted for plotting to blow up major Jewish and African American monuments in the

Boston area. They were also plotting the assassinations of Steven Spielberg and Jesse Jackson. On July 26, 2003, Felton was convicted and sentenced to twenty years in prison; Chase, who was repentant, received a five-year sentence.
* Temple Beth El in Syracuse, New York, was destroyed in an arson attack on October 13, 2000.

The rise of anti-Jewish incidents on campus has been a particularly troubling development. The ADL recorded 106 such incidents in 2002; this number did not include anti-Israel rallies unless there was an overt anti-Jewish manifestation during the event. On May 7, 2002, Jewish students at a rally at San Francisco State University (SFSU) were cornered and physically threatened. Some assailants shouted, "Hitler should have finished the job." (*San Francisco Chronicle,* July 29, 2002, A1) The incident sent a chill throughout the Jewish and university communities. SFSU's president assured the community that any students involved in the assault would face expulsion and possible prosecution.

A few months earlier, a cement block was thrown through a window at the University of California–Berkeley Hillel Center at the same time that anti-Jewish graffiti appeared on the building. A swastika defaced a sukkah (a temporary structure used to commemorate a Jewish holiday) at the University of Colorado, and the campus's Jewish fraternity house was vandalized. On July 7, 2002, Daniel Aghion, a Jewish student at the University of Michigan who wore a yarmulke, was hit with a bottle and verbally harassed while walking near the campus. The court issued an enlightened verdict for the perpetrator: Ghassan Issa, eighteen years old, was sentenced to perform 100 hours of community service, write an essay about anti-Jewish hatred, and send a letter of apology to the victim.

The situation for Jewish students on campuses became so serious that more than 300 college and university presidents signed an ad appearing in the October 7, 2002, issue of the *New York Times.* The ad stated: "In the past few months, students who are Jewish or supporters of Israel's right to exist—Zionists—have received death threats and threats of violence." Although some pro-Arab supporters claimed the ad tried to stifle criticism of Israeli policies, the statement explicitly acknowledged the right to free speech and strong dissent. The signers, however, specifically condemned violence, harassment, and threats of violence directed against Jewish students, who have been the overwhelming number of hate crime victims on college campuses.

Gay Men, Lesbians, and Transgendered People

In a 1988 case involving the beating death of a gay man, a circuit court judge in Broward County, Florida, jokingly asked the prosecuting attorney, "That's a crime now, to beat up a homosexual?"

The prosecutor replied, "Yes, sir. And it's also a crime to kill them."

The judge reportedly replied, "Times have really changed." (Jenness, 1997, 50)

Prior to the passage of the Hate Crime Statistics Act in 1990, no federal statute had addressed the problem of antigay violence. Similarly, very few laws at the state and local levels had specifically addressed these types of crimes. Only recently has violence against gay men and lesbians been considered a hate crime by the federal government and by most state and local law enforcement agencies. Despite a tide of new legislation concerning the issue, the number of reported crimes against gays has continued to increase in some years.

On October 9, 1986, the U.S. House of Representatives Judiciary Subcommittee on Criminal Justice convened the first congressional hearings on antigay violence throughout the United States. Physicians, psychologists, sociologists, and other health professionals offered testimony on the nature, extent, and consequences of antigay violence.

The first national study focusing exclusively on the topic of antigay violence was conducted by the National Gay and Lesbian Task Force in 1984. Interviewing almost 1,500 gay men and 654 lesbians in eight U.S. cities (Boston, New York, Atlanta, St. Louis, Denver, Dallas, Los Angeles, and Seattle), the respondents reported the following:

- 19 percent of the respondents reported having been punched, hit, kicked, or beaten at least once in their lives because of their sexual orientation;

- 44 percent had been threatened with physical violence; and
- 92 percent of those who had been targets of antigay verbal abuse had experienced such harassment "more than once or many times."(Herek and Berrill 1992, 19–25)

These survey results also highlight another issue involving bias crimes against homosexuals: Statistics on antigay crimes vary greatly in reports issued by gay rights activists and law enforcement authorities. In 2001, the National Coalition of Anti-Violence Programs (NCAVP) recorded 2,210 attacks on gay men and lesbians; the FBI, however, cited 1,555 incidents in its annual report. Phyllis B. Gerstenfeld notes that the "actual discrepancy is actually much greater because the FBI data purport to include almost all of the United States, whereas the NCAVP report included only a dozen reporting regions with a combined population of about 51 million." (Gerstenfeld 2004)

When comparing the FBI figures with those from nongovernmental monitoring groups, it is important to remember that the private advocacy groups have been monitoring hate crimes for a longer period of time than has the government. Whereas the FBI's first *Hate Crime* report covered the year 1991, the National Gay and Lesbian Task Force (NGLTF) conducted annual surveys of antihomosexual violence from 1985 to 1995. The NCAVP later assumed this duty in 1997.

From 1985 to 1989, the NGLTF gathered statistics from a wide range of community groups and media sources. Since 1990, these reports have focused on major metropolitan areas, including Boston, Chicago, Denver, Minneapolis, St. Paul, New York City, and San Francisco. Gay rights organizations have consistently claimed that antihomosexual hate crimes are vastly underreported and that this is true for several reasons. The primary is that lesbians and gay men are often reluctant to report these incidents, fearing that such publicity would adversely affect their employment or relations with family members who are unaware of their sexual orientation.

"While victims may want to prosecute their assailants, they are too vulnerable as homosexuals in American society to be exposed in this manner," asserts law scholar Teresa Eileen Kibelstis. She cites a 1994 incident in Los Angeles in which eight men were arrested for assaulting two others with baseball bats. Although the police termed the incident "a gay bashing" and arrested the assailants with the aid of witnesses, the victims quickly left the scene of the crime and were never located. "Gay bashing crimes involve gay victims, and for some lesbians and gay men, that label can have too many repercussions," Kibelstis concludes. (Kibelstis 1995)

Many gays and lesbians have been distrustful of police departments nationwide, both historically and in recent times. The Stonewall riot, which occurred at a gay bar in New York's Greenwich Village in 1969 and is considered the founding event in the birth of the modern gay liberation movement, involved a police assault against gay and transgendered men.

Violent hate crimes committed against gays and lesbians are also notable in another respect: These incidents are especially brutal. According to one study, "an intense rage is present in nearly all homicide cases involving gay male victims. A striking feature . . . is their gruesome, often vicious nature. Seldom is the homosexual victim simply shot. He is more apt to be stabbed a dozen or more times, mutilated, and strangled."

A hospital official in New York City remarked, "Attacks against gay men were the most heinous and brutal I encountered. . . .They frequently involved torture, cutting, mutilation . . . showing the absolute intent to rub out the human being because of his (sexual) preference" (Winer 1994)

In recent years, gay men and lesbians have broadened their civil and political rights concerns to include transgendered people. (According to the *Oxford English Dictionary*, the word refers to "a person whose identity does not conform unambiguously to conventional notions of male or female gender." The term is very broad and includes transsexuals, individuals who undergo sex-change operations.)

Transgendered individuals in particular have been subjected to hate-motivated violence, and occasionally murder. According to the winter 2003 issue of the Southern Poverty Law Center's *Intelligence Report*, fourteen transgendered individuals were murdered in 2002 in the United States; by the end of September 2003, at least another thirteen had been slain. The death of Brandon Teena, a girl who passed as a man, was the first anti-transgender murder to receive media attention. The award-winning film *Boys Don't Cry* tells the story of Teena's life and tragic death. The FBI *Hate Crimes Statistics* does not include separate statistics for anti-transgendered crimes.

In recent years, the most widely reported hate crime against gays occurred in Wyoming. On October 6, 1998, Matthew Shepard, a twenty-two-year-old gay student at the University of Wyoming, was lured from a local bar by two men, kidnapped, beaten with a .357 Magnum, and tied to a wooden fence. He hung there for almost eighteen hours until a passing bicyclist noticed his bloodied body. He lay in a coma in a hospital in Fort Collins, Colorado, until he died on October 12.

Sadly, there have been many other grotesquely violent incidents directed against gays and lesbians—or those thought to be gay—both before and after Shepard's murder.:

- In Atlanta, Georgia, Gregory Love was attacked with a baseball bat by a fellow Morehouse College student because he believed Love was making a sexual pass at him in a dormitory shower. A jury found Aaron Price, a nineteen-year-old sophomore at Morehouse, guilty of aggravated assault and aggravated battery in the November 3, 2002, beating. Price received ten years on each count, to be served concurrently. Price, who was subsequently expelled from Morehouse, was acquitted of a hate crime after prosecutors failed to convince jurors that Price's action was motivated by antigay feelings. Love also testified that he was not gay. This violent incident aroused great fears among gay students at Morehouse, a historically black men's college. As a result, many black gays and lesbians spoke out for the first time about antigay prejudice in the African American community. This trial was the first case involving Georgia's recently passed hate crimes enhancement penalty statute.
- On July 1, 1999, Gary Matson and Winfield Scott Mowder, a gay couple, were shot to death in their home outside Redding, California. James Tyler Williams, the killer of the gay couple, was sentenced to twenty-nine years to life in prison for the murders, plus a nineteen-year sentence for the firebombing of three Sacramento-area synagogues. His brother, Benjamin Williams, who was an accomplice in the crimes, committed suicide in his Shasta County jail cell on November 17, 2002.

Benjamin Williams reportedly said that the murder of the gay couple was "God's will."

- In May 1988, a lesbian couple, Rebecca Wright and Claudia Brenner, were victims of a gruesome murder in Pine Grove State Park in Pennsylvania. Stephen Ray Carr was convicted of first-degree murder and sentenced to life imprisonment.
- Also in May 1988, a college freshman committed a grisly murder of two gay men, Tommy Trible and Lloyd Griffin, in a Dallas, Texas, neighborhood. Although the prosecutor requested life imprisonment for the murderer, Richard Lee Bednarski, the trial judge imposed a thirty-year sentence and callously declared, "I put prostitutes and gays at about the same level and I'd be hard put to give somebody life for killing a prostitute." (Belkin 1988)
- Vietnam War veteran James Zappalorti was brutally beaten in Staten Island, New York, on January 21, 1990. The murderers, Phillip Sarlo and Michael Taylor, later defiantly declared that they had "only killed a gay." (*Newsday*, November 4, 1990, p. 8)
- On October 27, 1992, Seaman Allen Schindler, while serving on a U.S. Navy ship stationed in Japan, was murdered outside his base. The assailant, Navy Airman Terry Helvey, who had recently learned of Schindler's homosexuality, stomped on his face and chest with his feet. Schindler's body was so disfigured by the brutal attack that seasoned Navy medics were sickened at the sight of the body.

The latest FBI annual report on hate crimes in the United States placed the number of antigay incidents at 1,454 for 2003. According to the report, the number of sexual orientation bias victims constituted 16.6 percent of all hate crime victims. As noted earlier, the FBI does not record statistics on hate crimes committed against transgendered individuals. Gay rights groups believe the following FBI figures are gross underestimates. The FBI breaks down the antigay crimes in this way:

- 881 (61.6 percent) of those offenses were anti–male homosexual;

- 220 (15.4 percent) were anti–female homosexual;
- the remaining crimes were classified as general "antihomosexual" or "antibisexual."

As of July 2004, thirty states and the District of Columbia have passed hate crime laws that include sexual orientation as a protected class.

Despite the generally gloomy news, Valerie Jenness, a sociologist who has written extensively about hate crimes, was heartened when U.S. Attorney General John Ashcroft held a nationally televised news conference on April 10, 2002, to announce that Darrell David Rice was to be charged with a federal hate crime for the murder of Laura Winans and Julianne Marie Williams, two lesbians who were found dead on June 1, 1996, in Shenandoah National Park in Virginia. (Although later evidence required the government to dismiss the case against Rice, the U.S. Department of Justice was still pursuing leads about the murder in 2004.)

This was the first case in which the federal government used the Hate Crimes Sentencing Enhancement Act (1994) to prosecute a hate crime based on gender and sexual orientation. In his news conference, Ashcroft noted that he had met with the parents of the victims and learned about their lives. He declared that the Department of Justice would "pursue, prosecute, and punish those who attack law-abiding Americans out of hatred for who they are."

Arab Americans and Muslim Americans

Following the Arab terrorist attacks on the United States on September 11, 2001, there appeared to be a sizable increase in anti-Arab and anti-Muslim prejudice throughout the country, resulting in widely reported incidents of harassment, vandalism, and occasionally violence.

According to the annual FBI *Hate Crimes Statistics,* in the last several years anti-Muslim incidents have generally accounted for the second-smallest number of religious-bias crimes. (Anti-Jewish crimes accounted for the highest number of such incidents, followed by anti-Catholic, anti-Protestant bias, and then bias directed against other religions.) In 2001, however, anti-Islamic hate crimes accounted for the second-highest number of religious crimes (27.2 percent), after anti-Jewish incidents (55.7 percent). According to the FBI report, there were 481 incidents and 554 victims in 2001, a seventeen-fold increase over the previous year. In 2002, however, there was a dramatic 70 percent decrease to 155 incidents and 174 victims.

Most of the deadliest hate crimes ostensibly aimed against Muslims were, in fact, committed against Sikhs, who wear turbans, and others who look Middle Eastern but are not necessarily Arab or Muslim. (See *Asian-American* section above.)

The following list includes some of the most violent incidents directed against American Arabs or Muslims:

- On March 25, 2002, Charles D. Franklin crashed his pickup truck into the Islamic Center of Tallahassee, Florida, after evening prayers. No one was inside the mosque when the truck smashed into the doorway, causing about $1,000 in damage to the building.
- On September 12, 2001, 300 angry protestors tried to storm a mosque in Bridgeview, Illinois, a Chicago suburb. More than 100 police controlled the demonstrators and arrested three people.
- On September 11, 2001, the Islamic Center of Irving, Texas, which serves as a school and a mosque, was fired upon, leaving thirteen to fourteen bullet holes in the building. No one was injured. In the following week, there were also gunshots and vandalism directed at mosques in Toledo, Ohio; Bridgeport, Connecticut; Claremont, California; Lexington, Kentucky; and Sterling, Virginia, among other places.
- In October 2002, hundreds of leaflets containing anti-Islamic obscenities and threats were distributed at the Muslim Association of Honolulu mosque. The FBI investigated the incident as a hate crime.
- In Salt Lake City, Utah, James Herrick, thirty-two, was sentenced to more than four years in prison after pleading guilty to setting fire to the "Curry in a Hurry," a Pakistani American–owned restaurant, on September 13, 2001.
- On December 17, 2002, in what federal officials described as the most stringent penalty for a post–September 11, 2001, hate crime, Patrick Cunningham, fifty-four, was sentenced to six and a half years for an assault on the Islamic Idriss mosque in Seattle two days after the

terrorist attacks. He admitted to trying to set fire to parked vehicles and to threatening two worshipers with a loaded .22-caliber pistol. In an emotional plea before U.S. District Judge Barbara Rothstein, Cunningham said that on the night of the assault he was drunk and distraught over the terrorist attacks. He apologized to his victims and thanked God "for intervening" before things got worse. Although Cunningham maintained he had fired his pistol only once, the prosecutors said that he had fired three additional times but that the weapon had misfired. No one at the mosque was injured. Judge Rothstein acknowledged the defendant's apologies and his crime-free record, but she also denounced his crime: "The greatest flaw of human nature is when you extend hatred of an individual to a group." (*Seattle Times,* December 18, 2002, p. B1)

- Vandals hit all three floors of the Islamic Foundation of Central Ohio in Columbus on the evening of December 29, 2001, shredding copies of the Koran and breaking water pipes to cause damage to the building. According to a November 2002 Human Rights Watch report, the damage was estimated at $379,000.

- On August 24, 2002, federal authorities arrested Dr. Robert Goldstein, a thirty-seven-year-old Tampa, Florida, podiatrist, for plotting to bomb local mosques and an Islamic cultural center in south Florida. He pleaded guilty and was later sentenced to twelve and a half years in prison. The defendant wanted to get revenge for the September 11 terrorist attacks.

- During the last week of August 2003, a fire at the Islamic Center in Savannah, Georgia, destroyed a building that had been used as a mosque by approximately 100 of the estimated 400 to 500 Muslims in the area. Early evidence indicated that the arson was motivated by hate.

During the first Gulf War, from 1990 to 1991, there were several recorded incidents of harassment and vandalism directed against Arab and Muslim Americans in cities throughout the country. On September 24, 1990, President George H. W. Bush declared that "death threats, physical attacks, vandalism, religious violence and discrimination against Arab-Americans must end."

Despite these disturbing hate crime incidents, there was much heartening news in the wide range of expressions of concern and support throughout the country that no group would be scapegoated for the murder of some 3,000 Americans in the September 11 terrorist attacks. The support ranged from the president of the United States to elementary-school children:

- Only a day after the terrorist attack, President George W. Bush wrote, in published remarks to Mayor Rudolph Giuliani: "Our nation should be mindful that there are thousands of Arab-Americans who live in New York City, who love their flag just as much as we do. . . . we treat Arab-Americans and Muslims with the respect they deserve." The president also visited the Islamic Center of Washington, D.C., and issued similar supportive remarks.
- In 2003, both the U.S. Senate and House of Representatives passed a resolution "condemning bigotry against Arab-Americans, Muslim-Americans, South Asian-Americans, and Sikh-Americans."
- Governors, mayors, and town officials appeared publicly with Arab Americans and Muslims to condemn hate crimes and ensure the prosecution of perpetrators, according to a Human Rights Watch report, "We are Not the Enemy: Hate Crimes Against Arabs, Muslims, and Those Perceived to be Arab or Muslim After September 11," issued in November 2002. The authors of the report noted that this type of solidarity was uniformly expressed in every area of the country.
- The Anti-Defamation League (ADL), the largest Jewish civil rights organization in the U.S., publicized anti-Arab and anti-Muslim hate crimes on its Web site and worked with law enforcement officers to prosecute these crimes.
- Dearborn, Michigan, which has a large Arab American population, experienced only two September 11–related assaults. Some officials credit an ongoing community-police cooperative relationship with stemming any potential violence.

The following incidents also were indicative of the attitudes of most Americans after the September 11 attacks:

- According to the October 18 , 2001, issue of the *Seattle Post-Intelligencer*, a bus driver in Seattle posted a sign on his bus exhorting riders to beware of Muslims. When a passenger filed a complaint, the driver was suspended from work and the sign was removed.
- Elementary school students at the Park Day School in Montclair, California, organized a "Walk of Acceptance" to raise money for a hate crimes information hotline.
- In Cambridge, Massachusetts, members of a local synagogue joined other religious groups in a march against hate. "I'm inundated with calls from rabbis," said Tahir H. Chaudhry, president of the Islamic Center of Boston, a Wayland, Massachusetts mosque. (*Boston Globe*, September 17, 2001, B1)
- Harvard University president Larry Summers addressed a regular Friday prayer meeting for the school's Muslim community, emphasizing the university's commitment to its Islamic students. "We cannot tolerate any failure to respect individuals as individuals," he said. His expression of concern was typical of other college and university officials throughout the United States.
- In addition, local synagogues, churches, and community groups around the country demonstrated their concern in a variety of interreligious activities, congregational visits, and local programs.

Although the press seemed to publicize—and, some would argue, exaggerate—the extent of anti-Muslim hate crimes, some Muslim Americans criticized their coreligionists for wrapping themselves in the "mantle of victimhood." In an open letter to his fellow Muslims, M. A. Muqtedar Khan criticized the attitudes of many of his coreligionists. Writing in the electronic journal Salon.com on October 18, 2001, the Adrian College (Michigan) professor wrote: "Muslims love to live in the U.S. but also love to hate it. As an Indian Muslim, I know for sure that nowhere on earth, including India, will I get the same sense of dignity and respect that I have received in the U.S. . . . In many places hundreds of Americans have gathered around Islamic centers in symbolic gestures of protection and embrace of American Muslims. In patience and in tolerance ordinary Americans have demonstrated their extraordinary virtues." (Khan 2001)

Similar sentiments have been expressed on the Internet and in newspaper and magazine articles by a growing number of Muslim and Arab Americans. The founding of the American Islamic Congress (AIC) (see entry for this organization in chapter 6) raises hopes for better mutual understanding among Muslims and other Americans. On its Web site, the AIC explicitly notes its dual concerns: "We must work to guarantee our equal rights and prevent hate crimes. At the same time, we must condemn hate speech and calls for violence by Muslims. Hateful statements and actions by fellow Muslims threaten the reputation of our entire community. We must censure intolerance, whatever its source."

References

Belkin, Lisa. 1988. "Texas Judge Eases Sentence for Killer of 2 Homosexuals." *New York Times*, December 17, 8.

Fumento, Michael. 1996. "A Church Arson Epidemic? It's Smoke and Mirrors." *Wall Street Journal*, July 8, 8.

Gellman, Susan. 1991. "Sticks and Stones Can Put You in Jail, but Can Words Increase Your Sentence? Constitutional and Policy Dilemmas of Ethnic Intimidation Laws." *UCLA Law Review* (December): 333–396.

Gerstenfeld, Phyllis. 2004. *Hate Crimes: Causes, Controls and Controversies.* Thousand Oaks, CA: Sage Publications.

Greenawalt, Kent. 1992–1993. "Reflections on Justifications for Defining Crimes by the Category of Victim." pp. 617–628 in *Annual Survey of American Law*. New York: New York University School of Law.

"Hate Crime Charged in Death of Thung Phetakoune." 2001. *AsianWeek*, August 17–23. http://www.asianweek.com/2001_08_17/news_deathhate.html

Herek, Gregory M., and Kevin Berrill, eds. 1992. *Hate Crimes: Confronting Violence against Lesbians and Gay Men*. Newbury Park, CA: Sage Publications.

Human Rights Watch. November 2002. "We Are Not the Enemy: Hate Crimes against Arabs and Muslims and Those Perceived to be Arabs and Muslims." http://www.hrw.org

Jacobs, James B., and Kimberly A. Potter. 1997. "Hate Crimes: A Critical Perspective." Pp. 1–50 in *Crime and Justice: A Review of Research 22*, Michael Tonry, ed. Chicago: University of Chicago Press.

Jenness, Valerie, and Kendal Broad. 1997. *Hate Crimes: New Social Movements and the Politics of Violence.* New York: Aldine de Gruyter.

Khan, M. A. Muqtedar. October 18, 2001. "A Memo to American Muslims." http://www.salon.com

Kibelstis, Teresa Eileen. 1995. "Preventing Violence against Gay Men and Lesbians: Should Enhanced Penalties at Sentencing Extend to Bias Crimes Based on Victims' Sexual Orientation?" *Notre Dame Journal of Law, Politics and Public Policy,* 9 no. 1: 309–343.

Lawrence, Frederick M. 1999. *Punishing Hate: Bias Crimes under American Law.* Cambridge, MA: Harvard University Press.

National Asian Pacific American Legal Consortium (NAPALC). 2002. *2002 Audit of Violence Against Asian Pacific Americans: Tenth Annual Report.* http://www.napalc.org/literature/annual_report/2002_Audit.pdf.

———. 2000. *2000 Audit of Violence Against Asian Pacific Americans: Eighth Annual Report.* http://www.napalc.org/files/2000_Audit.pdf

"Why Are Churches Burning?" 1996. *USA Today* (June 28–30). (See other articles on church burning in these three issues.)

Winer, Anthony S. 1994. "Hate Crimes, Homosexuals and the Constitution." Pp. 387–438 in *Harvard Civil Rights Civil Liberties Review* (Summer).

2

Hate Crimes around the World

A ccording to a recent study, several dozen violent ethnic conflicts currently rage throughout the world. Some of these
conflicts are widely known: Catholics and Protestants in
Northern Ireland; Muslims and Christians in Pakistan; and Israeli Jews and Palestinian Arabs in Israel and the Palestinian National Authority. Other ethnic strife is not as well reported, but
the violence is nonetheless severe: Sinhalese and Tamils in Sri
Lanka; Chechens and Russians in the former Soviet Union; and
Berbers and Arabs in Algeria, to name only a few.

How do these conflicts—often involving violence directed at
individuals because of their race, religion, or ethnic background—differ from the type of violence we term "hate crimes"?
Although the distinction is not always easy to make, the above-
mentioned conflicts have been more accurately defined, by some
social scientists, as "ethno-national violence." Phyllis Gerstenfeld, the author of *Hate Crimes: Causes, Controls and Controversies,*
cites several differences. One significant distinction is that hate
crimes—as defined by U.S. statutory law and social science
scholars—are usually violations of criminal laws and are not acts
committed during a civil war or to achieve political sovereignty
or independence.

Gerstenfeld also notes that much of the literature on hate
crimes outside the United States focuses on Europe, whereas
Asia, Africa, and South America receive relatively little attention. Since it is impossible to cover the huge range of hate crimes
committed in almost 200 countries around the globe, the mater-

ial covered in this chapter is necessarily more limited and hopefully more comprehensive. This chapter focuses on the most statistically frequent victims of violent hate crimes around the world, both historically and in modern times: gay men and lesbians and Jews.

Gays and Lesbians

In 2001, Amnesty International issued one of the first human rights reports focused solely on the torture and mistreatment of gay men and lesbians around the world. Entitled *Crimes of Hate, Conspiracy of Silence: Torture and Ill-Treatment Based on Sexual Identity* (Amnesty Report # ACT 40/016/2001 available in print and on the Internet), the report includes some of the following disturbing information:

- In October 2000, the Namibian home affairs minister Jerry Ekandjo, according to state television, urged the police "to eliminate" gay men and lesbians from "the face of Namibia." (p. 5)
- In a widely reported September 1999 directive, President Yoweri Musevani of Uganda ordered the Criminal Investigations Department of this African country "to look for homosexuals, lock them up and charge them." (p. 1)
- Robert Mugabe, the dictatorial president of Zimbabwe, has allowed gay people to be harshly repressed for many years and has derided them "as less than human." (p. 4) He has also declared: "I don't believe that they [gays] have any rights at all." When the organization Gays and Lesbians of Zimbabwe set up a stall at the 1996 Zimbabwe International Book Fair in the capital city, Harare, the exhibit was set on fire by a student group. The Zimbabwe police did not arrest the arsonists and claimed the gays had brought the attacks on themselves.
- In Romania, there have been persistent reports of government-sanctioned abuse of homosexuals. In one instance, Mariana Cetiner, a Romanian lesbian, was beaten and tortured by prison guards in 1996 for "attempting to seduce another woman." (p. 13) Faced

with international pressure, the Romanian government released her from prison, and Cetiner left the country in 1998.

- Gay people have been subjected to both government and citizen abuse in Jamaica. In November 1996, four men arrested near the airport in Kingston were charged with gross indecency. Forced to remove all their clothes in public, the men were soon confronted by a threatening mob, which was reportedly incited by the police. Amnesty International claims that Jamaica's harsh laws against homosexuality encourage violence against gay people. In one instance, a young man whose gay relationship was discovered by his family was chased into a church by local residents, who shot and killed him. According to some reports, gay men who report attacks to the police are invariably met with indifference and are sometimes subjected to further abuse.

- A 1999 Amnesty International report on Afghanistan noted that a half dozen gay men were "crushed to death" by the former Taliban rulers.

- In Argentina, Brazil, Ecuador, France, Mexico, and other countries, Amnesty International has documented brutally violent attacks by police and prison officials against transgendered people.

- Some Russian lesbians have been subjected to police extortion and compulsory psychiatric treatment.

- Amnesty International has accused an Asian journalist organization for inciting hatred and advocating violence against gay people. In August 1999, in Sri Lanka, where homosexuality can be punished by a long prison sentence, the *Island* newspaper published a letter protesting a local lesbian conference. The letter writer called for police to "let loose convicted rapists among the jubilant but jaded jezebels when their assembly is in full swing so that those who are misguided may get a taste of the real thing." (p. 43) When the Sri Lankan lesbian and gay organization criticized the publication of the letter to the Sri Lankan Press Council, the media organization refused to condemn the newspaper. Indeed, the press council praised the letter writer's sentiments and claimed that lesbianism is an "act of sadism" and that "misguided and erratic women should be corrected and allowed to understand the true sense and reality of life."(p. 43)

Since the publication of the Amnesty International report in 2001, there have been a few positive developments but also several troubling incidents and trends. On the encouraging side, an international conference on antigay hate crimes took place in Sydney, Australia, in 2002. Organized in conjunction with the Sydney Gay Games held in October–November 2002, the Amnesty International Global Rights Conference sought to publicize incidents of ill treatment, discrimination, and torture directed at lesbians, gay men, bisexual, and transgendered people throughout the world. This Nobel Prize–winning organization actively lobbies national governments to investigate antigay hate crimes and demands that the perpetrators or government officials responsible should be brought to justice.

It is only in the last decade that international human rights organizations have publicized violence and discrimination against gay people around the world. In 1991 Amnesty International broadened its mandate to include people imprisoned because of their sexual orientation. A few years later, Human Rights Watch, another international human rights organization, began to publish reports on discrimination and violence committed against gay men and lesbians around the world. Although many Western countries—including the United States, Canada, Germany, the United Kingdom, Australia, New Zealand, and Israel—specifically outlaw hate crimes and discrimination based on sexual orientation, many other countries—most notably those in the Middle East, Asia, and Africa—do not provide such legal protections. Human rights activists and organizations cite a variety of international treaties and conventions that would deter or prevent violence against gay people. These international conventions and agreements include the following:

- Article 2 of the Universal Declaration of Human Rights (1948) asserts all human beings are entitled to the rights described in the document "without distinction of any kind, such as race, colour, sex, language, religion, political or other opinion, national or social origin, property, birth or other status."
- The UN Convention against Torture and Other Cruel, Inhuman or Degrading Treatment or Punishment

includes declarations under Articles 21 and 22 that recognize the authority of the Human Rights Committee to consider individual complaints.

* Other international agreements often cited are the International Covenant on Economic Social and Cultural Rights, the UN Convention on the Elimination of All Forms of Discrimination against Women and the International Covenant on Civil and Political Rights (ICCPR). Human rights activists often cite Article 6 of the ICCPR to condemn governmental executions of individuals based solely on their sexual orientation: "Every human being has the inherent right to life. This right shall be protected by law. No one shall be arbitrarily deprived of his life."

Some legal scholars, however, complain that these conventions and covenants are too ambiguously worded. Writing in the law journal *Law and Sexuality,* Duke University professor Debra L. DeLaet notes that "the lack of specific language protecting gay, lesbian and bisexual persons from discrimination is indicative of the lack of intent on the part of signatories to the major human rights documents to extend protection on these grounds."(De-Laet, 1997, 35) However, James D. Wilets, writing in the *Albany Law Review,* suggests that the "breadth of the wording indicates that the categories listed as protected are not exclusive and that indeed, the provisions should be interpreted as expansively as possible."(Wilets 1997, 1033)

Regardless of how positively these international human rights documents may be interpreted, many countries around the world still harshly deny such rights to their citizens. Iran, Mauritania, Pakistan, Saudi Arabia, Sudan, United Arab Emirates, and provinces of northern Nigeria impose the death penalty for individuals who engage in same sex relations. Occasionally, these brutal punishments are enforced. (A useful chart listing the legality of same-sex relationships of countries throughout the world can be found at http://www.sodomy-laws.org.) Amnesty International has documented some of these cases and syndicated columnist Jack Anderson has written that "three homosexual men were publicly beheaded in one of the city squares of Nahavand (Iran) and two accused lesbians were stoned to death in Langrood (Iran). (Wilets, p. 997, cited in footnote 29; *San Francisco Chronicle*; January 22, 1990, A17)

The laws of some countries are remarkably graphic in their description of the crime and the resultant punishment. Writing in the fall 1994 issue of the *Hastings International and Comparative Law Review*, James D. Wilets provides a translation of the Iranian statutes. (In addition, his article—although a bit dated—is an outstanding source for much hard-to-find information on violence against gays around the world.) The Islamic Penal Code of Iran declares that the punishment for sodomy is death. Article 121 provides that "punishment for Tafhiz (rubbing of the thighs or the buttocks) and the like committed by two men without entry shall be a hundred lashes for each of them." Article 129 provides that "punishment for lesbianism is a hundred lashes for each party," and Article 131 provides that "if an act of lesbianism is repeated three times and punishment is enforced each time, death sentence will be issued a fourth time." (Wilets 1994, 28)

Government-sanctioned punishment is not the only type of violence committed against gay people around the world. Although Australia has strict laws against hate crimes, a study conducted and released in 2002 by the Australian Institute of Criminology noted that there were seventy-four homicides over the previous twenty years committed against homosexuals. The institute's director Adam Graycar said these homicides were particularly disturbing: "We discovered so much more brutality than in other kinds of homicides. These killings were more likely to be done as sport." (Pollard 2002, August 13) Some of the murder weapons included a hammer, saw, spade, fire extinguisher, and crossbow. Many victims died from intense pummeling and beatings.

Brazil has reportedly the largest number of murders committed against homosexuals. The Gay Group of Bahia (Grupo Gay da Bahia-GBB), the oldest gay rights group in Brazil, reports a total of 2,092 such murders between the years 1980 and 2001, an average of 104 homicides each year. Compiled from a variety of sources—there are no official government statistics of these crimes committed in Brazil—these figures indicate a very disturbing phenomenon in the largest South American country. According to GGB publications, transvestites are proportionately the most vulnerable group; the total population of transvestites in Brazil is under 10,000 individuals, yet although their population is relatively small, they are subjected to a larger number of crimes. Like similar crimes in Australia and other countries, many crimes against gays in Brazil are marked by excessive brutality, including multiple stabbings, strangulation, suffocation, and even torture. Luiz Mott, a professor of anthropology at the Federal University of Bahia and the president of GGB, noted that "only 10 percent of those responsible are brought to justice and only 4 percent are sentenced. Impunity encourages the boldness of the criminals."("Brazil: World Champion in the Murder of Homosexuals")

The issue of the rights of gay men and lesbians in the Muslim and Arab world has been a particularly bitter debate. On the one hand, many Islamic countries charge that Western Christian Europe has colonized their lands and religiously persecuted and negatively stereotyped Muslims for centuries. Yet many gay and lesbian Muslims living in predominantly Islamic nations accuse their own societies of rampant discrimination, resulting in often brutal government-sponsored and local citizen violence directed against them. Indeed, many Muslims have fled to Western countries in order to avoid the persecution in their native lands.

The Organization of the Islamic Conference, which represents the more than fifty predominantly Muslim countries in the world, has been vociferous at international conferences in its condemnation of homosexuality. In addition, the rise of Islamic fundamentalism has enhanced the conservative views of many traditional Muslims on the nature of human sexuality. Human rights organizations, which have been in the forefront of defending the rights of persecuted Muslims in Western countries, have recently begun to publicize the plight of gay Muslims. As noted above, the Islamic Republic of Iran metes out very severe punishment for homosexual behavior. In March 2004, Human Rights Watch issued a report entitled *In a Time of Torture: The Assault on Justice in Egypt's Crackdown on Homosexual Conduct*. This report examined the police entrapment of gay male Egyptians in May 2001 and the general treatment of this minority in the world's largest Arab country.

Despite the ongoing conflict between Palestinian Arabs and Israeli Jews, many gay Palestinian men risk their lives to cross into Israel, asserting that they feel much safer there. According to an October 22, 2003, BBC report, there are approximately 300 gay Palestinians secretly living and working in Israel. Several other journalistic accounts describe the plight of these young men who fled the Palestinian National Authority because they feared the police, their neighbors, and even their own families. In June 2004, two British gay rights organizations were attacked at a pro-

Palestinian rally in London. Peter Tatchell, a leading British gay rights advocate, who, ironically, has been an active supporter of Palestinian Arabs for many years, complained that "gay Palestinians live in fear of arrest, detention without trial, torture and execution at the hands of Palestinian police and security services. They also risk abduction and so-called honor killing by vengeful family members and vigilante mobs, as well as punishment beatings and murder by Palestinian political groups such as Hamas and Yasser Arafat's Fatah movement."("Gays Attacked at Palestine Rights Protest" 2004)

In June 2004 intolerance toward homosexuals was openly manifested several thousand miles away in predominantly Hindu India. Some movie theaters in the western state of Gujarat stopped showing a film about a lesbian love affair because of fears of attacks by religious Hindus. The film censorship came shortly after violent protests by right-wing Hindus who vandalized cinemas in several Indian cities, claiming the Bollywood movie *Girlfriend* violated India's traditional culture.

In neighboring Nepal, members of the gay rights group the Blue Diamond Society charged that they were abused and beaten by local police in July 2004. The organization claims that gays and transvestites are frequently attacked and sexually abused by local law enforcement officers.

Hate crimes against gay people, unfortunately, span the globe. Yet many local cultures and various religions claim that the secular and modern West is trying to impose its own morals and values on their venerable religious traditions. The situation seems particularly acute in many parts of Europe. The so-called clash of civilizations between Islam and the West has been increasingly heightened in recent years. Pim Fortuyn, the gay Dutch candidate for prime minister, was assassinated on May 6, 2002, because of his reportedly critical views of recent Muslim immigrants and their attitudes toward other religions and lifestyles, which he vigorously denounced in the months leading up to the election. A few years ago, a leftist German newspaper, *Taz*, published a front-page article about Muslims perpetuating hate crimes against gays. The article claimed that 39 percent of reported antigay violence in Berlin is committed by young men from Muslim communities.

While the debate about homosexuality in the United States has mostly focused on whether gay men and lesbians should enjoy the same social and economic rights as their fellow citizens—

such as marriage, child adoption, and employee benefits—the situation is qualitatively different in many parts of the world. Some international gay rights organizations would not consider raising such issues in countries where the major battle is to obtain rudimental rights and protections: combating state-sanctioned and religiously approved violence against gay men, lesbians, and transgendered people.

Jews

"In fighting anti-Semitism, we fight for the future of humanity," declared Kofi Annan, secretary-general of the United Nations, on June 21, 2004. The chief UN official added:

> Anti-Semitism has flourished even in communities where Jews have never lived, and it has been a harbinger of discrimination against others. The rise of anti-Semitism anywhere is a threat to people everywhere. . . . And a human rights agenda that fails to address anti-Semitism denies its own history. . . . We owe it to ourselves, as well as to our Jewish brothers and sisters, to stand firmly against the particular tide of hatred that anti-Semitism represents. And that means we must be prepared to examine the nature of today's manifestations of anti-Semitism more closely. ("Throughout History" 2004)

Annan was speaking at the first UN conference ever held to combat anti-Jewish hate and violence. Established only a few years after the Holocaust, the UN has hosted many conferences against racism, discrimination, and unfair treatment of women but never a meeting solely devoted to the "longest hatred"— the term coined by Hebrew University professor, Robert Wistrich—contemporary violence and prejudice directed against Jews.

Since the breakdown of the Oslo Agreement between Palestinian Arabs and Israeli Jews in September 2000, there has been an alarming increase in anti-Jewish incidents throughout the world. Some commentators try to minimize these incidents as manifestations of critical attitudes toward Israeli government policy, which, they claim, will subside when the Arab-Israeli dispute is finally resolved. Yet, as the following short random list demonstrates, the incidents are rarely related to the conflict in the Middle East: a violent attack on Jewish students leaving a Paris school; swastika daubings on Jewish cemetery monuments in New Zealand, on a grocery store in Germany and on the walls of the Jewish community building in Caracas, Venezuela; and the firebombing of a Jewish library in Montreal. Even more alarming, women, children, and elderly Jewish men have been beaten in Lausanne, Antwerp, Vienna, Berlin, and London.

In 2003 the Stephen Roth Institute for the Study of Contemporary Anti-Semitism and Racism recorded a total of 360 "serious" incidents worldwide: 30 major attacks (including shootings, knifings, bombings, and arson) and 330 major violent incidents (i.e., vandalism and physical aggression without the use of a weapon). This number indicates a small increase compared to 2002, when 311 serious incidents were recorded. Unlike the Federal Bureau of Investigation's annual hate crime report, which records only the number and type of incident without using adjectives such as *serious*, the Stephen Roth Institute uses such loosely defined terms in its year-end world summary. Nevertheless, the institute does itemize and classify defined types of hate crimes by country. The five countries with the highest number of anti-Jewish incidents in 2003–2004 were France, the United Kingdom, Russia, Germany, and Canada.

A report by the French Interior Ministry recorded 503 anti-Jewish acts in 2003, whereas 510 such incidents had already been recorded in the first six months of 2004. The major French Jewish organization, Conseil Représentatif des Institutions Juives de France, noted that the number of violent attacks against Jews rose from 185 in 2002 to 233 in 2003; assaults on individuals increased from 75 in 2002 to 100 in 2003. Moreover, 50 percent of all incidents in 2003 were directed against Jewish youngsters under the age of eighteen. Hardly a week passes without the news media reporting a disturbing anti-Jewish incident occurring somewhere in France. The situation has become so alarming that a few hundred French Jews moved to Israel in July 2003. Despite regular denunciations of anti-Jewish violence by French government officials, including President Jacques Chirac, many French Jews have expressed disgust toward the tardy and weak response of their government. Although there has been some recent vandalism against Muslim sites, including a few mosques, the vast majority of hate crimes in France have been directed against Jews by mostly North African Muslim young people.

According to the Community Security Trust (CST), a British Jewish communal organization, there were 532 anti-Jewish incidents in 2004, including 83 assaults. This total was 42 percent higher than the 2003 figure. In March 2004 alone, the CST reported 100 incidents. In the worst incident, a Jewish adolescent had his jaw shattered in Southampton, an English coastal city. According to the Stephen Roth Institute, five incidents in 2002 were considered life threatening, and seven victims required hospitalization. There were 55 incidents involving physical damage and vandalism of communal property, including the desecration of seven Jewish cemeteries. In June 2002, four juveniles were convicted for the desecration of the Rainsough Jewish cemetery in January of that year. They were ordered to pay compensation and damages.

In March 2003, in partial reaction to these and other hate crimes, the Crown Prosecution Service—the national agency responsible for bringing criminal cases to court—issued a document to explain hate crimes legislation to prosecutors, victims, and the general public. In addition, the government was planning a new procedure to record statistics on the ethnicity of the criminals charged with hate crimes and their victims. London's Metropolitan Police also promoted an advertising campaign against hate crimes, which was soon followed by a police crackdown that resulted in more than 100 arrests for racist and antigay offenses.

Russia, which has a long and ignoble anti-Jewish history, still has a festering problem of violent and other types of prejudice against Jews. The number of anti-Jewish incidents has risen since 2002. Since that time, at least four Jews have been murdered but the motivation has not been firmly established and may have been criminal, not religious. In 2002, there were eighteen incidents in which booby traps, both real and fake, were attached to anti-Jewish signboards. On May 27, 2002, Moscow resident Tatiana Sapunova was severely injured when she tried to pull down such a signboard. Particularly disturbing are the violent attacks against Jewish clergy. On January 14, 2005, Rabbi Alexander Lakshin, a U.S. citizen, and Rabbi Reuven Kuravskii were attacked while walking with two children near a Jewish center in Moscow. The perpetrators shouted anti-Jewish epithets and injured Lakshin, who was hospitalized with head injuries and a broken bone. Only a few hours earlier, a Jewish couple had been attacked in the same place. Jewish organizations expressed their concern over the frequency of these attacks and called on the police to ensure the safety of members of their community. (www.tau.ac.il/Anti-Semitism/updates.html) In March 2002, a group of Moscow skinheads attacked a Jewish youth, inflicting severe injuries that resulted in his death.

The Stephen Roth Institute notes that the number and severity of anti-Jewish incidents in Russia may be underreported. The organization cites various problems, including the troubled relations between the members of the Jewish communities throughout Russia and the local authorities, as well as the lack of effective monitoring techniques that are well-established in longtime democratic countries.

Unlike European countries and Russia, which have witnessed age-old religious and ethnic prejudice against Jews, Canada does not share this historical intolerance. Yet, disturbingly, the number of anti-Jewish incidents increased 27 percent from 2002 to 2003 and has doubled since 2001. Almost 600 cases of harassment, vandalism, and violence were reported in 2003, including fifteen cases of assault mostly directed against young people. According to the Canadian League for Human Rights of B'nai Brith Canada, the number of incidents in 2003 was the highest recorded by the League in its twenty-one years of recordkeeping.

In March and April 2004, a spate of anti-Jewish hate crimes occurred in Toronto and Montreal, including cemetery and synagogue desecrations. The most serious incident was the firebombing of the United Talmud Torah elementary school in Montreal on April 5, 2004, the eve of the Jewish holiday of Passover. The Canadian Prime Minister Paul Martin vehemently condemned the attack declaring, "This is not my Canada. This is not our Canada." (Toronto Star, April 7, 2004, p. A26)

The alarming rise of anti-Jewish incidents and overt prejudice throughout the world has evoked consternation among many governments and human rights organizations. In March 2004, the Vienna-based European Monitoring Centre on Racism and Xenophobia (EUMC) issued two reports on anti-Semitism in Europe. The main report, *Manifestations of Antisemitism in the EU 2002 –2003*, analyzes data up to October 2003 and proposes policies to counter anti-Semitism. The second report, *Percep-*

tions of Antisemitism in the European Union, contains interviews with members of the Jewish community.

Although the 345-page main report details the rise of anti-Jewish violence in several countries, including Belgium, England, France, Germany, and the Netherlands, some critics charge that the report's authors were negligent in not assigning responsibility for these crimes. Serge Cwajgenbaum, secretary-general of the European Jewish Congress, declared that it is "contradictory that the EUMC puts an emphasis on 'white, right-wing perpetrators', where as the report reveals that the majority of attacks in most countries are committed by young Muslims of North African origin." He concludes, "How can we effectively fight anti-Semitism when we refuse to identity the true perpetrators?" ("A Report Halfway There" 2004)

Amir Zaidan, the director of the Islamic Religious Studies Institute in Vienna, Austria responded, however, that the report contained an unfair description of the two groups of perpetrators. "Religion is mentioned for Muslims," he said, "but no religion is attached to white young people." (http://www/euro-correspondent.com, April 3, 2004)

In April 2004, two months before the first UN conference on anti-Semitism, the Organization for Security Cooperation in Europe held a conference in Berlin that was attended by fifty-five countries. At the conference's conclusion, the leaders of these nations unveiled a landmark "Berlin Declaration" against anti-Semitism, pledging to intensify efforts to combat anti-Jewish prejudice and violence in all its manifestations and to promote and strengthen tolerance and nondiscrimination.

In response to the global upsurge of anti-Jewish violence, the U.S. Congress passed the Global Anti-Semitism Review Act of 2004, which became law on October 16, 2004. This legislation (Public Law 108-332) mandated the U.S. Department of State to a) issue a one-time report surveying the extent of anti-Jewish activity throughout the world, b) include sections on anti-Semitic acts and incitement in both of the following State Department publications: *Country Reports on Human Rights Practices* and the *Annual Report on International Religious Freedom*, and c) establish within the State Department a special Office to Monitor and Combat Anti-Semitism, to be headed by a special envoy. The one-time Report on Global Anti-Semitism covered the period from July 1, 2003 to December 15, 2004. (http://www.state.gov/g/drl/rls/40258.htm)

References

"A Report Halfway There." 2004. Press release, March 31. European Jewish Congress website, http://www.eurojewcong.org/english/press/press.php?code_communique=33

"Brazil: World Champion in the Murder of Homosexuals." International Gay and Lesbian website, http://www.igla.info

DeLaet, Debra L. 1997. "Don't Ask, Don't Tell: Where Is the Protection against Sexual Orientation Discrimination in International Human Rights Law?" *Law and Sexuality* 7: 31–53.

"Gays Attacked at Palestine Rights Protest." 2004. Press release, May 15. OutRage Organization website, http://www.outrage.org.uk/pressrelease.asp?ID=189.

Pollard, Ruth. 2002. "Attacks on Gays Extraordinarily Brutal: Report." *The Age* [Australia], August 13, 2002.

"Throughout History Anti-Semitism Unique Manifestation of Hatred, Intolerance, Persecution Says Secretary-General in Remarks to Headquarters Seminar." United Nations Press Release SG/SM/9375 HR/4774 PI/1590. http://www.un.org/News/Press/docs/2004/sgsm9375.doc.htm

United Nations. The United Nations International Covenant on Civil and Political Rights. http://www.hrweb.org/legal/cpr.html

———. Universal Declaration of Human Rights. http://www.un.org/Overview/rights.html

Wilets, James D. 1997. "Conceptualizing Private Violence against Sexual Minorities as Gendered Violence." *Albany Law Review* 60, no. 3: 989–1050.

———. 1994. "International Human Rights Law and Sexual Orientation." *Hastings International and Comparative Law Review* 18, no. 1: 1–120.

3

Chronology

Because the number of individual violent hate crimes committed in the United States during the past few decades is too large for a comprehensive list, the following chronology is necessarily selective. The list has been compiled to demonstrate the wide range of these crimes and to illustrate why some groups are calling for legislation to deter and prevent their future occurrence. The chronology also contains notable events in the legislative and judicial history of hate crimes laws. Much of the information regarding crimes committed before 1979 has been adapted from the outstanding reference work *Racial and Religious Violence in the United States: A Chronology* (New York: Garland, 1991) by Michael and Judy Ann Newton.

The chronology begins in 1955, the year Emmett Till was lynched in Mississippi, an event many historians consider the beginning of the modern civil rights movement. In spring 2004, the U.S. Department of Justice reopened this historic case to investigate new information about other possible perpetrators. (For an outstanding cultural history of this incident, see Stephen J. Whitfield, *A Death in the Delta: The Story of Emmett Till* [Free Press, 1988].)

1955   May 7. The Reverend George W. Lee, an official of the National Association for the Advancement of Colored People (NAACP), is shot and killed on a highway in Belzoni, Mississippi.

August 13. Lamar Smith, a vocal supporter for black voter registration, is shot and killed on the lawn of the county courthouse in Brookhaven, Mississippi.

1955, August 28. Emmett Till, a fourteen-year-old black boy, is
cont.   kidnapped, shot, and drowned in a river near Money,
        Mississippi, for allegedly whistling at a white man's
        wife. His killers are acquitted after a controversial trial.
        This notorious incident is often considered the catalyst
        for the modern civil rights movement. Two books pub-
        lished in 2002 and 2003 and a television documentary re-
        veal possibly new information on this case.

        October 22. John Reese, a sixteen-year-old African Amer-
        ican, is killed and two other black youths are wounded
        by white gunmen at a café in Mayflower, Texas. The at-
        tack is one of several violent incidents aimed at discour-
        aging the black community from building a new school.

1956   January 30. A bomb explodes at the Montgomery, Al-
        abama, home of the Reverend Martin Luther King Jr.

        February 3–4. The admission of black student Autherine
        Lucy to the University of Alabama sparks a riot from lo-
        cal Ku Klux Klan (KKK) members and white students.
        Another riot occurs on February 6, which leads univer-
        sity administrators to suspend and later expel Lucy
        from the university. In April 1988, the university re-
        voked her expulsion and she re-enrolled. More than
        thirty-five years later, Autherine Lucy received an M.A.
        degree in elementary education at the University of Al-
        abama.

        April 11. Six Klan members assault singer Nat "King"
        Cole during a performance at the Birmingham, Alabama,
        municipal auditorium.

1957   January 23. Willie Edwards, a black truck driver, is ab-
        ducted by Klan members in Montgomery, Alabama.
        They accuse Edwards of attacking white women and
        force him at gunpoint to leap from a river bridge. His
        death, considered accidental until 1976, is charged as a
        homicide when a Klan member confesses to the crime.
        Three other Klan members are indicted, but the charges
        are dismissed when the prosecution fails to prove that
        the cause of Edwards's death was drowning. In 1998

Montgomery district attorney Ellen Brooks orders an exhumation, and the coroner finds the death was indeed caused by drowning.

1958 March 16. The Jewish Community Center in Nashville, Tennessee, is dynamited.

August 24–25. Two formerly all-white schools in Deep Creek, North Carolina, are destroyed by fire after they were scheduled to be integrated.

June 29. A black miner removes a package of dynamite from a Baptist church in Birmingham, Alabama, whose pastor is civil rights leader Reverend F. L. Shuttlesworth. The dynamite explodes in the street, breaking windows in a four-block area.

July 7. An early morning explosion damages the home of the Reverend Warren Carr, the white chairman of the Durham, North Carolina, Human Relations Committee, a local group devoted to improving racial relationships.

October 12. The Temple, a synagogue in Atlanta, is bombed at 3:30 A.M., causing an estimated $200,000 in damage. The blast tears an eighteen-square-foot hole in a side entrance of the building and shatters windows of a nearby building and apartment house. Twenty minutes after the blast, a caller says it was the "last empty building I'll blow up in Atlanta." The bombings and phone calls parallel similar attacks on synagogues in Miami and Jacksonville, Florida, and Birmingham, Alabama, during this time.

1959 April 25. Mack Parker, a black truck driver, is taken from his jail cell, where he was being held for suspected rape, and is lynched by a mob of whites in Poplarville, Mississippi. An area prosecutor refuses to accept evidence by the Federal Bureau of Investigation (FBI) naming several of the lynchers. When the state trooper who arrested Parker offers his gun to the husband of the rape victim so that he can shoot Parker, the husband refuses because his wife's description of the perpetrator is unclear.

1960   January 7–8. Teenage vandals are arrested in a wave of anti-Jewish vandalism at synagogues and other buildings in New York, Philadelphia, Chicago, Boston, and more than a dozen other cities.

April 23. William Moore, a northern white civil rights advocate, is shot and killed in Attalla, Alabama, during a one-man civil rights march from Tennessee to Mississippi. On April 27, a local white man is charged with the murder.

1961   September 25. Herbert Lee, a cotton farmer and black voter registration organizer, is shot and killed by E. H. Hurst in the town of Liberty, Mississippi. Hurst, a white neighbor and state legislator, is never brought to trial.

1962   April 9. Roman Ducksworth, a black soldier, is shot and killed by a white policeman for refusing to sit in the back of a bus in Taylorsville, Mississippi.

1963   June 8. The county sheriff and police chief of Winona, Mississippi, and three other whites are indicted on federal charges of brutalizing black prisoners.

June 12. Medgar Evers, a black NAACP leader, is killed by a sniper in the driveway of his home in Jackson, Mississippi. The FBI finds that the murderer is Byron De La Beckwith, a member of the Ku Klux Klan and White Citizens' Council. However, two trials for the murder result in hung juries. In 1967 Beckwith runs for governor of Mississippi with the backing of the Klan. After prosecutors try Beckwith a third time, he is convicted on February 5, 1994, and sentenced to life imprisonment at the Central Mississippi Correctional Facility.

September 4 . The home of Arthur Shores, a black attorney in Birmingham, Alabama, is bombed a second time, touching off a riot that results in one death and eighteen injuries. On the same day, 125 members of the National States Rights Party, a neo-Nazi racist organization, scuffle with police outside a recently integrated school.

September 15. A bomb explodes at the Sixteenth Street Baptist Church in Birmingham, Alabama, during Sunday services. Four black girls are killed: Addie Mae Collins, Cynthia Wesley, Carole Robertson, and Denise McNair. Another person is blinded. African Americans riot in response to the explosion. Alabama state troopers, under the command of Al Lingo, a "good friend" of the Klan, try to disperse the rioters. During the outbreak, a police officer kills Johnny Robinson, a black youth. Another black youth, thirteen-year-old Virgil Ware, is also fatally shot by two white youths.

1964   January 31. Louis Allen, a witness to the 1961 murder of Herbert Lee, is shot and killed in the front yard of his home in Liberty, Mississippi.

April 7. The Reverend Bruce Klunder, a white minister from Cleveland, Ohio, is crushed to death by a bulldozer while protesting the construction of a segregated school.

May 2. Henry Dee and Charlie Moore, two African American teenagers, are abducted by Klan members in Meadville, Mississippi. Two months later, their bodies are pulled from a nearby river. Although murder charges are filed against two Ku Klux Klan members, the charges are later dismissed.

June 10. A white mob hurling bricks and sulfuric acid breaks through police lines to attack black demonstrators in St. Augustine, Florida. Police use tear gas to disperse the rioters.

June 21. Civil rights workers Michael Schwerner, James Chaney, and Andrew Goodman are arrested for allegedly speeding in Philadelphia, Mississippi. They are released to a waiting group of Klan members, who murder the men on a rural road and bury them in an earthen dam. On August 4, their bodies are recovered. Although the state of Mississippi refuses to file murder charges, the seven Klan members are later convicted of federal civil rights violations.

1964, June 25. A black church in Longdale, Mississippi, is dam-
cont. aged by a firebomb.

June 26. Arsonists burn a black church in Clinton, Mississippi.

July 6. Two black churches in Raleigh, Mississippi, are
burned to the ground.

July 10. Three rabbis active in black voter registration
programs in Hattiesburg, Mississippi, are assaulted with
metal clubs. On August 8, two white men plead guilty to
the attacks, pay $500 fines, and receive ninety-day sus-
pended sentences.

July 11. Klan members in Colbert, Georgia, ambush a carload of black army reserve officers returning home from
summer training exercises. Lt. Col. Lemuel Penn is killed
by shotgun blasts; his companions escape unharmed.
Two Klan members are acquitted of murder charges, but
both are later sentenced to prison for federal civil rights
violations.

1965 February 10. Deputies armed with electric prods force
civil rights marchers out of Selma, Alabama, leaving
them stranded more than a mile from town.

February 17. A voter registration headquarters is set on
fire by Ku Klux Klan members in Laurel, Mississippi.

February 18. Jimmy Lee Jackson, a black civil rights
worker, is beaten and fatally shot in Marion, Alabama,
when state law enforcement officers attack about 400
black demonstrators. While Jackson lies in a Selma, Alabama, hospital, police serve him an arrest warrant. He
dies on February 26.

March 9. In Selma, Alabama, violent racists attack the
Reverend James Reeb, a Boston minister active in the
civil rights movement. He is fatally beaten. The defendants are acquitted by a jury that had earlier discussed
their verdict with Sheriff Jim Clark, a professed racist.

March 21. A desegregated cafe is firebombed in Vicksburg, Mississippi.

March 25. Viola Liuzzo, a white civil rights worker from Detroit, is ambushed and killed by Klan members in Lowndesboro, Alabama.

March 29. Members of the Klan hurl a tear gas grenade at blacks in Bogalusa, Louisiana.

May 13. An African American church in Oxford, Alabama, is bombed.

May 17. A gas station and a motel owned by vocal Klan opponents are bombed in Laurel, Mississippi.

June 2. Oneal Moore and Creed Rogers, two black sheriff's deputies, are ambushed while on patrol in Bogalusa, Louisiana; Rogers is wounded, and Moore is fatally injured. On June 5, gunshots are fired at the home of the law enforcement official investigating the murder. Although Klan member Ray McElveen was arrested for the murder, he was released a few weeks later because local authorities claimed not to have enough evidence for a trial. Since that time, no one has been arrested or prosecuted for these crimes. In June 2002, 100 people gathered in Moore's hometown to honor his memory and his surviving partner, Creed Rogers, who was then eighty years old. The FBI is still offering a $40,000 reward for information leading to a conviction of the murderer.

June 16. Klan members shoot at a black-owned nightclub and also at the state vice president of the NAACP in separate incidents in Laurel, Mississippi.

July 1. In Laurel, Mississippi, Klansmen burn the headquarter of a civil rights organization and thirteen homes occupied by civil rights workers.

July 15. Willie Brewster, a black man, is shot and killed in Anniston, Alabama, by night riders following a rally organized by the National States Rights Party.

1965,   July 16. While police stand and watch, white mobs attack
cont.   black protesters in Bogalusa, Louisiana. After the seventh
assault, police arrest two white attackers. On July 17,
whites spray water and hurl rocks and bottles at black
demonstrators.

In Greensboro, Alabama, about seventy-five black
demonstrators are attacked by a white mob armed with
clubs, hammers, and rubber hoses. Seventeen demonstrators require hospitalization.

July 18. An African American church in Elmwood, Alabama, is burned. Arsonists also burn two black churches
in Greensboro, Alabama. The Imperial Wizard of the
Klan, Sam Bowers, boasts that the Klan is responsible for
more than sixteen arson fires in Laurel, Mississippi.

July 27. Two black homes are firebombed in Ferriday,
Louisiana. The office of the Congress of Racial Equality
(CORE) is firebombed in New Orleans, Louisiana.

July 31. The headquarters of the Council of Federated Organizations, in Columbia, Mississippi, is damaged by fire
and subjected to gunfire in a predawn attack.

August 20. Jonathan Daniels, a white seminary student
on leave from the Episcopal Theological School in Cambridge, Massachusetts, is shot and killed by a part-time
deputy sheriff and Klan member in Hayneville, Alabama. Robert F. Morrisoe, a Catholic priest from
Chicago, is also seriously wounded in the same attack.

August 23. The Reverend Donald A. Thompson, a Unitar-
ian minister who is involved in civil rights work in Jackson, Mississippi, is seriously wounded in an ambush.

August 26. At a rally in Plymouth, North Carolina, Klan
members beat twenty-seven black protesters.

August 27. George Metcalfe, an NAACP official, is
maimed when a bomb explodes in his car in Natchez,

Mississippi. Although FBI agents find Klan members responsible, no one is prosecuted for the explosion.

September 26. A black church in Jones County, Mississippi, is burned by arsonists.

October 4. In Crawfordsville, Georgia, the Grand Dragon of the KKK assaults a black demonstrator.

November 18. Gunshots are fired at four civil rights workers in Victoria, Virginia, injuring one person.

November 29. Three persons are injured from a car bomb planted near a black-owned grocery store in Vicksburg, Mississippi, close to the site of a local civil rights meeting.

December 15. Lee Culbreath, a black newspaper carrier, is shot and killed by two white men in Hamburg, Arkansas. Police charge two Klan members with the murder.

December 31. A store owned by John Nosser—the mayor of Natchez, Mississippi, and a vocal opponent of the Klan—is destroyed by arson.

1966 January 2. An African American church in Newton, Georgia, is burned. Anonymous callers threaten the life of the local sheriff if he investigates the incident.

January 3. Samuel Younge Jr., a black college student, is shot and killed in Tuskegee, Alabama, for trying to use a "whites only" restroom.

January 10. After volunteering to pay the poll taxes for black voters, civil rights activist Vernon Dahmer is fatally burned in a firebomb attack in his Hattiesburg, Mississippi, home. Imperial Wizard Sam Bowers of the Ku Klux Klan is to be tried four times for the murder; the trials resulted in deadlocked juries. On August 21, 1998, a multiracial jury convicted Bowers of murder and arson.

1966,   January 30. The Atlanta-based Southern Regional Coun-
cont.   cil issues a report stating that southern whites had killed
         a total of fourteen blacks and civil rights workers in 1965
         and three blacks thus far in 1966.

February 24. A recently integrated high school in Elba, Alabama, is damaged by two dynamite blasts.

April 2. Bombs explode at two swimming pools in Baton Rouge, Louisiana, that were scheduled to be integrated facilities.

April 9. Bombs destroy a black church in Ernul, North Carolina.

June 6. Civil rights worker James Meredith is wounded by three gunshots during a one-person "march against fear" in Hernando, Mississippi. The hospital treating Meredith receives threats from a caller describing himself as a Klan member.

June 10. Ben White, an elderly black man, is kidnapped, shot, and killed in Natchez, Mississippi, by Klan members who believe the murder will attract the Reverend Martin Luther King Jr. to the area. The Klan members are acquitted of murder charges on December 9, 1967. White's relatives file a civil suit for wrongful death and win more than $1 million in damages on November 13, 1968. The defendant, Ernest Avants, avoided paying any money by placing his assets in his first wife's name.

June 17. News reporters covering a civil rights rally in Greenwood, Mississippi, escape injury after two poisonous snakes are tossed into their vehicle.

June 21. Civil rights marchers are assaulted by white mobs in Philadelphia, Mississippi, while police watch.

June 24. A mob of whites pelt the Reverend Martin Luther King Jr. and other demonstrators with eggs and missiles in Philadelphia, Mississippi. Arsonists destroy a Catholic church in Carthage, Mississippi.

July 1. Klan members bomb a store in Milwaukee, Wisconsin, owned by the former president of the Wisconsin Civil Rights Congress.

July 3. Klan members pelt police with stones in Lebanon, Ohio, after two Klan members are arrested for violating the state's antimask law.

July 10. Two whites are arrested after firing a submachine gun at a federal officer and two civil rights workers outside an African American church in Grenada, Mississippi.

July 18. Jeering whites assault civil rights marchers in Jacksonville, Florida.

July 20. A black-owned store in Jacksonville, Florida, is firebombed.

July 28. Following a rally of the National States Rights Party, white gangs invade a black neighborhood in Baltimore, Maryland. Three members are charged with inciting a riot and are sentenced to a two-year prison term.

July 30. Charles Triggs, a black bricklayer, is shot and killed by two white gunmen in Bogalusa, Louisiana.

July 31. White mobs stone a civil rights procession led by the Reverend Martin Luther King Jr. in Chicago. Fifty-four persons are injured, including two police officers.

September 12–13. A mob of almost 400 whites riot in Grenada, Mississippi, in opposition to school integration. Police stand by while blacks and news reporters are beaten with ax handles, chains, and steel pipes. Two black youths are hospitalized with serious injuries.

September 24. Arsonists destroy the Cleveland, Ohio, home of the Reverend John Compton, a black minister.

October 5. A black church in Richmond, Virginia, is bombed.

1966, November 8. Violent incidents against blacks participat-
cont. ing in local elections occur in Lowndes County, Alabama, and in Amite County, Mississippi.

November 20. James Motley, a black man, is beaten to death in a jail cell in Wetumpka, Alabama. A jury acquits Sheriff Harvey Conner of murder on April 12, 1967.

1967 January 10. Vandals desecrate more than 100 graves at two Jewish cemeteries in New Orleans, Louisiana.

April 25. Bombs damage the home of the mother of Judge Frank Johnson in Birmingham, Alabama. Judge Johnson, a vocal opponent of the Ku Klux Klan, had issued several decisions in support of school integration.

May 14. A black-owned home in a predominantly white suburb of Cleveland, Ohio, is bombed.

July 18. FBI agents arrest twelve whites, including at least seven Klan members, for violent racist acts committed over a twenty-one-month period in Rowan and Cabarrus counties, North Carolina. In a separate incident in Greensboro, North Carolina, two Klan members are jailed for a cross burning.

August 28. White mobs shouting "We want slaves!" and "Get yourself a nigger!" stone NAACP demonstrators in Milwaukee, Wisconsin. Marchers are again attacked the next day and the local NAACP Freedom House is destroyed by arsonists. Milwaukee Mayor Henry Maier issues a proclamation banning evening demonstrations and rallies.

September 18. Temple Beth Israel in Jackson, Mississippi, is bombed. As FBI agents pursue suspects, their vehicle is rammed from the rear by a carload of armed Klan members.

October 6. Snipers fire into the home of an NAACP worker in Carthage, Mississippi.

November 21. The home of Rabbi Perry Nussbaum in Jackson, Mississippi, is bombed. Nussbaum and his wife, Arene, narrowly escape death.

1968   February 8. Three black students—Henry E. Smith, Delano H. Middleton, and Samuel Hammond Jr.—are killed and at least thirty-four others are wounded when state police fire on rioters at South Carolina State College in Orangeburg. Campus unrest began when college demonstrators started picketing a segregated local bowling alley.

April 4. The Reverend Martin Luther King Jr. is assassinated by a sniper on the eve of a scheduled protest demonstration in support of sanitation workers in Memphis, Tennessee. Rioting erupts in more than 125 U.S. cities over the next week, leaving 46 persons dead, 2,600 injured, and 21,270 arrested. Damage from arson and vandalism is estimated at $45 million.

August 14. The church of the Reverend A. D. King is bombed in Louisville, Kentucky.

August 16–17. Two white men murder the black female proprietor of a tavern in Cincinnati, Ohio. A riot erupts, and one black youth is critically shot while stoning police cars.

November 25. A Hebrew school in the Bronx, New York, is damaged in a suspicious fire. It is the tenth attack on Jewish institutions in New York City in the past three months.

November 27. The Yeshiva of Eastern Parkway in Brooklyn, New York, is destroyed in a fire. Four teenagers under sixteen years old are charged with arson. Mayor John Lindsay announces a six-point program for more police surveillance at religious institutions and the creation of a special arson squad.

December 24. Gunshots are fired into the home of a black Office of Economic Opportunity administrator in

1968, Monroe, Louisiana. Although a Ku Klux Klan member is
cont. arrested, he is set free in February 1969.

1970 January 19. Fire damages a Bronx, New York, synagogue that had been vandalized four times in the past year.

January 28. Vandals paint swastikas and start a fire at the Intervale Jewish Center in the Bronx, New York.

March 3. A mob of whites attack school buses carrying black students to recently integrated schools in Lamar, South Carolina. Three rioters are convicted on February 17, 1971.

August 30. Ten buses scheduled for use in desegregating schools in Pontiac, Michigan, are bombed. Six members of the Ku Klux Klan are arrested, including Robert Miles, a major national neo-Nazi leader.

September 10. A bomb with more than a dozen sticks of dynamite is found under a Jacksonville, Florida, school bus and defused.

1973 September 16. Ku Klux Klan member Byron De La Beckwith is arrested; firearms and a time bomb are found in his automobile. Beckwith was planning a raid on the home of A. I. Botnick, a local Jewish leader. The Louisiana Klan conducts a fundraising campaign for Beckwith's legal defense, and he is acquitted of all charges on January 16, 1974.

October 2. Evelyn Walker, a white woman, is doused with gasoline and burned to death by black youths after her car breaks down in a black neighborhood in Boston, Massachusetts.

October 6. Kirk Miller, a white cab driver, is the victim of a racially motivated murder in Boston.

October 19. Members of the San Francisco–based Black Muslim splinter group the Death Angels assault white victims Richard and Quita Hague with machetes, killing

Quita Hague and leaving her husband severely injured. Members of this violent group reportedly earn their "angel wings" by killing white men and women. The killings begin in October and continue for about six months, resulting in the deaths of fourteen men and women and leaving seven wounded. (The case was nicknamed "Zebra" because a special police task force used the last radio frequency, Z, for communication.)

October 29. Frances Rose, a white woman, is shot and killed in another "Zebra" killing in San Francisco, California. Jessie Cooks, a member of the Death Angels, is arrested near the scene and sentenced to life in prison for the murder.

November 21. The Sephardic Institute for Advanced Learning in New York City is damaged and one employee is killed during an arson attack. Twelve hours later, a second fire destroys the institute.

November 26. The Reverend Edward Pace, a black minister in Gadsden, Alabama, is shot and killed in his home. Bruce Botsford, a Klan member, is convicted of second-degree murder by an all-white, all-male jury on March 9, 1974, and sentenced to thirty years in prison.

1974 January 28. Death Angel members kill Tana White and Jane Holly in random, racially motivated attacks in the San Francisco, California, area.

April 14. Ward Anderson and Terry White are shot by Death Angel gunmen at a San Francisco bus stop.

April 19. Frank Carlson, a white grocer, is murdered and his wife is beaten and raped by an African American who claims to be one of the "Zebra" killers. Police arrest seven Death Angel suspects on May 1; four are convicted and sentenced to life in prison.

July 27. Shootings are reported during a local Klan recruiting drive in Kokomo, Indiana.

1974,   August 16. Judge Arthur Gamble, who signed the mur-
cont.   der indictments against three Klan members involved in
the murder of white civil rights activist Viola Liuzzo on
March 25, 1965, is injured by a car bomb in Greenville,
Alabama.

September 19. Dr. Charles Glatt, who worked for the city
of Dayton, Ohio, to prepare school desegregation plans,
is shot and killed at work. Police arrest Neal Bradley
Long, who had been linked to a series of racially motivated murders of seven local blacks since 1972.

November 11. In the Boro Park section of Brooklyn, New
York, two synagogues, a Jewish school, and the homes of
two Hasidic Jews are firebombed.

1976   February 26. Four members of the Ku Klux Klan are indicted for the murder of Willie Edwards in Montgomery,
Alabama, in 1957 (*see* 1957: January 23). The judge later
dismissed the charges. Diane Alexander, the widow of
Henry Alexander, who was accused of the crime but
never tried, said her husband confessed to the murder
before his death in 1992. Mrs. Alexander wrote a letter of
apology to Sarah Salter, Mr. Edwards's widow, who then
lived in Buffalo, New York, and met her in person on
September 4, 1993, to express her remorse.

April 6. In Boston, Massachusetts, Theodore Landsmark,
a black attorney, is attacked by a white youth who attempted to stab him with the staff of an American flag.
The Pulitzer Prize–winning photograph of this incident
is published in newspapers around the world.

September 8. White youths shouting racial epithets ran-
domly attack blacks and Hispanics in Washington Square
Park in Greenwich Village, New York. Marcus Mota is
killed, and several others are injured. Five youths are
sentenced to prison terms ranging from three to twenty-
five years.

1977   February 14. Fred Cowan, a professed hater of Jews and
blacks and member of the racist National States Rights

Party, kills six persons—Frederick Holmes, Joseph E. Hicks, James Greene, Pariyarathu Varghese, Allen Mc-Cleod, and Joseph Russo—and wounds five others before committing suicide in New Rochelle, New York. His victims were three blacks, an Asian Indian immigrant, and two whites, including a policeman. He was previously suspended from work after a conflict with a Jewish supervisor.

April 15–17. In a series of violent incidents in Elwood, Indiana, Klan members burn crosses and scatter garbage on the lawns of local residents. The mayor's home is also sprayed with shotgun pellets.

1978   April 28. Roy Keith Palmer, seventeen, pleaded guilty to burning down two black churches in Wilkes County, Georgia, in December 1977. At Palmer's sentencing, a black deacon and a minister from the destroyed churches asks that the defendant be treated leniently for the crime.

August 7. Alphonse Manning and Toni Schwenn, an interracial couple, are killed by Joseph Paul Franklin, in Madison, Wisconsin. Franklin is a former member of the Ku Klux Klan and the American Nazi Party.

September 5. A white youth wearing a Nazi armband fires on black picnickers in Jonesville, North Carolina, killing one man and wounding three. A second victim dies on September 7. The gunman commits suicide.

October 8. A sniper, later believed to be Joseph Paul Franklin, kills Gerald Gordon while he is leaving a bar mitzvah in Richmond Heights, a suburb of St. Louis, Missouri.

November 18. Former Klan member Robert Chambliss is convicted of murder in the bombing of the Sixteenth Street Baptist Church in Birmingham, Alabama, on September 15, 1963, which killed four black girls.

1979   December. The Anti-Defamation League (ADL) issues its first *Audit of Anti-Semitic Incidents*.

1979, October 21. Jessie Taylor and Marion Bresette, an interra-
cont. cial couple, are shot and killed in a parking lot in Oklahoma City. Joseph Paul Franklin is later charged in the
case, but the indictments are dismissed in 1983.

1980 January 8. Joseph Paul Franklin kills Larry E. Reese, an
African American man, at a local fast-food restaurant in
Indianapolis, Indiana.

August 19. Joseph Paul Franklin, a former member of the
Ku Klux Klan and American Nazi Party, murders David
Martin and Theodore Fields, two black men who were
jogging alongside two white women in a park in Salt
Lake City, Utah. Franklin was later connected to other
crimes, including the bombing of Beth Shalom synagogue in Chattanooga, Tennessee, on July 29, 1977; the
shooting of former National Urban League director Vernon Jordan on May 29, 1980; the murders of Darrell Lane
and Dante Evans Brown in a vacant lot in Cincinnati,
Ohio, on June 6, 1980; and the murders of Kathleen
Mikula and Arthur Smothers in Johnstown, Pennsylvania, on June 15, 1980. Franklin was reportedly involved
in the slaying of twenty-one people who were either interracial couples or Jews.

1981 The Anti-Defamation League drafts the first Model Hate
Crimes legislation.

1982 June 19. Vincent Chin, a young Chinese American, is brutally murdered in Detroit by unemployed autoworkers,
who apparently believed he was Japanese. The case receives national attention when the judge places the assailants on probation and requires them each to pay a
$3,000 fine.

1984 The National Gay and Lesbian Task Force issues its first
report on antigay violence in the United States.

June 18. Alan Berg, a popular Denver, Colorado, radio
talk show host, is murdered in a machine-gun attack in
the driveway of his home. His assailants are members of
a neo-Nazi group.

1985   March 21. The U.S. House of Representatives Committee on the Judiciary holds its first congressional hearing to discuss the passage of a law to require the U.S. Justice Department to collect and publish statistics on hate crimes.

December 24. Charles Goldmark, a Seattle, Washington, attorney, is brutally murdered by a drifter named David Lewis Rice, who had close ties with racist and anti-Jewish groups. Rice thought that Goldmark, a prominent liberal lawyer, "looked Jewish."

1986   July 16. The U.S. House of Representatives Committee on the Judiciary holds hearings to examine reports of harassment and violence directed against Arab Americans.

October 9. The U.S. House of Representatives Committee on the Judiciary holds hearings to examine the problem of violence against gay men and lesbians.

December 20. A gang of white teenagers in the Howard Beach section of Queens, New York, attack Michael Griffith, an African American who was passing through their neighborhood. They beat him and then chase him to his death on a nearby highway. His stepfather, Cedric Sandiford, is also severely beaten.

1987   November 10. The U.S. House of Representatives Committee on the Judiciary holds hearings on the causes of and possible responses to recent violent acts committed against Asians and Asian Americans.

1988   May 11–July 12. The U.S. House of Representatives Committee on the Judiciary holds hearings to consider legislation to establish a Commission on Racially Motivated Violence and to examine the prevalence of violence against members of minority groups.

May 15. Eighteen-year-old Richard Lee Bednarski and his friends look for gay men to harass in Dallas, Texas. Bednarski kills thirty-four-year-old Tommy Trimble and twenty-seven-year old Lloyd Griffin in a gruesome mur-

1988, der. He was found guilty, but Judge Jack Hampton said
cont. that killing gays was not a serious crime and gave the defendant a lenient sentence for the murders. His remarks stirred a major controversy, and Hampton was censured by his judicial colleagues. He was later defeated for reelection in December 1992.

June 21. The U.S. Senate Committee on the Judiciary holds hearings to consider proposed legislation to require the U.S. Justice Department to collect and publish statistics on hate crimes.

1989 January 17. Patrick Purdy enters an elementary school yard in Stockton, California, and fires 105 rounds from an AK-47, killing three Cambodian girls (Ram Chun, Sokhim An, and Oeun Lim); a Cambodian boy (Rathanan Or); and a Vietnamese girl (Thuy Tran). The gunman also wounds thirty others, including a teacher, and then kills himself. The twenty-four-year-old Purdy had an obsessive hatred of Cambodians, Indians, Pakistanis, and especially Vietnamese.

July 29. Two brothers in Raleigh, North Carolina, beat to death Ming Hai "Jim" Loo, a twenty-four-year-old Chinese American. Witnesses told police that the men thought Loo was Vietnamese. They apparently sought revenge for their brother who served in the U.S. military in Vietnam and never returned.

August 23. A white gang armed with baseball bats and guns attack four black youths on a street in Bensonhurst, a neighborhood in Brooklyn, New York. Yusuf Hawkins is beaten and shot to death in the attack. Seven suspects are arrested.

November 5. A memorial sculpture made of black granite is dedicated on the grounds of the Southern Poverty Law Center in Montgomery, Alabama. Designed by Maya Lin, who also created the Vietnam Veterans Memorial in Washington, D.C., the sculpture commemorates the more than forty people—black and white; men, women, and children—who were killed during the civil rights movement. More than 600 relatives of the victims attend the dedication.

1990   January 21. James Zappalorti, a gay Vietnam war veteran, is brutally murdered in Staten Island, New York, by two teenagers.

March 15. Henry Lau, a thirty-one-year-old Chinese immigrant, is fatally stabbed on a New York City subway train. Prior to the stabbing, the assailant called Lau an "egg roll."

April 23. President George H. W. Bush signs into law the Hate Crime Statistics Act, which mandates the FBI to compile annual statistics on hate crimes throughout the United States.

August 9. Two skinheads shouting "white power" murder Hung Truong, a fifteen-year-old Vietnamese youth, in Houston.

1991   March 3. Rodney King, an African American motorist, is beaten by four white Los Angeles police officers after he is stopped for speeding. When police finally reach the car, they deliver more than fifty baton blows and six kicks to King in two minutes, resulting in eleven skull fractures as well as brain and kidney damage. The incident is captured on videotape by a bystander and gains national media attention.

August 19. A Hasidic Jewish driver is involved in a traffic accident in Brooklyn, New York, that kills Gavin Cato, a seven-year-old African American. Following the accident, black youths murder Yankel Rosenbaum, a visiting Australian Jewish scholar. During three days of rioting in the Crown Heights section of Brooklyn, crowds roam the streets, yelling, "Get the Jews."

1992   April 29. A jury in suburban Simi Valley, California, acquits four white Los Angeles police officers on all but one charge stemming from the beating of black motorist Rodney King in March 1991.

1992, April 30–May 3. Following the controversial jury verdict
cont. in the Rodney King case, the south central section of Los
Angeles is engulfed in widespread burning, looting, and
violence. Fifty-eight people are killed in the rioting, 2,383
are injured, and damage estimates range as high as $1
billion. According to Yumi Park, former director of the
Korean American Grocers Association, 800 Korean-
owned establishments are damaged in the rioting. Tensions between African Americans and Korean Americans
had risen following the November 15, 1991, trial of Soon
Ja Du, a Korean grocer who had shot to death a fifteen-
year-old black girl, Latasha Harlins. Even though the
grocer was convicted of manslaughter, the judge had refused to send her to prison.

May 11. The U.S. House of Representatives Committee
on the Judiciary holds hearings on crimes motivated by
prejudice against the racial, ethnic, religious, or sexual
orientation of the victim.

June 22. In the case of *R. A.V. v. City of St. Paul,* the U.S.
Supreme Court strikes down a hate crime ordinance in
St. Paul, Minnesota.

July 29. The U.S. House of Representatives Committee on
the Judiciary holds hearings on the use of penalty enhancement for hate crimes and also examines the implications of the June 22, 1992, U.S. Supreme Court decision.

August 5. The U.S. Senate Committee on the Judiciary re-
views implementation of the Hate Crime Statistics Act of
1990 by the FBI, state crime reporting agencies, and local
law enforcement agencies under the direction of the U.S.
Department of Justice.

August 18. Luyen Phan Nguyen, a nineteen-year-old
premed student at the University of Miami, is beaten to
death by five men in Coral Springs, Florida, who made
disparaging remarks about his Vietnamese ancestry.

October 27. Seaman Allen R. Schindler, serving on a U.S.
Navy ship, is brutally murdered by shipmates outside a

military base in Sasebo, Japan, after they learn of his homosexuality. One assailant later pleads guilty to murder and his accomplice receives a lighter sentence for cooperating with investigators. The cable station Lifetime airs *Any Mother's Son* in August 1997, a docudrama based on the murder.

1993   January 4. The FBI releases its first official report containing nationwide hate crime statistics for 1991.

June 11. The U.S. Supreme Court unanimously upholds Wisconsin's penalty enhancement hate crimes statute in the case *Wisconsin v. Mitchell.*

November 16. The U.S. House of Representatives Committee on the Judiciary discusses proposed legislation that would make crimes of violence motivated by gender actionable under civil rights and hate crime laws.

December 7. Colin Ferguson, a black Jamaican immigrant, murders Mi Kyung Kim, James Gorycki, Dennis McCarthy, Marita Theresa Magtoto, Amy Federici, and Richard Nettleton on the Long Island Rail Road. He had previously written notes expressing hatred of Asians and whites.

1994   February 5. In his third and decisive trial in Jackson, Mississippi, Byron De La Beckwith is found guilty by a jury of eight blacks and four whites of murdering Medgar Evers on June 12, 1963. (*See* 1963: June 1 and September 16)

March 1. Rashid Baz, a Lebanese immigrant, shoots at a van carrying fifteen Hasidic Jewish students over the Brooklyn Bridge. One student, Aaron Halberstam, is killed; another, Nachum Sasonkin, is severely injured. The murderer once vowed to "kill all Jews."

April. National Asian Pacific American Legal Consortium issues its first *Audit of Violence against Asian Pacific Americans.*

September 1. A mosque in Yuba City, California, is gutted in a suspected anti-Muslim arson case.

1994,   September 13. The Violent Crime Control and Law En-
cont.   forcement Act directs the U.S. Sentencing Commission to
         devise sentencing guidelines to incorporate a federal sen-
         tence enhancement for hate crimes.

         The Violence against Women Act (Title IV of the Violent
         Crime Control and Law Enforcement Act of 1994) pro-
         vides civil rights remedies for gender-motivated vio-
         lence, explicitly stating that all "persons within the
         United States shall have the right to be free from crimes
         of violence motivated by gender."(42 United States Code
         13981)

1995   December 7. African Americans Michael Jones and Jackie
         Burden are murdered in a random shooting by soldiers
         from Fort Bragg, North Carolina, who are affiliated with
         white supremacist groups.

         December 8. In previous weeks, picketers argued that
         Freddy's Fashion Mart, a store in Harlem, should be
         owned by blacks, and they made antiwhite and anti- .
         Jewish statements during their protests. Roland Smith,
         who had previously picketed the Jewish-owned store,
         enters the store, shoots four people, and then douses the
         premises with lighter fluid. The ensuing blaze kills seven
         people: Garnette Ramautar, Mayra Rentas, Cynthia Mar-
         tinez, Angelina Marrero, Luz Ramos, Kareem Brunner,
         and Olga Garcia. Smith also dies in the blaze.

1996   January 29. Thien Minh Ly, a twenty-four-year-old
         Vietnamese American, is kicked, stomped, and stabbed
         more than a dozen times on a tennis court in Tustin,
         California, in a racially motivated attack by white skin-
         heads.

         June 25. The U.S. House of Representatives Committee
         on National Security holds hearings on the participation
         of current or former U.S. military personnel in antigov-
         ernment or racist hate groups.

         June 27. The U.S. Senate Committee on the Judiciary
         holds hearings on the rash of arsons directed against

black churches and other acts of violence against houses of worship.

1997   February 23. Ali Abu Kamal, a sixty-nine-year-old Palestinian Arab teacher who arrived in the United States in December 1996, opens fire on the eighty-sixth floor observation deck of the Empire State Building in New York City, killing Chris Burmeister, a Danish tourist, and wounding six others before taking his own life. In a pouch around Abu Kamal's neck, police found a letter stating his intention to kill as many "Zionists" as possible in their "den" in New York City.

November 18. Oumar Dia, an immigrant from Mauritania, is murdered at a Denver, Colorado, bus stop by Nathan Thill, a skinhead who later said he hated blacks. (Dia, a black African, had fled his native country because he was persecuted by Arabs.) Jeannie VanVelkinburgh, a white woman who comes to his aid, is also shot and is consequently paralyzed from the waist down. Thill pleads guilty to first-degree murder and is serving a life sentence plus thirty-two years. His accomplice, Jeremiah Barnum, also pleads guilty as an accessory to the murder and is sentenced to twelve years.

1998   February 23. Members of the New Order, a neo-Nazi group, are arrested in their homes in southern Illinois, where police find guns, pipe bombs, and hand grenades. The FBI says the suspects were plotting to bomb the Southern Poverty Law Center in Montgomery, Alabama, and the Simon Wiesenthal Center, the New York headquarters of the Anti-Defamation League. Authorities learned of the plot when the suspects attempted to recruit a man who then became a federal informant.

Also on this date, in the largest hate crime judgment in Illinois history, a jury awards $6 million to the family of Ricardo Arroyo of Waukegan, Illinois, who died from injuries inflicted by another motorist. After Arroyo's and the other motorist's cars collide, the assailant kicks Arroyo in the stomach three times and shouts at him, "Mexicans, go back to Mexico!"

1998, March 13. Brian Wilmes falls into a coma after being
cont. beaten outside a San Francisco, California, gay bar by an
attacker who uttered antigay slurs. In November 1998, a
municipal court judge rules that the alleged assailant,
Edgard Mora, must stand trial for murder with a hate
crime enhancement.

April 5. Five white men in Orange County, California, are
beaten by five Iranian males attending an Iranian New
Year's party. The Iranian men jump the victims—whose
names were not released by police—from behind,
yelling, "What are you white guys doing here?" A witness captures the attack on videotape; the footage shows
one of the perpetrators kicking a victim with steel-toed
boots.

April 14. In Biddeford, Maine, Anthony Cabana is sent to
jail for threatening to "snap" a woman's neck. He is reportedly the first person ever charged in Maine with a
gender-based hate crime.

April 27. Steven Goedereis, a gay man, is brutally beaten
to death in West Palm Beach, Florida, by two teenagers,
Bryan Donahue and William Dodge, who were angered
by an allegedly sexually suggestive comment Goedereis
made to them.

May 9. In Rutherfordton, North Carolina, two men with
Ku Klux Klan ties attack Isaiah Edgerton, his wife, and
their two-year-old daughter in their home. The men,
both in their twenties, are charged with a hate crime. Police suspect that the local chapter of the American
Knights of the KKK ordered the shooting.

May 20. A cross is burned in front of a Jewish family's
home in Huntington Beach, California. It is the second
anti-Jewish crime committed against the family; in an
earlier incident, someone stamped a swastika on their
front lawn.

June 7. James Byrd Jr., a forty-nine-year-old black man, is
chained to a pickup truck in Jasper, Texas, and dragged

along an asphalt road for almost two miles. His head, neck, and right arm are later found on the road. His attackers, who claimed membership in the white supremacist group Aryan Nations, reportedly said to Byrd, "We're starting the *Turner Diaries* early." This book, widely disseminated among white racists and neo-Nazis, advocates the murder of African Americans and Jews. President Bill Clinton issues a statement condemning the grisly murder.

September 20. In the South Ozone Park neighborhood of Queens, New York, Rishi Maharaj, the twenty-one-year-old son of Trinidadian immigrants of Indian descent, is beaten by three young men who utter anti-Indian slurs. He suffers severe head trauma, facial fractures, and other injuries. The Queens district attorney condemns the incident as an unprovoked hate crime and charges the assailants with attempted murder.

October 6. Matthew Shepard, a gay college student in Laramie, Wyoming, is tied to a fence and savagely beaten with a gun by two men he met in a bar. Left for dead, he is found by a passerby eighteen hours later. He remained in a coma for several days and died October 12. His funeral is protested by the Reverend Fred Phelps and his followers from Topeka, Kansas, who carry signs saying "God hates fags" and "Fags deserve to die."

October 12–15. President Clinton condemns the murder of Matthew Shepard; the U.S. House of Representatives passes a resolution condemning the murder as a hate crime.

1999   February 19. In Sylacauga, Alabama, Billy Jack Gaither is bludgeoned to death with an ax handle and his body is burned. Steven Eric Mullins and Charles Monroe Butler murdered Gaither because he allegedly propositioned the two men.

May 16. James Longenbach deliberately drives his car into Austin Hansen-Tyler and Dontrell Langston, two African-American teenagers who are riding bicycles in

1999, Kenosha, Wisconsin. Longenbach was sentenced to 176
cont. years in prison for this racially motivated hate crime.

June 18. Congregation B'nai Israel and Knesset Israel
Torah Center in Sacramento and Congregation Beth
Shalom in Carmichael, California, are set ablaze, causing
an estimated $3 million in damage.

July 1. Gary Matson and Winfield Scott Mowder, a gay
couple, are shot to death in their Happy Valley home,
outside Redding, California, in an antigay hate crime.

July 2–4. Benjamin Nathaniel Smith, a twenty-one-year-
old white supremacist involved with the World Church
of the Creator, goes on a murderous rampage in Illinois
and Indiana, killing Ricky Birdsong, a black coach at
Northwestern University, and Won-Joon Yoon, a graduate student at Indiana University. He also shot at Orthodox Jews, African Americans, and Asians, leaving nine
people injured. He shoots and kills himself in Indiana
during a car chase with local police.

August 10. Buford O. Furrow Jr., a self-professed white
supremacist, shoots and wounds five people at the North
Valley Jewish Community Center in Los Angeles and
murders Joseph Santos Ileto, a Filipino American postal
worker.

2000 April 28. Richard Baumhammers, a white immigration
attorney who professed hatred of minorities, murders
Anil Thakur and paralyzes Sandip Patel at the India Grocers store in Pittsburgh. He begins his rampage by killing
Anita Gordon, a Jewish neighbor, and later goes to a Chinese restaurant and kills Thao Q. Pham and Ji-Ye Sun.
His last victim is Garry Lee, a twenty-five-year-old
African American. On May 11, 2001, a jury deliberates for
three hours and convicts Baumhammers of killing five
people and paralyzing a sixth. He is currently on death
row in a Pennsylvania prison.

May 17. Thirty-seven years after the crime, Thomas Blanton Jr. and Bobby Frank Cherry are charged with plant-

ing a bomb at the Sixteenth Street Baptist Church in Montgomery, Alabama, that killed four black schoolgirls. They are both later sentenced to life imprisonment for the murders by mixed-race juries. (*See* 1963: September)

2001   April 19. Leo V. Felton and Erica Chase, members of a white supremacist group, are arrested for passing counterfeit money in Boston and are later indicted for plotting to blow up major Jewish and African American monuments in the Boston area. (They were also plotting the assassinations of Steven Spielberg and Jesse Jackson.) On July 26, 2003, Felton is convicted and sentenced to twenty years in prison; Chase, who is repentant, receives a five-year sentence. The *Boston Globe* (November 3, 2002) publishes a feature story revealing that Felton had a black father and a white mother.

September 12. Three hundred men and women chanting "U.S.A., U.S.A." try to storm a mosque in the Chicago suburb of Bridgeview, Illinois. More than 100 police restrain the demonstrators and arrest three people.

September 15. Balbir Singh Sodhi, a Sikh gas station owner, is murdered by Frank Roque in Mesa, Arizona, who vows vengeance for the September 11 terrorist attacks.

September 30. Swaran Kaur Bhullar, a Sikh woman, is stabbed twice in the head by two men when she stops her car at a red light in San Diego. The attackers, who are never caught, probably assumed she was a Muslim.

December 11. Federal prosecutors charge Irv Rubin, the head of the Jewish Defense League, and his associate Earl Krugel with plotting to blow up the King Fahd Mosque in Culver City, California, and bomb the office of Congressman Darrell Issa (R-CA), a Lebanese American. Rubin reportedly commits suicide in prison in November 2002.

2002   May 18. Stephen J. Kinney attacks a group of three Chinese families at Harrah's casino in Lake Tahoe, Nevada,

2002,
cont.

shouting racial epithets and injuring three people. Kinney is charged with aggravated assault and committing a hate crime. The sentence will be suspended for three years, however, if Kinney completes fifty-six hours of community service with the Chinese Historical Society and pays the costs of the prosecution in this case.

August 10. Mizanor Rahman, a thirty-seven-year-old Bangladeshi photojournalist, is beaten to death in his Brooklyn neighborhood. Although Michael Gabriel, the inspector with the New York City Police Department, reportedly says the murder may have been motivated by racial bias, no hate crime statute is invoked against the murderers, Rafael Santos and Hardy Marston.

November 11. Mohammed Sakawat Hossain, a nineteen-year-old Bangladeshi immigrant, is beaten to death in his Brooklyn neighborhood by Javier Amigan and Charles Durante. Police do not charge the perpetrators with a hate crime, but some members of the Bangladeshi community feel the attack is racially motivated. Dr. Iftekhar Ahmed Chowdhury, a Bangladeshi diplomat, joins with community leaders, charging that this incident, along with the August 10, 2002, murder of Mizanor Rahman (*see* August 10, above), are hate crimes.

2003

March 27. James Tyler Williams, the killer of gay couple Gary Matson and Winfield Scott Mowder (*see* 1999: July 1), is sentenced to twenty-nine years to life in prison for the murders. Williams also receives a nineteen-year sentence for the firebombing of three Sacramento-area synagogues (*see* 1999: June 18). His brother, Benjamin Williams, who is an accomplice, commits suicide in his Shasta County jail cell on November 17, 2002. Benjamin Williams reportedly says that the murder of the gay couple was "God's will."

May 1. The Carbondale Islamic Center near Southern Illinois University is spray-painted with graffiti in English and Hindi. The FBI investigates the vandalism as a hate crime.

May 1. Sen. Edward Kennedy (D-MA) and Sen. Gordon Smith (R-OR) reintroduce the Local Law Enforcement Enhancement Act, formerly called the Hate Crimes Prevention Act, which died in congressional committee in 2001. This legislation, which has forty-nine cosponsors, provides additional federal support to local law enforcement agencies to prosecute hate crimes. The law would also add sexual orientation, gender, and disability as hate crime categories; current statutes cover only race, national origin, and religion.

May 11. Sakia Gunn, fifteen, is fatally stabbed in the chest at a bus stop in Newark, New Jersey. She and her two friends were being harassed by three men and attempted to rebuff their advances by claiming to be lesbians.

June 11. A jury finds Aaron Price, a nineteen-year-old sophomore at Morehouse College in Atlanta, Georgia, guilty of aggravated assault and aggravated battery in the November 3, 2002, beating of his fellow student Gregory Love in a dorm shower. Price, who thought that Love was gay and was making a pass at him, attacked Love with a baseball bat. Price receives ten years on each count, to be served concurrently. Price is acquitted of a hate crime after prosecutors fail to convince jurors that his actions were motivated by antigay feelings. Love testified that he was not gay. This trial is the first case involving Georgia's recently passed hate crimes enhancement penalty statute.

November 13. An arson fire destroys the CANDLES Holocaust Museum in Terre Haute, Indiana. (CANDLES stands for Children of Auschwitz Nazi Deadly Experiments Survivors.) The museum was founded in 1995 by Holocaust survivor Eva Kor and housed artifacts from Auschwitz and documents relating to Dr. Josef Mengele, the infamous Nazi doctor who experimented on human beings. "Remember Timothy McVeigh" is scrawled on a nearby wall. McVeigh, the Oklahoma City bomber, was executed at a prison near Terre Haute.

2003, December 17. Raussi Uthman, a U.S. citizen born to
cont. Palestinian parents, is convicted of hate crimes for bur-
glarizing and burning down Temple Beth El in Syracuse,
New York, on October 13, 2000. He is sentenced to
twenty-five years in prison for the fire, which caused
more than $700,000 in damage but no injuries. His ac-
complice, Ahed Shehadeh, is sentenced to five years for
aiding and abetting the arson.

2004 April 5. The library of the United Talmud Torah elementary school in Montreal is firebombed. Rouba Fahd
Elmerhebi and her son, Sleiman, are charged with plant-
ing the bomb, which destroyed the library. In December
2004, Sleiman Elmerhebi pleaded guilty and was later
sentenced to forty months in prison. His mother, an
accessory to the crime, is still awaiting sentencing.

June 9. Brian Williamson, a leading gay rights activist in
Jamaica, is murdered in his home in the capital city of
Kingston. A crowd soon gathered outside the murder
scene and chanted, "boom, bye bye," a lyric from a popular Jamaican song advocating the murder of gay people.

June 22. A California judge declared a mistrial for the
three men accused of the brutal murder of seventeen-
year-old Eddie Araujo, a transgendered male, in Newark,
California, on October 4, 2002. The jury was deadlocked
but prosecutors plan again to try the accused men for
first degree murder.

September 2. Thousands of demonstrators in Kath-
mandu, Nepal riot, burn down a mosque, and attack local Muslims after twelve Nepalese hostages are executed
in Iraq.

September 29. Fanny Ann Eddy, the thirty-year-old
founder of the Sierra Leone Lesbian and Gay Association, is found dead in her office in the capital, Freetown.
According to the organization Human Rights Watch, she
had been repeatedly raped and stabbed, and her neck
was broken.

November 2. Theo Van Gogh, a Dutch filmmaker who produced a controversial movie on the treatment of Muslim women, was murdered while cycling through Amsterdam. Police later arrested a twenty-six-year-old man who had dual Dutch-Moroccan nationality and was suspected of having links to radical Islamic groups. The murder evoked a furious backlash among some Dutch citizens and several mosques were burned down in the following weeks. In retaliation, a few Dutch churches were later destroyed.

November 26. The ABC television newsmagazine program *20/20* features an investigative report claiming that the murder of Matthew Shepard, a gay Wyoming college student (see 1998: October 6), was not a hate crime, but a botched robbery committed by men high on drugs. Some gay rights organizations denounce the show and question the veracity and motives of the perpetrators who were interviewed on the show from their prison cells.

December 20. The Mississippi Religious Leadership Conference offers a $100,000 reward for information leading to the arrest and conviction of the murderers of three civil rights workers—James Chaney, Andrew Goodman, and Michael Schwerner—killed in Philadelphia, Mississippi on June 21, 1964.

2005   January 15. In Jersey City, New Jersey, four Copt Christians immigrants from Egypt—Hossam Armanious, his wife, Amal Garas, and their daughters, Sylvia and Monica—are murdered in their home. The killings enrage Copts in Jersey City—a community with a large Egyptian Copt and Muslim population—who blame the local Egyptian Muslims for the crime. Many Copts fled Egypt because of religious persecution.

March 11. A Santa Fe, New Mexico, grand jury issued indictments against six men in the severe beating of twenty-one-year-old James Maestas, a gay man, outside a local hotel on February 27. His companion, twenty-three-year-old Joshua Stockham, received minor injuries. The perpetrators reportedly shouted antigay epithets during the assault. New Mexico Attorney General Patricia Madrid announced that the accused perpetrators would be prosecuted under the state hate crimes penalty enhancement statute—the first such prosecution since the law went into effect in July 2003.

4

Biographical Sketches

Much information on hate crimes and violent extremist groups comes from the research and publications of human rights activists and organizations, college and university professors, and investigative journalists and authors. Because their work often involves exposing the activities of violent individuals and organizations, some of these human rights activists prefer to remain out of the public eye. Their legitimate concerns have been respected, and they have not been included in this chapter. The following are brief biographies of some notable experts on hate crimes, racial and religious bigotry, and political extremists.

Zainab Al-Suwaij (1971–)

Zainab Al-Suwaij is the executive director of the American Islamic Congress. This new organization represents the diverse political and cultural interests of Muslim Americans and aims to combat both hate crimes committed against Muslims and those crimes perpetrated by their coreligionists.

Born in Basra, Iraq, Al-Suwaij comes from a religious Muslim family. She was on a visit to Kuwait in 1990 when Iraq invaded that country. In 1991 she returned to Iraq, participated in the failed uprising against Saddam Hussein's regime, and fled to Jordan. According to a *Boston Globe* story on April 7, 2003, she bears a thin scar from an Iraqi army attack during the rebellion.

After the first Gulf War, she fled to the United States to complete her studies. She has worked as a refugee case manager and a teaching fellow in Arabic at Yale. On April 4, 2003, Al-Suwaij and other prominent Iraqi Americans met with President George W. Bush at the White House.

Al-Suwaij has written articles in support of the coalition war against Hussein's tyranny and has also published essays against Muslim intolerance for the *New York Times, Boston Globe,* and *Wall Street Journal.* She helped organize a Boston memorial service for slain *Wall Street Journal* reporter Daniel Pearl—which were also held in London, New York, and Los Angeles—and observed that "to remember Daniel Pearl is to remind ourselves of the human side of terror and intolerance." In addition to her work with the American Islamic Congress, she is involved in developing education programs in Iraq.

Chip Berlet (1949–)

A senior analyst at Political Research Associates (PRA), Chip Berlet has spent over thirty years studying prejudice, conspiracy theories, and authoritarianism. He has investigated far right hate groups, reactionary backlash movements, theocratic fundamentalism, civil liberties violations, police misconduct, government and private surveillance abuse, and other antidemocratic phenomena.

PRA is an independent, nonprofit research center that publishes extensive reports on hate group activities aimed against blacks, Jews, gays, lesbians, and other minority groups.

Berlet has written chapters in several scholarly books, reviewed articles for sociology journals, and prepared entries in encyclopedias on fundamentalism, millennialism, and criminal justice. He was coauthor with Matthew N. Lyons of *Right-Wing Populism in America: Too Close for Comfort* (Guilford Press, 2000) and also has written op-ed pieces for the *Boston Globe,* the *New York Times,* and other major newspapers and magazines.

Following the terrorist bombing in Oklahoma City, Berlet frequently appeared in the media to discuss the nature and overlap of right-wing populism, the patriot movement, and armed militias. He has personally attended meetings held by right-wing patriots, armed militia activists, white supremacists, Holocaust deniers, the Ku Klux Klan (KKK), and neo-Nazis. He also was among the first researchers to warn of the attempt by anti-Jewish and other white supremacist hate groups to recruit financially failing Midwest farmers in the late 1970s and early 1980s. A longtime critic of the extremist ideologue Lyndon LaRouche, Berlet has been sued twice by the LaRouche movement for his characterization of it as a conspiracist neo-Nazi movement engaged in illegal fundraising activities. LaRouche's organization lost both cases.

In 1985 Berlet cofounded the Public Eye BBS, the first computer bulletin board system designed to challenge the information circulated by the KKK and neo-Nazis on racist and anti-Jewish bulletin boards. He has worked on joint projects with many groups, including Facing History and Ourselves, Planned Parenthood, the National Gay and Lesbian Task Force, the Massachusetts chapter of the American Jewish Congress, and the Chicago chapter of the American Jewish Committee.

Kathleen M. Blee (1953–)

A sociology and women's studies professor at the University of Pittsburgh, Kathleen Blee has written widely on race, racism, social movements, and the sociology of women. Her most recent book is *Inside Organized Racism: Women in the Hate Movement.* (Berkeley: University of California Press, 2002) She has also written books on Appalachia and women and radical movements. She won an award from the Gustavus Myers Center for the Study of Human Rights in North America for her book *Women of the Klan: Racism and Gender in the 1920s* (University of California Press, 1991). This work offered pioneering research on the little-known fact that women in the 1920s constituted almost half of the Klan membership in some states. Most surprising, some of these women were simultaneously involved in such progressive movements as women's suffrage. Blee's current projects include the ethnography of anti-Jewish crimes and the micropolitics of new social movements.

Professor Blee has served as the director of the women's studies program at the University of Pittsburgh. Previously, she was an associate dean and director of the women's studies program at the University of Kentucky and has done extensive research on poverty in eastern Kentucky. Blee has an undergraduate degree in sociology from Indiana University and a PhD from the University of Wisconsin–Madison.

Floyd Cochran (1956–)

Floyd Cochran is the founder and director of Education & Vigilance, a Pennsylvania-based grassroots group that monitors and exposes white supremacist activity.

Born in rural Cortland, New York, Cochran, like many individuals involved in racist hate movements, came from a troubled background. His mother was jailed for armed robbery and his father physically abused him. He was eventually placed in a foster home.

Early on, Cochran developed an interest in Nazism and Adolph Hitler. After high school, he became a member of the Ku Klux Klan. He married and soon divorced his wife after they had two sons.

In 1990 he moved to the Pacific Northwest and became active in the largest neo-Nazi group in the United States, Aryan Nations, whose headquarters were in northern Idaho. He soon became a major spokesman for the group, recruiting skinheads and other disaffected individuals. "In six months," he once boasted, "I went from milking cows in upstate New York to being in *Newsweek*. There are very few racists who could smile and make hatred sound as palatable as I could."

At a 1992 youth festival, however, he was shocked when he heard someone talking about killing disabled people. His son, then four years old, had been born with a cleft palate. He became disillusioned, left the movement, and eventually met with two individuals who had formerly been his most bitter adversaries: Lenny Zeskind and Loretta Ross, a Jewish man and an African American woman who worked with the Center for Democratic Renewal.

After several meetings with Zeskind and Ross, Cochran eventually renounced his racist and anti-Jewish views. He soon emerged as a leading national speaker warning against the dangers of racist hate movements. He now tours the country, speaking to civic groups and on radio and television. He recounts his odyssey in the racist movement, especially aiming his message at susceptible young people. Cochran recalls indoctrinating one youth who was later convicted of firebombing the Tacoma, Washington, office of the National Association for the Advancement of Colored People.

Although his life has been repeatedly threatened by former comrades, Cochran continues to give public talks. He often ends his speeches with a heartfelt sentiment: "If my racism harmed you in any way, directly or indirectly, I am sorry."

Rabbi Abraham Cooper (1950–)

The associate dean of the Simon Wiesenthal Center in Los Angeles, Rabbi Cooper came to California with Rabbi Marvin Hier to help establish the organization in 1977. A longtime human rights and Jewish activist, Cooper has been extensively involved in the Soviet Jewry movement including visiting refuseniks in the 1970s.

Since the early 1980s, Rabbi Cooper has administered the Wiesenthal Center's international program, including the battle against worldwide anti-Semitism, remaining Nazi war criminals, violent extremist groups, hate on the Internet, terrorism, and tolerance education.

Rabbi Cooper has coordinated international conferences on anti-Semitism at the United Nations Educational, Scientific, and Cultural Organization's headquarters in Paris, on Holocaust restitution in Geneva, and on digital hate in Berlin. He has been particularly active in Asia and has worked with government officials and other individuals in Japan, the People's Republic of China, and India on intergroup relations. He was a leader of the Simon Wiesenthal Center mission that brought the first Jewish-sponsored exhibition to China in 1992.

In 2001, Rabbi Cooper was a delegate at the controversial United Nations conference in Durban, South Africa, where he spoke against the upsurge in anti-Jewish violence and hate throughout the world.

Rabbi Cooper is the editor-in-chief of *Response*, the center's quarterly magazine. He has written a children's book and authored exhibitions on prominent individuals, including Simon Wiesenthal and Jackie Robinson.

Morris S. Dees (1936–)

The son of an Alabama farmer, Morris Seligman Dees gave up a successful career running a mail order and book publishing business to pursue his commitment to civil rights.

A graduate of the University of Alabama Law School, Dees filed a suit in 1967 to stop the construction of a white university in an Alabama city that already had a predominantly black state college. In 1969, he filed a suit to integrate the all-white Montgomery YMCA. Dees and his law partner Joseph Levin Jr. saw the need for a nonprofit organization dedicated to seeking justice and, with civil rights activist Julian Bond, founded the Southern Poverty Law Center (SPLC) in 1971.

As chief trial counsel for the SPLC, he filed suit against white supremacist Tom Metzger and his White Aryan Resistance group for their responsibility in the beating death of a young Ethiopian student in Portland, Oregon. His second book, *Hate on Trial: The Case against America's Most Dangerous Neo-Nazi* (Villard Books, 1993) chronicles this case, which resulted in an unprecedented $12.5 million judgment against a U.S. hate group.

His autobiography, *A Season for Justice* (Charles Scribner) was published in 1991, and the American Bar Association released it in 2001 as *A Lawyer's Journey: The Morris Dees Story*. His third book, *Gathering Storm: America's Militia Threat*, exposes the danger posed by today's domestic terrorist groups (HarperCollins Publishers, 1996).

Steven Emerson (1954–)

Steven Emerson is an expert on terrorism and national security and an author who also serves as the executive director of a consulting firm, The Investigative Project. He was one of the earliest researchers to warn about the dangers posed by Islamic extremists who were living in the United States and preaching violence against Americans here and abroad.

Emerson started The Investigative Project in late 1995, following the broadcast on public television of his documentary film *Jihad in America*, which portrayed the clandestine operations by militant Islamic terrorist groups on U.S. soil. This film later received the George Polk Award in 1994 for best television documentary. Since the mid-1990s, Emerson has testified before Congress and has briefed the National Security Council at the White House as well. He has won three awards from the organization Investigative Reporters and Editors for magazine journalism.

Emerson's latest book is *American Jihad: The Terrorists Living Among Us* (Simon & Schuster, 2002). He has authored or coauthored four other books: *Terrorist: The Inside Story of the Highest-Ranking Iraqi Terrorist Ever to Defect to the West* (Villard/Random

House, 1991); *The Fall of Pan Am 103: Inside the Lockerbie Investigation* (Putnam, 1990); *Secret Warriors: Inside the Covert Military Operations of the Reagan Era* (Putnam, 1988); and *The American House of Saud: The Secret Petrodollar Connection* (Franklin Watts, 1985).

Between 1990 and 1993, Emerson served as a special investigative correspondent for CNN, where he was an international reporter. He has also served as a senior editor for *U.S. News & World Report*. He has a BA and an MA from Brown University.

Gregory Herek (1954–)

Gregory Herek is an authority on hate crimes, prejudice against lesbians and gay men, and AIDS-related stigma. A research psychologist at the University of California at Davis, he was one of the earliest researchers to conduct empirical research on hate crimes based on sexual orientation. Herek has testified on behalf of the American Psychological Association on antigay hate crimes at hearings before the House Subcommittee on Criminal Justice in 1986. He also organized and cochaired a research workshop on antigay violence for the National Institute of Mental Health (NIMH) and has been involved with a four-year NIMH empirical study of the mental health consequences of violence directed against gay men and lesbians. Herek was also a participant at the White House Conference on Hate Crime in November 1997. He and Kevin Berrill coedited *Hate Crimes: Confronting Violence against Lesbians and Gay Men* (Sage Publications, 1992). He writes widely for psychological and social science journals.

Herek received a BA from the University of Nebraska at Omaha in 1977 and later, his PhD in social psychology from the University of California at Davis in 1983. He was a postdoctoral fellow and a faculty member at Yale and the Graduate Center of the City University of New York before returning to the University of California at Davis.

James B. Jacobs (1947–)

James Jacobs is the director of the Center for Research in Crime and Justice and the Chief Justice Warren E. Burger Professor of Constitutional Law and the Courts at the New York University School of Law. A leading critic of hate crimes legislation, he has written widely on the topic in many law and academic journals, including the *Journal of Criminal Law & Criminology, Annual Survey of American Law, Criminal Justice Ethics,* and *The Public Interest.*

Jacobs is the coauthor, with Kimberly Potter, of *Hate Crimes: Criminal Law and Identity Politics* (Oxford University Press, 1998). He has a JD and a PhD in sociology from the University of Chicago. His first book, *Statesville: The Penitentiary in Mass Society* (University of Chicago Press, 1977), is a standard textbook in college and university classrooms.

Valerie Jenness (1963–)

Valerie Jenness, the chair of the Department of Criminology, Law and Society and an associate professor in the Department of Sociology at the University of California at Irvine, has written widely on sociological aspects of hate crimes and hate crime legislation. Her research focuses on the links between deviance and social control (especially law), gender, and social change. She is the coauthor of two recent books on hate crimes: *Making Hate a Crime: From Social Movement to Law Enforcement Practice* (Russell Sage Foundation, 2001) and *Hate Crimes: New Social Movements and the Politics of Violence* (Aldine de Gruyter, 1997). She has also written for academic journals on a variety of subjects, including the politics of prostitution, AIDS and civil liberties, hate crimes and hate crime law, the gay/lesbian movement, and the women's movement in the United States. She has served as an associate editor for the journal *Social Problems* and is active on several committees of the American Sociological Association.

Brian Levin (1963–)

A civil rights attorney, Brian Levin is an associate professor of criminal justice and the director of the Center for the Study of Hate and Extremism at California State University, San Bernardino, where he specializes in the analysis of hate crimes, and terrorism.

Previously, Levin served as the associate director of legal affairs of the Southern Poverty Law Center's Klanwatch/Militia Task Force in Montgomery, Alabama; legal director of the Center for the Study of Ethnic and Racial Violence in Newport Beach,

California, and as a corporate litigator for a law firm. He was also a New York City policeman in the drug-plagued sections of Harlem and Washington Heights during the 1980s.

Levin began his academic career in 1996 as an associate professor at Stockton College in New Jersey. A graduate of Stanford Law School, he was awarded the Block Civil Liberties Award for his work on hate crime. An author or coauthor of many publications on extremism and hate crime, he also wrote briefs in the U.S. Supreme Court case of *Wisconsin v. Mitchell* in 1992–1993, analyzing criminological data that established the severity of hate crimes.

Jack Levin (1941–)

Jack Levin is the Irving and Betty Brudnick Professor of Sociology at Northeastern University, where he has taught since 1970. He has authored or coauthored more than two dozen books; his most recent include *Dead Lines: Essays in Murder and Mayhem* (Allyn & Bacon, 2001) and *The Violence of Hate: Confronting Racism, Anti-Semitism and other Forms of Bigotry* (Allyn & Bacon, 2002). A social psychologist and media personality, Levin's research interests focus on prejudice. As the director of the Brudnick Center on Conflict and Violence at Northeastern, he is researching school violence, riots, celebrities in popular culture, and hate crimes.

Levin is the coauthor of *Hate Crimes: The Rising Tide of Bigotry and Bloodshed* (Westview Press, 1993) and the revised and updated work, *Hate Crimes Revisited: America's War against Those Who Are Different* (Westview Press, 2002). Levin has written extensively on hate crimes for academic and popular journals and lectures widely on the topic. He received a BA degree from American International College and a PhD from Boston University.

Daniel Levitas (1960–)

Daniel Levitas is a writer and researcher on the subject of extreme right-wing racist, anti-Jewish, and neo-Nazi organizations. Since 1986 he has testified as an expert witness or provided pretrial consulting expertise on the Ku Klux Klan, anti-Semitism, Holocaust denial, the skinhead movement, Aryan Nations, and hate-motivated violence. From 1989 to 1992, Levitas served as the executive director of the Center for Democratic Renewal in Atlanta, a nonprofit organization that monitors hate groups.

Levitas is the author of *The Terrorist Next Door: The Militia Movement and the Radical Right* (St. Martin's, 2002). He was also a contributing author to *Anti-Semitism in America Today* (Birch Lane Press, 1995). From 1991 to 1992 he edited *When Hate Groups Come to Town: A Handbook of Effective Community Responses,* a 192-page handbook about constructive responses to local hate group activity and violence. Levitas contributed articles to *Grolier's Multimedia Encyclopedia* on the history of American anti-Semitism, hate crimes, and the U.S. militia movement. He has written for the *Nation,* the *Los Angeles Times Book Review,* the *New York Times, Roll Call, Congress Monthly, Reform Judaism* magazine, and other publications.

Mark Potok (1955–)

As director of publications and information for the Southern Poverty Law Center's Intelligence Project (formerly known as Klanwatch), Potok is frequently interviewed in the national media about right-wing extremist and violence-prone groups. Before joining the center, Potok was the southwest correspondent for *USA Today,* covering the siege in Waco, Texas; the bombing in Oklahoma City; and the trial of Timothy McVeigh. Potok has also worked at the *Dallas Times Herald* and the *Miami Herald.* In early 2000, he presented a paper at a United Nations conference in Geneva on hate on the Internet and also testified at a U.S. Senate hearing on that topic. Potok is the editor of the widely praised journal *Intelligence Report,* a publication frequently consulted and quoted by journalists and law enforcement officials.

Kenneth Stern (1953–)

Attorney Kenneth S. Stern is a program specialist on anti-Semitism and extremism for the American Jewish Committee (AJC). Since joining the AJC in October 1989, Stern has written for a variety of publications on the militia movement, bigotry on campus, hate on talk radio, hate on the Internet, anti-Zionism, skinheads, David Duke, Louis Farrakhan, and the extremist Christian Identity movement. His AJC report *Militias: A Growing*

Danger, issued two weeks before the Oklahoma City bombing, predicted such attacks on government buildings. He also wrote *Holocaust Denial*, one of the earliest works on the dissemination of lies by anti-Jewish propagandists about the Nazi Holocaust. His investigative study of the PBS documentary *The Liberators: A Background Report* (American Jewish Committee, 1993) questioned the accuracy of the film; PBS later withdrew the documentary from distribution.

Stern's book *Loud Hawk: The United States vs. The American Indian Movement* (University of Oklahoma Press, 1994) surveys prejudice against Native Americans and *A Force upon the Plain: The American Militia Movement and the Politics of Hate* (Simon & Schuster, 1996) details the growth in that extreme right-wing movement.

As an attorney for the American Jewish Committee, he has written a critique of the court of appeals decision in the matter of Nazi war criminal John Demjanjuk and was of counsel on AJC's brief in *Wisconsin v. Mitchell*, the landmark hate crimes case decided by the U.S. Supreme Court. Mr. Stern was an adviser to the defense in the historic London-based Holocaust denial trial of *Irving v Penguin*. He has helped create two major Web sites to combat bigotry.

Most recently, Stern has written and spoken about the upsurge of anti-Jewish activities on college campuses following the collapse of the Arab-Israeli peace process. In 1997 Stern served as an invited presenter at the White House Conference on Hate Crimes and was an official member of the U.S. delegation to the Stockholm International Forum on Combating Intolerance in 2001. He also serves as a board member of the Gonzaga University Institute for Action against Hate, which publishes the *Journal of Hate Studies*.

Stern earned an AB at Bard College and a JD from Willamette University College of Law.

Lu-in Wang (1962–)

Lu-in Wang, a professor of law at the University of Pittsburgh Law School, has written extensively in the area of hate crimes law and is the author of *Hate Crimes Law* (Clark Boardman Callaghan, 1994, updated annually), the first textbook on that subject. Wang discusses the assumptions underlying the debate on the merits of hate crimes legislation and suggests a complex view of the dynamics of hate crimes. More recently, she has used psychological and sociological research to examine the social and behavioral attitudes that perpetuate discrimination in everyday life. Her articles have appeared in the *Boston University Law Review*, the *Michigan Journal of Race and Law*, the *Ohio State Law Journal*, and the *Southern California Law Review*.

Wang was the 2000 recipient of the Student Bar Association's Excellence in Teaching Award, the 2000 recipient of the Pitt Law Women's Association's Celebrating Women in the Law Award, and a recipient of the University of Pittsburgh 2001 Chancellor's Distinguished Teaching Award.

Wang previously practiced law with firms in Chicago and Ann Arbor, Michigan, and she is a former staff attorney for the Center for Social Gerontology, a national support center on law and aging. She has a BS and a BA degree from Pennsylvania State University and a JD from the University of Michigan.

Bill Wassmuth (1941–2001)

A leading activist against neo-Nazi and white supremacists in the Northwest region of the United States, Bill Wassmuth was praised by Idaho governor Dirk Kempthorne as an "early voice for human rights and human dignity in our state." (News Release, Idaho Office of the Governor, August 28, 2002) Born in Green Creek, Idaho, a small farming community, Wassmuth later entered the Catholic priesthood and became a well-known activist. He was appointed chairman of the Kootenai County Task Force on Human Relations, a civil rights group formed in 1981 in response to the harassment of a multiracial family. In September 1986, a pipe bomb exploded at Wassmuth's Coeur d'Alene home, causing extensive damage but no injuries. Local authorities determined that the bombing was carried out by neo-Nazi members of the Aryan Nations in retaliation for Wassmuth's human rights work. They were later convicted of the crime.

After leaving the priesthood in June 1988, Wassmuth moved to Seattle and later became the first executive director of the Northwest Coalition against Malicious Harassment. This nonprofit Seattle-based human rights organization formed under his guidance, serves Washington, Idaho, Oregon, Montana,

Wyoming, and Colorado and is composed of approximately 100 smaller organizations and 2,500 individual members.

In his book *Hate Is My Neighbor* (Stand Together Publishers, 1999), written with Tom Alibrandi, Wassmuth said, "To ignore hate groups, even though they usually include relatively small numbers of people, is to miscalculate the impact that they can have on a community."

Wassmuth retired from the Northwest Coalition in December 1999 but remained active in human rights circles. He died of amyotrophic lateral sclerosis, commonly known as Lou Gehrig's disease, in 2001.

5

Documents and Reports

Statistics on Hate Crimes

When Congress passed the Hate Crimes Statistics Act of 1990, the Uniform Crime Reporting (UCR) Program of the Federal Bureau of Investigation (FBI) became the official U.S. government clearinghouse for the collection and sharing of data regarding hate crimes. Since 1991, the program has compiled and published statistics on offenses determined by law enforcement to have been driven by bias against race, religion, ethnicity, sexual orientation, and since 1994, disability. The following are edited excerpts from the 2003 edition of the F.B.I. Hate Crime Statistics (the full report can be accessed at http://www.fbi.gov/ucr/03hc.pdf).

Incidents and Offenses
Hate Crime Statistics—2003

The UCR Program collects data for crimes motivated by biases against a race, religion, sexual orientation, ethnicity/national origin, or disability. Each bias type is further broken down into a more specific bias. For example, when a law enforcement agency determines that a hate crime was committed because of a bias against an individual's race, the agency may then classify the bias as anti-white; anti-black; anti-American Indian/Alaskan Native; anti-Asian/Pacific Islander; or anti-multiple races, group, which describes a group of victims in which more than one race is represented.

Hate crime data collection guidelines stipulate that officers can identify single-bias incidents, i.e., those that involve one type of bias, and multiple-bias incidents, i.e., those that involve two or more offense types motivated by two or more biases. Additionally, the UCR Program collects multiple offenses, victims, and offenders within one hate crime incident.

During 2003, 11,909 law enforcement agencies provided the UCR Program with 1 to 12 months of hate crime reports. Of those agencies, 1,967 agencies (16.5 percent) reported 7,489 hate crime incidents involving 8,715 offenses, 9,100 victims, and 6,934 known offenders.

Incidents and Offenses

Among the 7,489 reported hate crime incidents in 2003, 7,485 were single-bias incidents. Investigators reported 4 multiple-bias hate crime incidents in 2003.

Within the 7,485 single-bias incidents reported in 2003, 51.4 percent of the hate crime incidents were committed because of the offenders' racial bias. Nearly 18 percent (17.9) were due to religious bias, 16.6 percent were attributed to sexual-orientation bias, and 13.7 percent occurred because of an ethnicity/national origin bias. Disability bias motivated 0.4 percent of single-bias incidents.

In 2003, the single-bias hate crime incidents reported to law enforcement involved 8,706 offenses. The 4 multiple-bias incidents that officers reported in 2003 encompassed 9 different offenses.

By Crime Category. The UCR Program categorizes offenses as crimes against persons, crimes against property, and crimes against society. Law enforcement agencies reported 5,517 offenses as crimes against persons, which accounted for 63.3 percent of reported hate crimes in 2003. Investigators determined that 3,139 offenses, 36.0 percent of reported hate crimes, were crimes against property. Fifty-nine offenses (0.7 percent) were crimes against society.

By Bias Motivation. Racial bias motivated more than half (52.5 percent) of the 8,706 single-bias hate crime offenses reported in 2003. Religious bias and sexual-orientation bias each accounted for 16.4 percent of all reported single-bias hate crimes. Ethnicity/national origin bias prompted 14.2 percent of offenses, and disability bias spurred 0.5 percent of bias-motivated offenses.

In 2003, law enforcement reported 4,574 single-bias offenses that were motivated by the offender's bias against race. Among those offenses, 66.3 percent were perpetrated because of an anti-black bias, and 21.2 percent were due to an anti-white bias. Just over 6 percent (6.1) of racially-motivated hate crimes were driven by an anti-Asian/ Pacific Islander bias, 1.8 percent involved a bias against American Indians/Alaskan Natives, and 4.7 percent were directed at groups of individuals in which more than one race was represented (multiple races, group).

Law enforcement reported that 1,426 single-bias hate crime offenses resulted from a religious bias: 69.2 percent were an anti-Jewish bias, 10.9 percent were an anti-Islamic bias, 8.3 percent were an anti-other (unspecified) religion bias, 5.5 percent were an anti-Catholic bias, 3.5 percent were an anti-Protestant bias, and 0.9 percent were an anti-atheism/agnosticism bias. Nearly 2 percent (1.8) of anti-religious hate crime offenses in 2003 were due to a bias against groups of individuals of varying religions (multiple religions, group).

Within the 1,430 single-bias hate crime offenses perpetrated due to a sexual-orientation bias, law enforcement identified 61.6 percent as having an anti-male homosexual bias. In addition, 21.3 percent were due to an anti-homosexual bias, 15.4 percent were committed because of an anti-female homosexual bias, 1.0 percent were driven by an anti-heterosexual bias, and 0.6 percent involved an anti-bisexual bias.

Law enforcement agencies classify hate crimes motivated by a bias against an ethnicity/national origin into one of two categories: anti-Hispanic or anti-other ethnicity/national origin. In 2003, investigators reported 1,236 single-bias hate crime offenses that were committed because of an ethnicity/national origin bias. Nearly 43 percent (42.8) were due to an anti-Hispanic ethnicity bias, and 57.2 percent were directed at other ethnicities/national origins. Among hate crimes committed because of a bias against a disability, investigators classify the offense as having an anti-physical disability bias or an anti-mental disability bias. Of the 40 single-bias hate crime offenses committed in 2003 because of a bias against a disability, law enforcement agencies reported that 30 were provoked by an anti-physical disability bias, and 10 were committed because of an anti-mental disability bias.

By Offense Type. An analysis of the 8,715 hate crime offenses that were reported in 2003 showed that intimidation accounted for 31.5 percent of the total. Destruction/damage/vandalism comprised 30.0 percent; simple assault, 20.8 percent; and aggravated assault, 10.6 percent. Crimes against society comprised 0.7 percent of all reported hate crime offenses in 2003. The remaining offenses collectively made up 6.5 percent of the total.

Law enforcement reported 14 murders that were bias motivated in 2003—6 resulted from a sexual-orientation bias, 5 were racially motivated, 2 were due to an ethnicity/national origin bias, and 1 was because of a disability bias.

Officers' investigations determined that 5 forcible rapes in 2003 were bias motivated. Three forcible rapes were committed because of a sexual-orientation bias, 1 forcible rape occurred because of a racial bias, and 1 involved a disability bias.

Fifty of the 107 robberies that law enforcement identified as being motivated by bias were committed because of the offender's racial bias, and 36 robberies were committed because of a sexual-orientation bias. Seventeen robberies were attributed to an ethnicity/national origin bias, and 4 robberies were committed because of a religious bias.

Of the 34 arsons that investigators reported as bias-motivated crimes in 2003, 17 were motivated by a bias against a race, 8 were the result of an ethnicity/national origin bias, 5 were based on a religious bias, and 4 were because of a sexual-orientation bias.

By Victim Type.   Law enforcement agencies reported 3,139 bias-motivated offenses against property during 2003. A review of these offenses by victim type revealed that 52.1 percent were directed at individuals, 11.2 percent were directed at a business or financial institution, and 7.4 percent were directed at a religious organization. In addition, 7.0 percent were directed against government, and 0.1 percent of these offenses were directed at society or the public. Law enforcement categorized the remaining 22.3 percent of offenses against property as those directed against other/unknown/multiple victim types.

Victims

In the hate crime data collection program, the term victim may refer to a person, a business, an institution, or, in some cases, society as a whole. For the 2003 report, law enforcement identified 9,100 victims of 8,715 criminal offenses within 7,489 separate incidents. The following summarizes the data concerning victims of hate crimes as contributed by participating agencies.

By Bias Motivation.   More than half (52.3 percent) of all hate crime victims of single-bias incidents in 2003 were the targets of racial prejudice. As percentages of the single-bias victim total, victims of religious bias and victims of sexual-orientation bias were nearly equal: 16.4 percent and 16.3 percent, respectively. Victims of ethnicity/national origin bias made up 14.6 percent of the total victims, and victims of a disability bias accounted for the remainder, 0.5 percent.

Racial bias motivated hate crimes against 4,754 victims in 2003. The majority of these victims—66.3 percent—were the objects of anti-black bias. Of the remaining victims of single-bias incidents motivated by racial bias, 21.2 percent were victims of anti-white bias, 6.1 percent were victims of anti-Asian/Pacific Islander bias, and 1.8 percent were victims of anti-American Indian/Alaskan Native bias. Victims of anti-multiple races bias, that is, groups in which more than one race was represented, accounted for 4.7 percent of the victims of single-biased racially motivated hate crimes.

Of the 1,489 victims of single-bias crimes motivated by religious intolerance during 2003, 68.8 percent were victims of anti-Jewish bias. Victims of anti-Islamic bias comprised 11.5 percent of religious-bias victims. Anti-Catholic bias prompted offenses against 5.4 percent of victims of religious bias, and anti-Protestant bias initiated crimes against 3.6 percent of the religious-bias victims. Biases against members of other religious groups (anti-other religion) and those directed at groups comprised of individuals from varying or multiple religious faiths (anti-multiple religions, group) motivated the crimes against 8.1 percent and 1.7 percent of victims, respectively. Anti-atheism/agnosticism biases accounted for nearly 1 percent (0.9) of victims of the crimes caused by a religious bias.

Antagonism toward a sexual orientation formed the motivation for crimes against 1,479 victims of single-bias incidents in 2003. Among victims of a sexual-orientation bias, 61.5 percent were the victims of anti-male homosexual bias, and 21.2 percent were targets of anti-homosexual bias (male and female). An anti-female homosexual bias contributed to crimes against 15.6 percent of victims of sexual-orientation bias. The remaining victims were targets of anti-heterosexual (1.0 percent) and anti-bisexual (0.7 percent) attitudes.

In 2003, there were 1,326 victims of single-bias incidents involving anti-ethnicity/national origin bias. Of these, 44.9 percent were victims of anti-Hispanic prejudice, and 55.1 percent were victims of anti-other ethnicity/national origin bias.

Law enforcement agencies reported that 43 victims in single-bias incidents were assailed because of an anti-physical or anti-mental disability bias in 2003. Of these, 32 were victims of an anti-physical disability bias, and 11 were victims of an anti-mental disability bias.

There were 9 victims of the 4 multiple-bias incidents reported in 2003.

By Offense Category. A review of the 9,100 hate crime victims reported for 2003 revealed that 60.6 percent were victims of crimes against persons, 38.7 percent were victims of crimes against property, and 0.6 percent were victims of crimes against society.

By Offense Type. For 2003, law enforcement reported 5,517 victims of crimes against persons. These victims were most often the objects of intimidation (49.7 percent), simple assault (32.8 percent), or aggravated assault (16.7 percent). Those who were murdered accounted for 0.3 percent of all hate crime victims, and those who were raped made up 0.1 percent. The remainder, 0.5 percent, were victims of other types of crimes against persons.

Of the 3,524 victims of crimes against property, 82.3 percent were the objects of destruction/damage/vandalism. Victims of other crimes against property included those of burglary, which accounted for 5.4 percent of victims; larceny-theft, 5.3 percent of victims; robbery, 4.3 percent of victims; and arson, 1.2 percent of victims. Victims of motor vehicle theft comprised 0.4 percent. The remaining victims, 1.0 percent, were targets of various other types of crimes against property.

Offenders

As defined by the UCR hate crime data collection program, the term *known offender* does not imply that the suspect's identify is known but that an attribute of the suspect is identified which distinguishes him or her from an unknown offender. On the *Hate Crime Incident Report* form, reporting agencies can specify the number of offenders and, when possible, the apparent race of the offender (or offenders as a group).

In 2003, a total of 6,934 known offenders were identified in 7,489 bias-motivated incidents. Of the known offenders, 62.3 percent were white and 18.5 percent were black. Groups comprised of individuals of varying races (multiple races, group) accounted for 6.3 percent of known offenders. Reporting agencies identified Asian/Pacific Islander as the race for 1.3 percent and American Indian/Alaskan Native for 0.9 percent of the known offenders. For 10.7 percent of known offenders, the attribute of race was unknown.

Of the 5,543 known offenders who perpetrated crimes against persons in 2003, 40.3 percent committed simple assault, 36.5 percent committed intimidation, and 22.3 percent committed aggravated assault. Of the 1,558 known offenders who perpetrated crimes against property, 66.9 percent carried out acts of destruction/damage/vandalism, 16.4 percent committed robbery, and 6.7 percent committed larceny-theft. In 2003, 92 known offenders committed 59 hate crime offenses that agencies reported as crimes against society.

Location

A review of hate crime incidents by location revealed that nearly one-third—32.0 percent—of all single-bias hate crime incidents occurred in or near residences or homes in 2003. Highways, roads, alleys, or streets were the locations of 17.6 percent of the total incidents, and schools or colleges were the sites of 11.8 percent of hate crime occurrences. Six percent of hate crime incidents happened in a parking lot or garage, and 3.8 percent took place at a church, synagogue, or temple. The locations of 12.5 percent of hate crime incidents were unknown or unspecified, and the remaining incidents, 16.3 percent, occurred in a variety of locations.

By Bias Motivation. An analysis of bias-motivated offenses with regard to location showed that of the 3,844 incidents sparked by racial prejudice, 33.8 percent occurred at a home or residence. Over 19 percent (19.2) occurred on a highway, road, alley, or street, and 12.5 percent happened at a school or college. Of the 1,343 incidents caused by religious intolerance, 29.8 percent occurred at a home or residence, and 16.9 percent took place at a church, synagogue, or temple. A school or college was the setting for 12.3 percent of the total incidents attributed to a religious bias. Incidents involving bias against a sexual orientation also occurred most often in homes or residences—30.3 percent of the 1,239 incidents reported in 2003. Highways, roads, alleys, or streets were the locations of 25.0 percent of the incidents motivated by a sexual-orientation bias, and schools or colleges were the locations for 11.9 percent of those incidents. A residence or home was the setting for 29.8 percent of the 1,026 hate crime incidents involving the victim's ethnicity/national origin. Highways, roads, alleys, or streets were the locations of 17.4 percent of such incidents, and schools or colleges were the scenes of 8.2 percent of those incidents. Of the 33 hate crime incidents in which the offender was driven by a bias against a disability, 13 took place at a home or residence. A school or college was the scene of 6 of these bias-motivated incidents, and a highway, road, alley, or street was the location for 4 incidents. The remainder of these hate crime incidents occurred in various other and unknown locations. Concerning the 4 multiple-bias incidents reported in 2003, 2 occurred at residences or homes, 1 happened at a restaurant, and 1 took place at a school or college.

Training Law Enforcement to Combat Hate Crimes

Published by the International Association of Chiefs of Police (IACP), this document provides succinct and useful information for law en-forcement officers, community officials, educators, and others about the general nature of hate crimes and methods to prevent them.

Responding to Hate Crimes: A Police Officer's Guide to Investigation and Prevention
by Nancy Turner

What Is a Hate Crime?

Hate crimes and hate incidents are major issues for all police because of their unique impact on victims as well as the community. This guidebook will explain the differences between hate crimes and hate incidents and how to respond to both.

A hate crime is a criminal offense committed against persons, property or society that is motivated, in whole or in part, by an offender's bias against an individual's or a group's race, religion, ethnic/national origin, gender, age, disability or sexual orientation. (Definition developed at the 1998 IACP Summit on Hate Crime in America.)

Legal definitions of hate crimes vary. The federal definition of hate crimes addresses civil rights violations under 18 U.S.C. Section 245.

As of 1999, 41 states and the District of Columbia have hate crime statutes that provide enhanced penalties for crimes in which victims are selected because of a perpetrator's bias against a victim's perceived race, religion or ethnicity. Many states also classify as hate crimes those in which a victim is selected based on a perception of his/her sexual orientation.

Hate crime definitions often encompass not only violence against individuals or groups but also crimes against property, such as arson or vandalism, particularly those directed against community centers or houses of worship. Check your state statutes for the definition of hate crime in your jurisdiction.

Accurate and comprehensive police reporting is essential to understanding the prevalence and patterns of hate crimes both locally and nationally.

The federal Hate Crimes Statistics Act of 1990 (Public Law 102–275 April 23, 1990) encourages states to report hate crime data to the Federal Bureau of Investigation (FBI). Twenty-three states and the District of Columbia require the collection of hate crime data. In 1997, 11,211 state and local law enforcement agencies voluntarily reported 9,861 hate crime offenses to the FBI.

Why Is It Important to Respond to Hate Crimes Quickly and Effectively?

Hate crimes differ from other crimes in their effect on victims and on community stability:

- Hate crimes are often especially brutal or injurious.
- Victim(s) usually feel traumatized and terrified.
- Families of victims often feel frustrated and powerless.
- Others in the community who share the victim's characteristics may feel victimized and vulnerable.
- Hate incidents can escalate and prompt retaliatory action.
- Hate crimes and hate incidents create communitywide unrest.

A swift and strong response by law enforcement can help stabilize and calm the community as well as aid in a victim's recovery. Failure to respond to hate crimes within departmental guidelines may jeopardize public safety and leave officers and departments open to increased scrutiny and possible liability.

What Is the Difference Between a Hate Incident and a Hate Crime?

Hate incidents involve behaviors that, though motivated by bias against a victim's race, religion, ethnic/national origin, gender, age, disability or sexual orientation, are not criminal acts. Hostile or hateful speech, or other disrespectful/discriminatory behavior may be motivated by bias but is not illegal. They become crimes only when they directly incite perpetrators to commit violence against persons or property, or if they place a potential victim in reasonable fear of physical injury. Officers should thoroughly document evidence in all bias-motivated incidents. Law enforcement can help to defuse potentially dangerous situations and prevent bias-motivated criminal behavior by responding to and documenting bias-motivated speech or behavior even if it does not rise to the level of a criminal offense.

What Is an Effective Police Response to Hate Crimes?

Police officers and investigators have important roles to play in responding to hate incidents and crimes. By doing the job efficiently and carefully, police can reinforce the message that hate crimes will be investigated aggressively, thus enhancing the likelihood of a successful prosecution.

Police Officers Arriving on the Scene Should Act Immediately to

- secure the scene
- stabilize the victim(s) and request medical attention when necessary
- ensure the safety of victims, witnesses and perpetrators
- preserve the crime scene; collect and photograph physical evidence such as
  - hate literature
  - spray paint cans
  - threatening letters
  - symbolic objects used by hate groups (e.g., swastikas, crosses)
- identify criminal evidence on the victim

- request the assistance of translators when needed
- conduct a preliminary investigation; record information on
  - identity of suspected perpetrator(s)
  - identity of witnesses, including those no longer on the scene
  - prior occurrences, in this area or with this victim
  - statements made by suspects—exact wording is critical
  - arrest the perpetrator(s) if probable cause exists

Note: In the presence of the victim, the officer should neither confirm nor deny that the incident is a hate crime—that determination will be made later in the investigative process.

After taking immediate action, police officers should

- assign only one officer to interview the victim(s) whenever practical in order to minimize trauma
- protect the anonymity of victim whenever possible
- explain to victim and witnesses the likely sequence of events, including contact with investigators and the possibility of media coverage
- refer victim to support services in the community; provide written resource lists when possible
- tell victim how to contact the police department to obtain further information on the case
- report the suspected hate crime to the supervisor on duty
- refer media representatives to the supervisor on duty or public information officer
- document the incident thoroughly on department report forms, noting any particular hate crime indicators and quoting exact wording of statements made by perpetrators
- assist investigators in making any other reports that may be required under federal or state guidelines and laws

When conducting a thorough follow-up investigation, officers should

- interview victim(s) and witnesses thoroughly and respectfully
- secure evidence by taking photos of offensive graffiti or other symbols of bias
- document the circumstances and apparent motives surrounding the event
- locate and arrest any suspected perpetrators not apprehended at the scene
- provide their supervisor or public information officer with information that can be responsibly reported to the media

- inform victim of what is likely to happen during the continuing investigation
- appeal to witnesses to come forward by canvassing the community
- offer rewards for information about the incident when possible
- coordinate with other law enforcement agencies in the area to assess patterns of hate crimes and determine if organized hate groups are involved
- collaborate with the responding officers to complete any written reports required by their department, state and federal agencies
- notify the FBI if further assistance with investigations is needed

What Are the Key Indicators that a Hate Crime May Have Been Committed?

The main difference between a hate crime and other crimes is that a perpetrator of a hate crime is motivated by bias. To evaluate a perpetrator's motives, you should consider several bias indicators:

- perceptions of the victim(s) and witnesses about the crime
- the perpetrator's comments, gestures or written statements that reflect bias, including graffiti or other symbols
- any differences between perpetrator and victim, whether actual or perceived by the perpetrator
- similar incidents in the same location or neighborhood to determine whether a pattern exists
- whether the victim was engaged in activities promoting his/her group or community—for example, by clothing or conduct
- whether the incident coincided with a holiday or data of particular significance
- involvement of organized hate groups or their members
- absence of any other motive such as economic gain

The presence of any of these factors does not confirm that the incident was a hate offense but may indicate the need for further investigation into motive.

A victim's perception is an important factor to consider, but be aware that victims may not recognize the crime as motivated by bias. Victims should not be asked directly whether they believe they were the victim of a hate crime, but it is appropriate to ask if they have any idea why they might have been victimized.

Victims and perpetrators may appear to be from the same race, ethnicity/nationality, or religion, but it is the perpetrator's perception of difference (whether accurate or not) motivating his or her criminal behavior that would constitute a hate crime.

What Are the Best Approaches for Working with Victims of Hate Crime?

Hate crimes are unique. Victims of hate crimes are targeted because of a core characteristic of their identity. These attributes cannot be changed. Victims often feel degraded, frightened, vulnerable and suspicious. This may be one of the most traumatic experiences of their lives. Community members who share with victims the characteristics that made them targets of hate (race, religion, ethnic/national origin, gender, age, disability or sexual orientation) may also feel vulnerable, fearful and powerless. In this emotional atmosphere, law enforcement officers and investigators must attend carefully to the ways they interact and communicate with victims, their families, and members of the community.

Effective Ways for Police to Support Victims While Investigating the Crime

- remain calm, objective and professional
- ask victim(s) how they want you to help them
- request the assistance of translators when needed
- let victim defer answering questions if they are too distraught
- ask them [if] they have any idea why this happened to them
- reassure victim that they are not to blame for what happened
- voice you[r] support of the actions the victim took to protect themselves and defuse the situation
- allow them to vent feelings about the incident or crime
- encourage victim to tell the story in their own words
- ask them to recall, [to] the best of their ability, the exact words of the perpetrator(s)
- ask victim if they have family members or friends who can support them
- inform them of what efforts can be made to enhance their safety
- reassure them that every effort will be made to protect their anonymity during the investigation
- tell victim about the probable sequence of events in the investigation

- provide information about community and department resources available to protect and support victim, their families and members of the community

Avoid:

- being abrupt or rushed
- telling victim(s) that you know how they feel
- asking them whether they think this was a bias or hate crime
- criticizing the victim's behavior
- making assumptions about the victim's culture, religion, sexual orientation or lifestyle choices
- allowing personal value judgements about the victim's behavior, lifestyle or culture to affect your objectivity
- using stereotyped or biased terms
- belittling the seriousness of the incident, especially if the perpetrator was a juvenile

Reasons Why Victims May Be Reluctant to Report or Participate in the Investigation of a Hate Crime:

- fear of re-victimization or retaliation
- fear of having privacy compromised
- for gays and lesbians, fear of repercussions from being "outted" to family and employers
- fear of law enforcement and uncertainty about justice agency responses
- for aliens, fear of jeopardizing immigration status, being reported to INS or deportation
- humiliation or shame about being victimized
- lack of a support system
- cultural and language barriers

What Is the Ongoing Role the Police Play with Hate Crime Victims and the Community?

By providing a continuing point of contact throughout the investigation and prosecution phase, police can facilitate a victim's cooperation with the justice system, assist with the healing process and promote law enforcement's credibility. In the following ways, officers and their departments can support hate crime victims and members of the community:

- Provide victim(s) [with] a point of contact in the department to whom they can direct questions or concerns.
- Inform them on case progress including the end result of the investigation and/or prosecution
- Help to connect them with appropriate support services, victim advocates and community-based organizations when needed
- Protect the privacy of victim[s] and their families as possible
- Engage the media as partners in restoring victimized communities through sensitive and accurate reporting
- Support or coordinate community clean-up efforts
- Participate in meetings or other forums designed to address the communitywide impact of hate incidents or crimes
- Share information, as appropriate, with schools about cases where students or staff were victims or perpetrators of hate crimes
- Collaborate with community leaders to mobilize resources that can be used to assist victims and prevent future hate incidents and crimes

Police Officers and Their Agencies Can Assume a Leadership Role in Their Community to Prevent Hate Incidents and Crimes

Police officers can . . .

- Help to ensure that victims of hate crimes will report their victimization by demonstrating that law enforcement will respond swiftly and compassionately to all reports
- Participate in hate crime training
- Serve as positive role models, exemplifying tolerance of and respect for others
- Maximize cultural awareness to better communicate and work with citizens from diverse ethnic, racial and religious backgrounds
- Collaborate with community leaders to increase tolerance and promote peaceful conflict resolution among community members
- Support and participate in school programs and curricula intended to reduce prejudice and prevent bias-motivated crimes
- Work with citizens and community organizations to identify and address bias incidents and make referrals to state and local agencies (housing, employment and civil rights) to resolve problems

- Encourage the media to highlight community successes in preventing and responding to hate crimes and incidents
- Contribute to tracking and monitoring organized hate groups by gathering, documenting and reporting information about their criminal activities in affected communities

Police agencies can . . .

- Establish a policy of "zero tolerance" for prejudice throughout the department
- Ensure police are trained to recognize and respond appropriately to hate crimes
- Provide officers with user-friendly hate crime incident report forms that comply with state and national reporting standards
- Sponsor and participate in community events and activities that promote diversity, tolerance, bias reduction and conflict resolution
- Track the criminal activities of organized hate groups
- Collaborate with community organizations, schools, and other public agencies to develop coordinated approaches to hate crime prevention and response
- Engage the media as partners in restoring victimized communities and preventing bias-motivated incidents and crimes
- Document the positive outcomes of hate crime prevention and response strategies

Police officers and their agencies can accomplish much by working in partnership with citizens to implement the American vision of diverse and tolerant communities that offer freedom, safety and dignity for all.

Hate Crimes on Campus: A Growing Problem

This excerpted report was issued by the U.S. Department of Justice's Community Relations Service (CRS) on June 1, 2000. The report surveys the problem of campus hate crimes and its impact on students, staff, and college and university administrators. The authors include case studies of incidents on a few campuses and discuss the police investigation, victim assistance, public relations, and community support. The report notes that the CRS offers mediation and conciliation assistance to affected campuses.

Responding to Hate Crimes and Bias-Motivated Incidents on College/University Campuses

The Community Relations Service, an arm of the U.S. Department of Justice, is a specialized Federal conciliation service available to State and local officials to help resolve and prevent racial and ethnic conflict. CRS offers its services to governors, mayors, police chiefs and school officials in their efforts to defuse racial crises. CRS assists local officials and residents design locally defined resolutions when conflict and violence threaten community stability and well-being. As directed by the Civil Rights Act of 1964, CRS conciliators use specialized crisis management and violence reduction techniques to provide assistance in identifying the sources of conflict and violence and creating a more cohesive community environment. CRS has no law enforcement authority and does not impose solutions, investigate or prosecute cases, or assign blame or fault. However, CRS conciliators are required by law to conduct their activities in confidence, without publicity, and are prohibited from disclosing confidential information.

Director's Message

Based on our work experience, there is no place where hate crimes are occurring with increasing frequency, more visibility and hostility, than in institutions of higher education. In the course of our casework, we searched the nation for expertise on the fallout from these incidents, and finding very few resources, decided that it would be beneficial to create a guide for systematic response to these terrible, hateful acts.

We created this guide by bringing together a cross-section of representatives from college campus law enforcement, college administrators, students, academicians and civil rights organizations from all across the nation. This focus group discussed how different campuses are handling hate crimes on topics including crime investigation, victim assistance, media relations and community healing. These discussions created this guide containing case studies and highlights of some of the best practices regarding this issue. We hope that this guide and CRS will continue to be a helpful resource.

Hate Crime

Definition: A hate crime can be generally defined as a crime which in whole or part is motivated by the offender's bias toward the victim's status. A hate incident [is] an action in which a person is made aware that her/his status is offensive to another, but does not rise to the level of a crime.

Hate crimes are intended to hurt and intimidate individuals because they are perceived to be different with respect to their race, color, religion, national origin, sexual orientation, gender or disability. The purveyors of hate use physical violence, verbal threats of violence, vandalism, and in some cases weapons, explosives, and arson, to instill fear in their victims, leaving them vulnerable to subsequent attacks and feeling alienated, helpless, suspicious and fearful. These acts of hatred can leave lasting emotional impressions upon their victims as well as entire communities.

Reporting Requirements

Federal and state reporting requirements vary in the definitions and victim categories for hate crimes. The FBI Uniform Crime Reporting Program (28 USC §534), Campus Security Act (20 USC §1092), state and local hate crimes legislation list specific crimes which are identifiable as a hate crime, including murder, manslaughter, robbery, aggravated assault, burglary, motor vehicle theft, arson, forcible and non-forcible sex offenses, intimidation, destruction, damage or vandalism of property, and other crimes involving injury to any person or property in which the victim is intentionally selected because of the actual or perceived race, gender, religion, sexual orientation, ethnicity, or disability of the victim. When they do not fall into one of the listed criminal categories, hate offenses are referred to as bias-motivated incidents. These incidents may include cases of minor harassment, verbal slurs, etc. and be precursors to more serious hate motivated violence.

Background

On college campuses around the country, the competition can be fierce. As a result, students don't always view one another as allies or friends, but sometimes as opponents or enemies with whom they must vie for scarce amounts of success both in and out of the classroom. Some students regard their minority classmates as the undeserving recipients of financial aid and compensatory programs—what they believe to be special attention and special treatment. Similarly, some students of color expect to find a racist behind every obstacle to their academic advancement. Moreover, there are some students who resent the challenge posed by a growing presence of successful female students and gay students. And some students resent the increasing number of Asian-American students on campus—all Merit scholarship winners in high school, at least according to the stereotype.

Unfortunately, inter-group conflict can result from the growing diversity among college students. Over the past three decades, there have been increasing numbers of women, blacks, Latinos, Asians, the disabled, international students, as well as gays and lesbians on campuses around the country. In a situation where everyone appears to have more or less the same background—where almost all students are, for example, white, straight, able-bodied, American, male, and Protestant—inter-group conflict does not become much of an issue. Under conditions of increasing cultural diversity, however, the differences between groups become salient on an everyday basis. For the first time, many students must learn to deal with classmates and roommates who are *different*.

For most students, whatever their racial identity, college is the first occasion to have extensive contacts with individuals who differ from them in socially significant ways. Because of the pervasive racial and ethnic segregation that characterizes many communities, most students grow up going to school and residing among only "their own kind." Then, they go off to college, where they might meet a broader range of humanity than they have ever encountered.

Of course, the first few months of college represent a particularly stressful and threatening period. It is often the first time away from home; and students are in an environment where they could fail and be forced to leave. For many students, it is difficult to make friends with someone who is different from you when you are terrified of being rejected yourself. Many students therefore react to this extremely stressful situation by seeking companions who are very much like themselves.

The process whereby students, fearing rejection, befriend other students with similar attitudes and similar previous life experiences can have another, more negative consequence. A small number of such students make themselves feel more secure by demeaning or attacking, either verbally or physically, those classmates they believe to be inferior by virtue of that group's background, race, or creed. The very presence of minority students on a campus may give rise to such behavior.

At a small four-year college in suburban New England, the administration decided not to tolerate what many would regard as a minor hate incident or merely a "prank," when two female students made an anti-Semitic phone call to Jewish students in another residence hall.

As soon as its administration had confirmed the charges, the college canceled classes for the day and held a mandatory session in the campus amphitheater—an all-day anti-hate program for all students (including the two offenders), administrators, and instructors. Speakers included the college president, a guest expert on prejudice, and a panel of young people representing diverse backgrounds who had been victimized by bigotry. In addition, students viewed one of several feature-length films dealing with hate and violence (e.g., Schindler's List, American History X, etc.). A special committee was formed to create anti-hate posters, which its members placed at strategic positions around campus. The entire effort was designed to send a message: hate is not "cool" and will not be tolerated on this campus! Apparently, it worked. For at least two years, there was not a single hate incident reported to the school's administration. Of course, the small size of the student body (fewer than 500 students) made possible a plenary session which included everyone on campus. At a college or university where thousands of students are enrolled, it might be more difficult, even impossible, for everyone on campus to meet together in the same place. Even at a large university, however, tactics and strategies can be created to assure that the appropriate message is sent to students, faculty, and staff.

Characteristics of Hate Episodes on Campus

Hate episodes, including those reaching the level of criminal behavior, can be classified in terms of offender motivations into three distinct types identified as reactive, impulsive, and premeditated.

Reactive Hate Episodes

In reactive hate episodes, the hatemongers seize on what they consider as a triggering incident to justify their expression of anger. They rationalize that by attacking someone they regard as an outsider they are in fact protecting their college, residence hall, fraternity, or group of friends. Indeed, they often cast their victims in the role of those actively threatening them, while they regard themselves as pillars of virtue on their campus.

Moreover, the perpetrators of reactive hate episodes tend to target a particular individual or set of individuals who are perceived to constitute a personal threat—the black student who has just moved into a previously all white dormitory, the white college student who has begun to date her Asian classmate, or the Latin professor who introduces her students to a Latin American perspective. The reactive attack is meant to send a signal not only to the primary victim but also to every member of the victim's group—"you and others from your group do not belong on this campus."

At first, the offense may consist of a relatively minor act—racist graffiti spray-painted on a door or ethnic slurs over the telephone. If the early warning is ignored, however, there often is an escalation of violence consisting of a direct threat to do bodily harm or an actual assault.

The perpetrators of reactive attacks on a college campus are usually not associated with any organized hate group. Typically, they have no prior history of overt bigotry. Their reaction may have a practical basis—they fear losing opportunities for success or advancement. Sometimes the perpetrators react instead to a symbolic loss of "turf" or "privilege"—for example, when "our women" begin to date "them" or when "they" come onto our campus and begin to "take over."

Recent research has identified the initial point of integration as a key to understanding hate violence. According to a 1997 survey conducted by the Klanwatch Project of the Southern Poverty Law Center in Montgomery, Alabama, about half of all racially-inspired acts of vandalism and violence are directed at blacks moving into previously white neighborhoods. More generally, Donald Green and his associates have shown that hate crimes occur most frequently in "defended" white neighborhoods—that is, in predominantly white areas which have experienced an in-migration of minorities.

Given the competitive nature of the workplace, it should come as no surprise that many reactive hate episodes also occur on the job. In their study of "ethnoviolence at work," sociologists Joan Weiss, Howard Ehrlich, and Barbara Larcom (1991–92) found that 27 percent of all respondents who reported "prejudice-based" episodes experienced them while at work.

The college campus is, of course, the "workplace" for hundreds of thousands of young Americans. Stretching the concept of "defended neighborhood" just a bit, it becomes clear that many college students might easily feel a need to protect their job experiences, social activities, educational opportunities, dormitories, fraternities, and classrooms from members of the much more diverse population with whom they now share their campuses. Thus, reactive hate episodes on campus tend to be committed by students residing in the same college community as their victims.

During recent years, campus hate attacks have apparently become more defensive; that is, they are committed by students in response to a particular student or campus event that they feel threatened by—Gay Pride Week, the first black student in a dormitory, hostilities in the middle-east, and so on. For example, at a large public university on the West Coast, after an unsuccessful attempt by some members of the student government to reduce funding for a minority-oriented campus newspaper, two of its Chinese American reporters received threatening phone calls. Identifying himself only as a member of the Ku Klux Klan, the caller suggested that "something drastic" would happen to them if they did not stop writing for the newspaper. Similarly, a first-year

Latin-American student at a prestigious East Coast college found the following anonymous note slipped under her dormitory door after she had complained about her test grade: "Hey S—. If you and your kind can't handle the work here, don't blame it on this racial thing. You are just making our school look bad to everyone else. If you can't handle it, why don't you just get out. We'd all be a lot happier."

Impulsive Hate Episodes

Impulsive hate offenses are committed by perpetrators who are looking for excitement. In the same way that some young men get together on a Saturday night to play a game of cards, youthful hatemongers gather to shout threats and obscenities, destroy property or to assault someone who is different. They look merely to have some fun and stir up a little excitement . . . but at someone else's expense.

In an impulsive thrill-seeking hate episode, there need not be a precipitating incident. The victim does not necessarily "invade" the territory of the assailant by walking across his campus or attending classes. On the contrary, it is the assailant or group of assailants, looking to harass those who are different, who searches out locations where the members of a particular group regularly congregate. The payoff for the perpetrators is psychological as well as social: In addition to gaining a sense of importance and control, the youthful perpetrators also receive a stamp of approval from their friends who regard hatred as "hip" or "cool" (Levin and McDevitt, 1993).

In an impulsive thrill-motivated hate episodes, a group of young people typically travels to another area to find victims. Thus, thrill-seekers might travel to a gay bar in the local community or target students at another college as something to do for fun when they are bored on a Saturday night.

It is also possible, of course, for thrill-seekers to focus on their own schoolmates. Just for the "kicks," several sorority members at a university located in the mid-west dressed in Indian costumes and parodied "Indian hollers" outside the Native American Center on campus.

Impulsive hate episodes satisfy the offenders' profound psychological need to feel important and gain a sense of belonging. Therefore, almost any member of a vulnerable group will usually "do" as a target. For example, if impulsive thrill-seekers fail to locate someone gay, they might easily decide to victimize someone who is black or Latino. If they can't find someone black or Latino, they might instead target someone who is Jewish or Asian.

Impulsive offenses tend to be finite in time and space. Inspired by some combination of boredom, hate, and sense of impotence, the offenders set out to have some fun at the expense of their "enemy."

Additionally, the use of alcohol and/or drugs frequently become a factor in this type of behavior. Similarly, reactive hate episodes are generally aimed against particular "outsiders"—those who are regarded as posing affront to a perpetrator's campus. As in impulsive thrill-seeking episodes, the defensive attack tends to be narrowly focused and of limited duration. Once the threat is perceived to subside, so does the criminal behavior.

Premeditated Hate Episodes

On occasion, however, hate occurrences go beyond what their perpetrators consider reaction, at least in the narrow sense. Rather than direct their attack at those individuals involved in a particular event or episode—moving into a residence hall, taking a seat at the next desk in a classroom, attending the same party—the perpetrators are ready to wage "war" against any and all members of a particular group of people. No precipitating episode occurs; none is necessary. The perpetrator is on a moral mission: His assignment is to make the world a better place to live for [him] and his friends.

Those who perpetrate a premeditated hate episode are convinced that all out-group members are sub-humans who are bent on destroying *our* culture, *our* economy, or the purity of *our* racial heritage. The offender therefore is concerned about much more than simply eliminating a few blacks or Latinos from his college or university. Instead, he believes that he has a higher-order purpose in carrying out his crime. He has been instructed by God or, in a more secular version, by the Imperial Wizard or the Grand Dragon to rid the world of evil by eliminating *all* blacks, Latinos, Asians, or Jews; and he is compelled to act before it is too late. Premeditated mission hate offenders are likely to join an organized group such as the KKK, World Church of the Creator, or the White Aryan Resistance. The mission motivation is likely to result in the commission of a vicious, even deadly, hate crime.

In July, 1999, Benjamin Smith, a former student at Indiana University, went on a shooting spree across Illinois and Indiana. Along the way, he shot and killed a black man who was a former Northwestern University basketball coach; he murdered a Korean graduate student at Indiana University; and he also wounded eight additional people including six orthodox Jews and two Asian Americans. Twenty-one year old Smith was a member of the World Church of the Creator, a white supremacist group based in East Peoria, Illinois, whose leader Matthew Hale preaches that Jews are parasites who control the finances, propaganda, media, and governments of the world, and that blacks and Asians are inferior to whites. The battle cry of the group is RaHoWa meaning racial holy war.

A few perpetrators of premeditated hate crimes operate alone, typically suffering from a profound mental illness which may cause hallucinations, impaired ability to reason, and withdrawal from contact with other people. This type of hatemonger intends to get even for the horrific problems that he has suffered. In his paranoid and delusional way of thinking, he sees a conspiracy of some kind for which he seeks revenge. His mission is in part suicidal. Before taking his own life, however, he attempts to eliminate the *entire category* of people he is absolutely convinced is responsible for his personal frustrations. There are rare cases in which a depressed and frustrated gunman has opened fire with the objective of eliminating *all* women, Asians, or white racists (See Fox and Levin, 1994). In 1989, for example, Marc LePine, after being rejected from the University of Montreal's School of Engineering, first executed 14 female students there and then took his own life. The young killer blamed "feminists" for all of his personal problems.

Increasingly, members of organized hate groups have targeted college campuses as a source of potential new members. For most students, such blatantly bigoted individuals and their organizations are dismissed almost immediately. Unfortunately, however, there are at least a few students who have been effectively persuaded that their personal problems are the result of the actions of a particular group. With the desire to maintain a free exchange of all ideas, many campus representatives have experienced a degree of frustration in arriving at the best way to handle these episodes when they occur.

Campus Mediation Services by CRS

CRS responds to provide mediation and reconciliation services when requested by school officials, faculty, students and law enforcement. Once alerted to potential tensions arising from racial, ethnic or national origin conflicts (jurisdictional mandate) on a school campus, CRS will conduct an assessment to determine if it can provide assistance to resolve the issues in the school community. Without the cooperation of the school and its community of students, faculty, law enforcement, and administration, the process of mediation cannot be initiated.

If all concerned parties are willing to work together to resolve their differences, CRS begins the process with discussions about the existing issues, and the history of race relations on campus. The CRS intervention process will be developed with the participation of all concerned parties on how the issues will be addressed, the selection of representatives, discussion guidelines, and goals for the mediation. These problem solving sessions create lines of communication and partnerships between students and the administration which can become institutionalized.

CRS has been highly successful in mediating school racial issues, all with outcomes designed by the interested parties not the mediator. The work of CRS mediators includes gaining the confidence of the participants; discussions are required by law to be confidential unless waived by the parties. Examples of outcomes mediated by CRS include: cultural diversity and anti-bias training for faculty and students, policy positions on hate crimes, development of multi-cultural student centers, student peer group disciplinary panels, college publication guidelines, law enforcement response policies, and victim assistance to hate crime victims.

CRS Case-Study—E-mail Hate at the University of Oregon

Campus episodes can frequently benefit from introducing the perspective and experience of an outside and impartial agency. The Community Relations Service has provided such a service to colleges and universities around the country. In May 1999, the University of Oregon experienced racial tensions in the wake of media reports of hate inspired e-mail between students and comments perceived to be racist in classroom debates. Consequently, a campus protest, organized by students of color, resulted in the arrest of 31 students who refused to leave the University administration building after eight hours. The Community Relations Service was contacted and conciliators were then asked to mediate relations between concerned students and the University President. In addition, CRS was available to offer its federal presence to defuse the escalation of tensions and possible retaliation. As a neutral outside agency, the CRS was able to assist in resolving at an informal level a situation that might easily have escalated into a full-blown campus crisis.

Preventive Practices

Universities should have a hate crime policy and procedural administration and law enforcement protocol in place to assist campus administrators and law enforcement authorities to react promptly and seriously to all hate motivated episodes.

Prevention policies require that Colleges and Universities take all episodes seriously. Offenders look for the reaction of the community. If their hate attack is ignored, they might easily conclude that other members of the college community are in sympathy with their bigoted ideology. Response time by the administration is crucial.

The prevention of hate crimes on college campuses requires an integrated approach that begins when a student arrives on campus and extends to include all members of the campus community: students, faculty, staff, campus law enforcement and the administration.

Many colleges have already implemented orientation programs which specifically deal with the diversity new students will encounter on the campus as well as facilitated discussions (often led by upper-class students) dealing with the prevention of racial and cultural conflicts. Follow-up programs during the school year assist in reinforcing the administration's policy and position against hate crimes and bias-related incidents.

In addition to broad based prevention programs, each college should have a policy in place specifying how campus authorities should react if a hate crime occurs on their campus. This hate crime response policy should acknowledge that each hate crime has many victims, not only the targeted individuals but other members of that group. This policy should first offer medical attention (if necessary), protection and counseling to the targeted individuals and at the same time deal with the fears and concerns of the entire campus community. The key to any successful campus hate crime policy involves communication to the broadest possible audience in the most timely fashion.

Frequently, the participation of an uninvolved third party can immediately serve to reduce tensions. The Community Relations Service of the U.S. Department of Justice offers both emergency assistance as well as ongoing technical assistance to campuses experiencing bias related tension. This assistance is provided by CRS staff who come to their assignment with substantial experience dealing with the fears and anxiety associated with bias motivated violence.

The University of Michigan policy highlighted below details such a campus wide approach.

Crime Prevention Model Policy—University of Michigan

"Hate crimes are viewed in the community not only as crimes against the targeted victim, but also as a crime against the victim's group as a whole. Working constructively with segments of this larger audience after such episodes is essential to help reduce fears that stem from possible retaliation, help prevent additional incidents and encourage any other previously victimized individuals to step forward and report those crimes. Towards this end, this department's community relations function, or officers so assigned, shall:

- *Meet with neighborhood groups, residents in target communities and other identified groups to [allay] fears, relay this department's concern over and response to this and related incidents, reduce the potential for counter-violence and provide safety, security and crime prevention information*

- *Provide direct and referral assistance to the victim and his family*
- *Conduct public meetings on hate threats and violence in general, and as it relates to specific incidents*
- *Establish a liaison with formal organizations and leaders*
- *Expand, where appropriate, existing preventative programs such as anti-hate seminars for school children"*

Reporting

Numerous hate crimes and bias motivated incidents occur on college and university campuses without ever being officially reported by the victim. In some cases, victims of hate episodes do not report because "they want to put the incident behind them." However, many other victims simply are not aware of, or do not have access to, the proper resources which can offer assistance in an episode of hate. In addition, cultural elements, such as language differences, and a distrust of law enforcement are also barriers to the reporting of hate episodes on campus.

In order to increase the reporting of hate crimes and bias motivated incidents by victims, colleges should establish procedures to make reporting as easy as possible, including the possibility of accepting confidential reports. Confidentiality provisions, such as anonymous reporting, are extremely helpful in many cases. For example, a student who is targeted because of perceived sexual orientation may not want to be identified because she has not yet "come out" to her friends and family. Some universities offer e-mail reporting, which has been instrumental in allowing those who are not entirely fluent English speakers an opportunity to express their experiences in written form. Most universities have also provided a number of different offices with the responsibility and resources to accept hate crime reports, i.e., the Dean of Students and the Affirmative Action officer. This has been helpful because students, who have not yet established ties with campus law enforcement, may have already developed a relationship of trust and confidence with officials elsewhere on campus.

Reporting may also be increased when campus police officers represent the diversity of the student body. Students of color, especially on campuses located in predominantly black or Latino neighborhoods, often complain that they are treated with suspicion by representatives of the campus police. In addition, the situation of white police officers confronting a student of color may be perceived as biased, even if it is not. Overall, increasing the diversity of the campus police force, as implemented in many local police agencies across the country, increases its credibility of campus police with students who might otherwise be reluctant to report a hate incident.

One additional element which has proven successful at most universities is to provide victims, in response to an act of hate, with the choice of pressing charges or taking some other action. Alternatives may include school sponsored discussion groups, hate crimes training, and outreach programs. The presence of an alternative tends to alleviate some of the pressures that are perceived to come along with the reporting of a crime, and results in increased campus dialogue and reporting of hate occurrences.

Some, but not all, campus law enforcement agencies are reluctant to get involved in cases where the victim wants to remain anonymous. It is important to note that many campus law enforcement agencies do take anonymous reports which assists the victim in dealing with the aftermath of an incident, allows the agency to offer protection to a member of the community who may be enduring some level of continued harassment, and most importantly sends a message to the entire university community that bias motivated acts of violence will not be tolerated.

Model Reporting Procedure—University of California, Berkeley

"Upon receipt of a reported Hate Motivated Crime or Incident, the Public Safety Dispatcher will:

1. *Notify the Division Commander immediately if on-duty*
2. *Dispatch a field unit as soon as reasonably practical, based on the nature of the call*
3. *Notify the Patrol Sergeant of the reported incident*

When a Patrol Officer responds to a reported Hate Motivated Crime or Incident, the Officer will:

1. *Apprehend the perpetrator(s) if applicable*
2. *Request that a Patrol Supervisor respond to the scene*
3. *Render assistance and comfort to the victim*
4. *Conduct a thorough preliminary investigation consistent with Department Policies and Procedures, including evidence collection and photographs when applicable*
5. *Provide assistance to the victim and/or referral to the appropriate legal or service agency*
6. *Provide relevant forms to the victim, i.e., "Victims of Violent Crimes" form*

The Patrol Supervisor, upon being notified of a possible Hate Motivated Crime or Incident, will:

1. *Respond to the scene, interview the Patrol Officer, and confirm whether or not a Hate Motivated Crime or Incident has occurred*
2. *Take whatever steps are necessary to ensure that the situation does not escalate*
3. *Render assistance and comfort to the victim*
4. *Supervise the preliminary investigation*
5. *The Supervisor will notify the Patrol Captain (if on-duty) or On-Call Captain, as appropriate*
6. *The Supervisor will notify the on-duty or on-call investigators, as appropriate*
7. *The Supervisor will see that a Patrol Incident Form is filed in addition to a police report*

The investigator of the Criminal Investigations Bureau will:

1. *Conduct a thorough follow-up investigation consistent with Department Policy and procedure including personal contact with victim(s)*
2. *Keep the Captain informed of the progress of the investigation*
3. *Prepare the case for prosecution in court*

Case wrap-up will include:

1. *A member of the Senior Staff to be designated to serve as the liaison between the Department and community, religious, and civic leaders, as appropriate*
2. *The Investigative and Support Service will ensure all necessary follow-up investigations are completed and shall brief the Chief regularly on the status of the investigations. He/she will also ensure that all Hate Motivated Crime or Incident statistics are reported in accordance with state and federal law"*

Important Questions During Initial Investigation— Stanford University

"Did the crime occur all or in part because of racial, ethnic, religious, gender, disability, or sexual differences between the persons or for other reasons?

Has the victim or victim's group been subjected to repeated attacks of a similar nature?

Is the victim the only minority group member in the neighborhood, or one of a few?

Did the victim recently move into the area: is the victim acquainted with neighbors [and]/or local community groups?

When multiple incidents occur at the same time, are all victims of the same race, ethnicity, religion, gender, disability or sexual orientation?

Has the victim been associated with recent or past activities relating to his/her race, ethnicity, religion, gender, disability or sexual orientation? (i.e., gay rallies, demonstrations, holiday celebrations, conferences, religious meetings, etc.)

Did the incident occur on a holiday or other day of significance to the victim's group or offender's group?

Has there been prior/recent news coverage of events of a similar nature?

What was the manner and means of account: i.e., the color of paint initiated or contributed to the act, could the act be retribution of some conflict with neighbors, juveniles, etc.?

Is there an ongoing neighborhood problem that may have initiated or contributed to the act (i.e., could the act be retribution for some conflict with neighbors, juveniles, etc.)?

Does the crime indicate possible involvement by an organized group? For example: Is the literature printed?

Does the name signify a "copy-cat" syndrome? Is there documented or suspected organized group activity in the area?

Are there other possible motivations for the attack?"

Resolution

There are very integral and distinct aspects of a campus-wide response system in the event of a hate crime or bias motivated incident. However, the notion of a "team approach" should set the foundation for all university efforts. Successful practices of some universities include the following procedures.

After the initial reporting takes place, the ability of the response teams to ensure the rapid and accurate collection of data and evidence has been key to the investigation and resolution of many cases. By taking immediate action on hate occurrences, the entire campus becomes aware of the severity of such acts and the university's intolerance for them. For example, if hateful graffiti is found on a college campus, it is in the best interest of the university to collect all evidence at the scene, including photographs, and then promptly clean up the damage to prevent any further hateful activity or retaliation. In a number of campus hate crimes, the existence of accurate evidence collected at the scene has been crucial in the ultimate prosecution of the purveyors of hate crimes and bias motivated incidents. The collection of photographs and the use of video cameras and voice recordings, have proven effective in identifying hate crime perpetrators.

At many institutions it has been useful to designate one member of the campus law enforcement staff to handle hateful activity. This responsibility is primarily given to someone who has been adequately trained in the area of hate crimes and bias motivated incidents and understands the importance of confidentiality, sensitivity and victim assistance. While this designated officer may have many additional responsibilities, having one officer who identifies hate crime activity as her/his responsibility reduces the likelihood that incidents will be ignored or that the response will fall short by the campus response policy.

Victim Assistance Resources

Victim assistance is one of the most important aspects of any hate crime and bias motivated incident response policy. Support should be made available to all victims of an incident whether they were directly [or] indirectly involved. Victims of hate occurrences need to be assessed both physically and emotionally. As hateful activity can tarnish an entire community, the victim's family and surrounding neighborhood should also be included in the healing process. In first approaching a hate crime or bias motivated incident, it is important to understand that although an occurrence may appear to be minor, the long term emotional impact upon the victim and the campus community may be immense.

While there is a variety of resources for victims of hate crimes and bias motivated incidents, some particularly helpful organizations that may be found on-campus include counseling centers, campus law enforcement, health services, cultural diversity advocacy groups, student groups, academic advisors, affirmative action offices, employee assistance programs, faculty and friends. Off-campus resources include local law enforcement, human rights associations, religious groups and institutions/churches, domestic violence shelters, state and county bar associations, the U.S. Department of Justice, and in particular the Community Relations Service, U.S. Attorney Hate Crime Working Groups, and civic groups such as the Anti-Defamation League, or the NAACP. In some cases an external group with experience dealing with these kind of cases, such as CRS, may be particularly effective because it is not part of any ongoing campus conflict that may surface in the aftermath of a hate motivated incident.

Victim Assistance Guidelines

Victims of hate crimes often experience feelings of shame, anger, fear, frustration and confusion. In helping the victim and surrounding community deal with the aftermath of a hate occurrence remember the following three points:

- *Conduct a **physical** evaluation performed by medical physicians.*
- *Conduct an **emotional** evaluation performed by counseling services.*
- *Offer peer, community and university support resources.*

Small v. Large Institutions of Higher Learning

The response capabilities of institutions vary primarily because the resources available to assist victims and investigate crime also vary widely. Large institutions tend to have more substantial resources than smaller institutions, and are, thus, more capable to respond to hate crimes and bias motivated incidents with less external support. However, even though resources for small universities may be limited, there are still pro-active measures that can be taken to ensure adequate response to hate crimes in any college setting. Among these are the formation of hate related policies, student awareness and training in rapid response to hate incidents, cooperation agreements with local law enforcement, and similar agreements with victim support agencies located in the community. Hate crime victims experience similar reactions and have similar needs for support regardless of the size of the campus.

Special Considerations

College communities are increasingly large diverse communities that include individuals with many different ideologies and experiences. Occasionally, campus staff members may fail to adequately implement the colleges' hate crime response policy. To prevent such failures, it is imperative that the university leadership, including the university president, have a strong public position in support of the university's hate crime response policy. Such action by those in leadership positions, demonstrates a commitment to preventing and resolving racial conflict and promoting a more racially harmonious campus environment.

The reluctance of many universities to take disciplinary action against the perpetrators of hate offenses poses another obstacle. Often, the lengthy investigation of hate crimes or bias motivated incidents can deter the institutions from taking a timely disciplinary stance. Once the perpetrators are identified, there are frequently varying degrees of participation and culpability among the students. Determining appropriate punishment for each of those involved can take substantial time. These delays may cause resentment to build and tensions to rise from victimized students and groups against campus administrators. In order to avoid such occasions, universities have emphasized the importance of timely and sensitive investigations, which result in appropriate disciplinary actions without undue delay.

International students also offer a different series of challenges to an effective campus hate crime response policy. Many foreign students may not be aware of their legal rights as a visiting student in the United States, leaving them reluctant to report any harassment or other criminal actions directed at them. Based on experiences in their native countries, some international students carry with them the fear of and animosity towards all law enforcement. In order to relieve some of these issues, many universities include staff from the International Students Office in their hate crime response team and have trained the International Students Office Staff to respond to a hate crime or bias motivated incidents that may come to their attention. This has proven to be effective because of relationships that have been developed between the foreign students and the university's administration.

Media Relations

Dealing with the media in times of racial tension on campus is quite complex. Many college officials would prefer to keep these episodes "quiet" to protect others who might feel intimidated if they became aware of the episode, or to prevent a tarnishing of the institution's reputation. This course of action is seldom successful and can often make the situation worse. Rumors, often full of misinformation, circulate across the campus and may cause some students to feel that if the university is not going to do anything, they should take matters into their own hands. A media policy that allows the university to provide accurate and timely information about the episode to the community should be an integral part of any campus response policy.

A key aspect of maintaining good relations with the press is the establishment of relationships with campus and off-campus reporters and editors *before* an episode occurs. This will facilitate communication and the factual reporting of episodes during the stressful atmosphere that often follows a campus hate crime. If the media are aware of the campus response policy and feel that the university will provide information to them once it is verified, they will be more likely to act in a supportive and responsible manner. While most universities agree that one university representative should be designated to speak with the press in order to minimize confusion. Some universities have also found it helpful to incorporate students and local community representatives into their media relations' policy.

Long-term Impacts

Hate crimes are among the most likely offenses to create or exacerbate tensions, which can trigger larger community-wide racial conflict, civil disturbances, demonstrations and even riots. Hate crimes can have a particularly detrimental effect upon college and university campuses. The negativity that comes with such hate motivated occurrences can impact the reputation of educational institutions, encouraging prospective students and faculty to look elsewhere. Ultimately, the diversity levels of universities which have experienced hate, may decline both within their student and faculty populations.

Hate crimes and bias-motivated incidents are also damaging to the campus environment where the free and open exchange of ideas is essential. If students fear retaliation for comments they make in class or in a casual conversation, the richness of the academic experience is significantly reduced. Campus administrators must create an atmosphere where all ideas and perspectives are respected and intellectual disagreements do not result in violence.

Similarly, college campuses are part of the broader community in which they are located. Hate crimes committed on campus, or near campus, strain the relationship between the college and the local community. Local residents fear that a rise in racial tension may cause their community to be labeled as intolerant and, thus, at-risk for serious social and economic consequences. Students may become afraid to interact with community neighbors fearing that they may become targets. To combat the negativity that may come about as a result of such hate occurrences, some communities have found themselves uniting with their local colleges and universities to fight the battle against intolerance. Many neighborhoods have formed support groups and networks that participate as part of the college response system and have contributed to the healing of entire communities after encountering a hate occurrence.

Additional Methods of Combating Campus Hate Crimes

Published in October 2001, this document was prepared by Stephen Wessler and Margaret Moss of the Center for the Prevention of Hate Violence at the University of Southern Maine. Although the report was funded by the Bureau of Justice Assistance, a division of the Office of Justice Programs in the U.S. Department of Justice, the ideas expressed do not necessarily represent the official views of the department. The full report can be accessed at: http://cphv.usm.maine.edu/monograph.pdf

Hate Crimes on Campus:
The Problem and Efforts to Confront It

When a hate crime occurs on a college campus, the ideal of a university as a place for learning and growth is ruptured. Bias-motivated violence or threats targeting students, staff, or faculty not only impair the educational mission of an institution of higher learning but also deprive young men and women of the chance to live and learn in an atmosphere free of fear and intimidation. No college campus is immune to the risk of hate violence. In the past 5 years alone, the U.S. Department of Justice has brought criminal civil rights actions against students attending institutions ranging from small liberal arts colleges in Massachusetts and Georgia to large state universities in Florida and California. This monograph examines four aspects of the problem of bias, prejudice, and hate crimes on our college and university campuses.

First, the monograph examines the prevalence of hate crimes on campuses, who is targeted, what kinds of crime are committed, and the frequency and impact of bias incidents. Second, the monograph identifies common problems college communities have experienced in responding to hate crimes and provides recommendations for prompt, effective, and appropriate responses. Third, the monograph describes several promising efforts to respond to campus hate crimes and implement prevention programs. Finally, the monograph explains the difference between hate crimes and bias incidents and discusses the factors police consider to determine whether a hate crime has been committed.

I. Introduction

Hate Crimes on Campus. Federal and State Enforcement Activity. Hate crimes on campuses involve a range of criminal conduct from threats to bombings to violent physical assaults. They occur at virtually every type of college and university and in every part of the nation. Perpetrators of these incidents include current and former students and nonstudents. Listed below is a sampling of recent federal and state enforcement actions involving bias motivated violence and threats on campuses.

United States v. *Samar.* James Samar, a college student, was indicted on three counts of using threats of force to interfere with the federally protected rights of three students attending a small Massachusetts college. Samar used anti- Semitic slurs, threatened two fellow students, and threatened to kill one fellow student. In addition, he delivered photographs of holocaust victims to one student and stated, among other things, that the photographs were "a reminder of what happened to your relatives because they too made a mockery of Christianity." Samar entered a plea agreement.

II. Hate Crimes and Bias Incidents on Campus

United States v. *Machado.* A former student was convicted of disseminating an e-mail containing racially derogatory comments and threats to 59 college students, nearly all of whom were of Asian descent.

State v. *Tozier.* A student at a small college in Maine yelled antigay slurs and threats at a fellow student who was working in a student lounge and, in three consecutive attacks, violently choked the student. The defendant signed a consent decree in a civil rights case brought by Maine's attorney general.

United States v. *Lombardi.* A nonstudent was charged with detonating two pipe bombs on the campus of a primarily African-American public university in Florida. After each of the bombings, violent racist telephone calls were made to the local television station.

State v. *Masotta.* Three white students at a university in Maine left an anonymous racist and threatening message on an African-American student's answering machine. The message ended with the following:

> I wonder what you're gonna look like dead? Dead. I wonder if when you die you'll lose your color. Like the blood starts to leave your body and you're gonna . . . start deteriorating and blood starts to leave your skin. . . . You get the picture? You're *** dead.

The defendants signed consent orders in a civil rights case brought by Maine's attorney general.

United States v. *Little.* The defendant, Robert Allen Little, was charged with igniting a homemade pipe bomb in the dorm room of two African-American students on a small campus in Utah. The letters "KKK" were painted in red fingernail polish on the bomb's firing device. The bomb caused extensive damage to the building and destroyed the belongings of both students. After the bombing, Little returned to the dorm and left a threatening and racist note on the door of another African-American student. Little was sentenced to 12 years in prison, fined $12,000, and ordered to pay restitution.

Campus Hate Crime Statistics. The available data on the prevalence of hate crimes and bias incidents on college campuses are not comprehensive, because they are based on information from relatively few reporting campuses. Three primary sources of data are the Federal Bureau of Investigation (FBI) Uniform Crime Reports on hate crime statistics, the U.S. Department of Education Campus Security Statistics, and the

International Association of College Law Enforcement Administrators (IACLEA) annual survey on campus crime statistics.

U.S. Department of Education data are collected pursuant to the Clery Act (20 U.S.C. § 1092(f)), which was enacted in 1992. This act requires colleges and universities across the nation to report campus crimes and security policies to both the campus community and the U.S. Department of Education. In addition to policy and reporting requirements, it specifies that schools must report separately those crimes that appear to have been motivated by prejudice. The U.S. Department of Education is currently working with colleges and universities to ensure that Clery Act data are complete and current.

Even statistics based on a relatively small number of reporting schools indicate that hate crimes on campus are a significant problem. Moreover, there are strong reasons to believe that the problem of hate crimes is more widespread than any statistics are likely to reveal. First, many students, faculty, and staff members are unsure of what to report, when to report an incident, and to whom they should report an incident. Second, and perhaps most important, victims of hate crimes often are reluctant to come forward because they feel isolated and fear the potential repercussions of a perpetrator. Gay and lesbian victims who attend schools in states that do not have laws protecting individuals from job or employment discrimination based on sexual orientation may fear that reporting a hate crime will place them at risk of further discrimination. For these and other reasons, reliable statistics regarding on-campus hate crimes are elusive.

As noted above, the FBI annual compilation of hate crime statistics and IACLEA annual survey of crimes on campuses are based on data from a relatively small number of reporting institutions. The limited number of reporting institutions and the varied survey instruments also account for a disparity in the results of the two surveys. Both reports indicate, however, that many schools experience hate violence.

The Federal Bureau of Investigation. *Uniform Crime Report on hate crime statistics.* The FBI report on 1998 hate crime statistics is based on reports from 450 colleges and universities from 40 states. Of these universities, 222 reported 241 incidents of hate crime during the year. The FBI data indicate that 57 percent of hate crimes were motivated by race, 18 percent were motivated by anti-Semitism, and 16 percent were motivated by bias based on sexual orientation.

The International Association of College Law Enforcement Administrators survey. The IACLEA report for 1998 surveyed 411 campuses.

Of these campuses, 88 reported experiencing at least one hate crime; in fact, these colleges experienced an average of 3.8 hate crimes each in 1998, for a total of 334 incidents. The reporting institutions designated the motivation for the alleged hate crimes under five categories: race, religion, disability, sexual orientation, and ethnicity/national origin.

The IACLEA report did not include a separate category for hate crimes motivated by bias based on gender. IACLEA statistics indicate that more than 80 percent of reported hate crimes were motivated by bias based on either race or sexual orientation.

Bias Incidents on Campus: The Prevalence and Impact of Prejudice and Harassment. Fortunately, hate crimes occur with relative infrequency on most campuses. Bias incidents (acts of prejudice that are not accompanied by violence, the threat of violence, property damage, or other illegal conduct) are far more common.

Bias incidents may violate some campus disciplinary or harassment policies (making them reportable under the Clery Act), but they do not violate civil or criminal hate crime statutes.

Based on discussions, workshops, and informal surveys with hundreds of students from institutions ranging from large state universities to small liberal arts colleges, students consistently report the widespread use of degrading language and slurs by other students directed toward people of color, women, homosexuals, Jews, and others who belong to groups that have traditionally been the target of bias, prejudice, and violence. Students report hearing degrading language about women, gays, and lesbians on a daily basis and racist, anti-Semitic, and other slurs on a regular but less frequent basis.

The widespread use of degrading language and slurs directed at traditionally targeted groups has two serious consequences. First, the use of such language creates an atmosphere that permits conduct to escalate from mere words to stronger words to threats and, ultimately, to violence. In a significant portion of campus hate crime cases, the illegal conduct appears to have escalated from lower levels of harassment, beginning with degrading language.

If not challenged or interrupted, the widespread use of this language sends the message—often unintended—that bias and prejudice are accepted within a campus community. Some students interpret this message to mean that more aggressive conduct may also be acceptable.

Second, even in the absence of escalation, bias incidents can have a traumatic impact on students, staff, and faculty. Members of a campus community often experience fear when they are on the receiving end of degrading language or slurs or see graffiti that targets groups in which they are members.

This fear can interfere with the ability of students to fully focus on their academic work. Some students who are the target of bias-motivated harassment do not react with fear but with anger. Campus or municipal police may be called to address physical confrontations between students who are experiencing bias-motivated harassment and their harassers.

III. Response to Campus Hate Crimes and Bias Incidents

The responses of campus administrators and campus and municipal police departments to hate crimes and bias incidents that occur on college campuses have varied greatly. Although there is no one correct way to handle every hate crime, the direct experiences of police officers and administrators make it possible to identify common problems they encounter in responding to campus hate crimes and those responses that permit effective investigation and appropriate community response.

Some of the most common problems in responding to hate crimes are that police are inadequately trained; students, staff, faculty, and administrators do not report the crimes; and administrators do not adequately disseminate information to the campus community. Listed below are descriptions of common problems, followed by recommended steps for effectively dealing with these frequently encountered challenges.

Problem 1: Campus Police Officers Need Adequate Training. Campus police officers who have not been trained to identify and respond to hate crimes may not be prepared to properly investigate incidents and recognize potential ramifications for the safety of students on campus. In addition, if police officers do not identify an act of campus violence as a possible hate crime and do not report it to the administration, the college or university may be hampered in its efforts to identify trends and begin appropriate prevention and intervention work.

Recommendations . Implement a training program for campus police. It is essential that all members of campus police departments (and municipal police departments that have colleges or universities within their jurisdictions) receive training in responding to and investigating hate crimes. All officers within a department, including command officers, patrol officers, and detectives, should attend training sessions. Police departments have an array of training programs available to them. In 1998, the U.S. Department of Justice launched its National Hate Crime Training Initiative. This initiative developed curricula for training police officers in how to respond to and investigate hate crimes and convened national train-the-trainer conferences around the nation. The initiative has taught trainers in every state to conduct half- or full-day courses. Additionally, the Bureau of Justice Assistance has developed a 20-minute training film for officers, titled Responding to Hate Crimes, and the International

Association of Chiefs of Police has developed a 12-page guide for officers that covers the major components of investigating and responding to hate crimes.

Designate a civil rights officer for each department. Every campus and municipal police department with colleges located within its jurisdiction should consider appointing at least one officer (preferably two) to serve as the designated civil rights officer. A designated civil rights officer is the primary liaison between campus administration, advocacy groups, and other law enforcement agencies (including prosecutorial offices). Appointing a designated civil rights officer lets the entire campus community know that responding to and investigating hate crimes is a priority, and hate crimes will be handled in a coordinated and consistent way. For more information about designating a civil rights officer, see *Addressing Hate Crimes: Six Initiatives That Are Enhancing the Efforts of Criminal Justice Practitioners* (February 2000, Bureau of Justice Assistance Hate Crimes Series).

Problem 2: Hate Crimes and Serious Bias Incidents Are Not Reported. Police believe that students, staff, faculty, and administrators often do not report possible hate crimes and serious bias incidents to the police. If police are not informed promptly of a possible hate crime, they cannot conduct an immediate investigation.

As a result, physical evidence (such as graffiti or recorded telephone messages) may be lost, and witnesses may not be identified and interviewed. The nonreporting of such incidents is particularly serious because many perpetrators of hate crimes repeat and escalate their behavior until they are confronted by authorities. Consequently, police are deprived of information that may enable them to halt this pattern of escalation before a more serious crime is committed.

Recommendation. Campus officials should develop a brochure that defines what should be reported, to whom an incident should be reported, and when an incident should be reported. The brochure should provide clear directives and be distributed broadly to faculty, staff, and students. It is particularly important that these brochures be distributed to those persons on campus who are most likely to learn about possible hate crimes. For example, individuals working for the campus housing and athletics departments, including student life staff, resident advisors, coaches, and team captains, should all receive and review the reporting guidelines. Student leaders throughout the university community, whether or not they are directly involved with the housing or athletics departments, should also receive and review reporting guidelines. The Recommendation section under Problem 4 sets forth guidelines.

Problem 3: Police Do Not Report Hate Crimes to Campus Administrators.   Some law enforcement agencies may not have a procedure for regularly informing college administrators of hate crimes or serious bias incidents that occur in or around a college campus, particularly when incidents occur on campus but not in campus housing. Inadequate reporting of such incidents by police deprives administrators of the opportunity to support students from the affected or targeted groups, provide reasonable warnings to members of the campus community, and put prevention efforts in place.

Recommendation.   Campuses should provide both campus and municipal police departments with clear and specific guidelines denoting who at the university or college should be contacted and under what circumstances. The reporting guidelines must be concise, identifying who should receive an initial report and who should receive followup information. The guidelines should include information on how to contact these individuals in the evening and on weekends, during campus holidays, and during vacations to avoid lapses in reporting.

Problem 4: Students, Staff, and Faculty Do Not Report Incidents Up the Administrative Ladder.   When students, staff, and faculty do not report (or do not report in a timely manner) possible hate crimes or serious bias incidents up the administrative ladder, senior college officials are denied critical information. If senior administrators are unaware of possible hate crimes, they will not be prepared to take action against perpetrators, initiate preventive measures, or respond knowledgeably to community and press inquiries.

Recommendation.   Campus administrators should work with campus and municipal police to develop and disseminate clear guidelines for reporting hate crimes. The guidelines should address the following:

- When and under what circumstances students, staff, and faculty should report hate crimes and bias incidents to campus or municipal police.
- When and under what circumstances students, staff, and faculty should report hate crimes and bias incidents to college administrators.
- When campus and municipal police should report hate crimes and bias incidents to college administrators.

The guidelines should include the names of individuals to contact during the week, as well as in the evenings, on weekends, and during campus holidays and vacations.

Problem 5: Administrators Do Not Disseminate Information to the Campus Community. When a hate crime occurs on campus, information about the incident spreads quickly throughout the campus community via informal avenues of communication. If college or university administrators do not inform the campus about the incident, several adverse consequences can occur. First, students, staff, and faculty may receive inaccurate information about what occurred. Second, the institution will lose the opportunity to send a strong message that bias and hate will not be tolerated on campus.

Finally, and often most destructive, when college administrators do not publicly comment on hate crimes, they may inadvertently create the impression that the institution is insensitive to the problem of hate crimes.

Recommendations. **Disseminate information about hate crimes.** Senior college and university administrators should consider promptly disseminating information through a campuswide letter or e-mail to provide details on alleged hate crimes and to strongly condemn bias-motivated violence, threats, and property damage. Often, it will be appropriate to follow this communication with an open campus meeting at which members of the campus community can ask questions and express their views. Campus disciplinary proceedings generally are confidential; therefore, any dissemination of information should take confidentiality restrictions into account.

Establish a hate crime response team. Administrators may want to establish a hate crime response team that recommends when and how the college or university should respond to an alleged hate crime. Hate crime response teams should include representatives from the president's office, the dean of students office, the multicultural office, the equal opportunity employer office, and campus and municipal police departments.

IV. Promising Efforts: Responding to and Preventing Hate Crimes

Colleges, universities, and nonprofit organizations are developing innovative ways to respond to and prevent hate crimes. The efforts described below are only a few examples of the creative programs being implemented around the nation to make our institutions of higher learning safe for all students. These programs are replicable and generally can be implemented without significant expense.

Campuswide Response to Hate Crimes. Many colleges and universities have responded to hate crimes on their campuses with a broad-based public condemnation of bias, prejudice, and violence. These responses have included the following:

- An open letter from the college or university president or dean to the campus community that explains the hate crime or bias incident that occurred on campus, the status of the police investigation of the alleged hate crime, and a strong condemnation of bias and violence.
- Meetings open to the entire campus community in which the president and other senior administrators explain what has occurred and restate the university's position against hate crimes. Students, staff, and faculty often are invited to ask questions and voice their opinions.

As a result of these and other actions, college administrators have calmed tensions and fears; addressed the need of students, staff, and faculty to receive reliable information; and gained the trust and confidence of the campus community.

Hate Crimes Awareness and Prevention Project.   Students at the University of California at Berkeley have developed a project to examine hate crimes and the underlying issues of bias and prejudice. Through education and training the project has increased awareness of the threat of hate crimes and fostered a campus climate that discourages hate crimes. The project includes a Web site that provides options for reporting hate crimes and lists additional campus and community resources. The project sponsored a Hate Crimes Awareness Week in spring 2000.

Combating Prejudice and Hate on Campus: A National Student Colloquium.   In March 2000, the Brudnick Center on Violence and Conflict at Northeastern University and the Center for the Prevention of Hate Violence at the University of Southern Maine cosponsored a national student colloquium to recognize those students, and their respective campus organizations, who are working to confront bias, hate, and violence. The event provided the students with the opportunity to build skills and learn from each other. More than 300 students and staff from more than 70 campuses throughout the country attended the colloquium. The colloquium was funded and supported by the U.S. Department of Education's Safe and Drug-Free Schools Program and the Bureau of Justice Assistance, U.S. Department of Justice.

Anti-Defamation League.   The Anti-Defamation League (ADL) formed its WORLD OF DIFFERENCE Institute in 1992 to "define and advance a discipline of diversity education." The institute's Campus of Difference Program provides training for students in groups of 25–40. Facilitated by two ADL staff members, the program's goal is to increase awareness of bias incidents and hate crimes and encourage university students to make proactive changes on campus. The Campus of Difference Program also offers train-the-trainer sessions of varying duration that enable a campus to develop 16–20 diversity trainers.

Peer Diversity Education. Several schools have implemented peer diversity education groups that promote understanding of diversity on campus. At Texas A&M University, University Awareness for Cultural Togetherness (U-ACT) is a peer diversity education group that requires participating students to take a semester-long course in social justice issues in higher education. Members of the group then conduct workshops and hold overnight retreats in an effort to bring students together and create an environment that is "safe, supportive, and educational."

New Jersey City University's Peers Educating Peers, or "PEP," program is based in the school's psychology department. About 25 students actively participate in PEP; they provide outreach on campus and to the community on a variety of issues. Other schools, including Bowdoin College in Maine and the University of Denver in Colorado, have successfully integrated peer diversity efforts into freshman orientation, using films, small group discussions, and campus speakers to increase awareness and promote safety.

Promising Efforts: Responding to and Preventing Hate Crimes. Campus Civility Project. The Center for the Prevention of Hate Violence at the University of Southern Maine has initiated the Campus Civility Project to address the climate of bias, prejudice, and harassment that exists on our nation's campuses. Administrators, faculty, staff, and student leaders (such as resident advisors and captains of sports teams) participate in 3-hour workshops that help them develop a fuller understanding of the harmful effects of degrading language and slurs. Most important, the workshops also provide participants with practical skills for intervening in low-key ways when students engage in conduct that demeans, degrades, or frightens others. The center conducts a 3-day training-of-trainers conference for representatives from each participating campus that will enable the campuses to conduct their own workshops for student leaders, staff, and faculty year after year.

V. Conclusion

The hate crimes and bias incidents that occur on this nation's college and university campuses not only leave scars on the targeted individuals but also on entire campuses. College administrators, police officers, students, and faculty members around the nation are devoting energy and creativity to responding to and preventing bias, prejudice, and hate violence. The cumulative impact of this work on campus will help ensure that all students—regardless of gender, race/ethnicity, sexual orientation, disability, religion, or age—are physically and emotionally safe.

VI. Appendix: Commonly Asked Questions About Hate Crimes and Bias Incidents

What Is a Hate Crime?. The Federal Government, more than 40 states, and the District of Columbia have hate crime statutes. These statutes vary in a number of ways. Generally, a hate crime is a crime of violence, property damage, or threat that is motivated in whole or in part by an offender's bias based on race, religion, ethnicity, national origin, gender, physical or mental disability, or sexual orientation.

Most jurisdictions that have hate crime laws cover bias based on race, religion, ethnicity, and national origin, and a smaller number of states cover bias based on gender, disability, and sexual orientation. In addition to criminal statutes, many states have civil statutes that authorize the state attorney general to seek restraining orders against persons who engage in bias-motivated violence, threats, or property damage. It is important to check the exact wording of the hate crime statutes applicable in your state.

What Are Hate or Bias Incidents?. Hate or bias incidents involve behavior that is motivated by bias based on race, religion, ethnicity, national origin, gender, disability, or sexual orientation. These incidents do not involve criminal conduct such as assault, threats, or property damage. Bias-motivated degrading comments often are considered to be bias incidents. They are not considered to be hate crimes, however, because the speaker of those comments has not engaged in criminal activity.

Why Do We Need To Focus on This Issue?. Police officers and prosecutors have learned that hate crimes can occur on any campus—urban or rural, large or small, public or private. Police and prosecutors have found that the lack of reported hate crimes only indicates that students, staff, or faculty are not reporting incidents, not that hate crimes are absent. Moreover, even if a campus has not experienced a reported hate crime, it is likely that students and other members of the campus community are hearing and using degrading language and slurs directed at those on campus who are of a different race, religion, gender, or sexual orientation. A campus culture in which the use of slurs becomes commonplace and accepted soon becomes an environment in which slurs can escalate to harassment, harassment can escalate to threats, and threats can escalate to physical violence. As noted previously in this monograph, an act of violence is the end result of this pattern. Even if violence does not occur, the degrading language alone has a negative impact on certain students, causing some to feel uncomfortable or unaccepted and others to feel scared.

How Do Police Officers Determine Whether a Hate Crime Has Occurred?. Police officers are trained to examine whether bias indicators exist. A bias crime indicator is an objective fact, circumstance, or pattern—standing alone or in conjunction with other facts or circumstances—that suggests that the offender's actions were motivated, in whole or in part, by bias. The presence of bias indicators does not establish that a hate crime has occurred. Rather, the presence of bias indicators prompts police to investigate the matter further to determine its motivation. The following factors may indicate bias motivation. Each factor is followed by one or more examples of bias indicators.

Racial, ethnic, gender, and cultural differences exist between the perpetrator and victim.

- The racial identity, religion, ethnic/national origin, disability, or sexual orientation of the victim differs from that of the offender.
- The victim is a member of a group that is overwhelmingly outnumbered by members of another group in the area where the incident occurred.
- The victim was engaged in activities promoting his or her group.
- The incident coincided with a holiday or date of particular significance to the victim's group.

Comments, written statements, and gestures were made. Bias related comments, written statements, or gestures were made by the offender either during, before, or after the alleged hate crime.

Drawings, markings, symbols, and graffiti were left. Bias-related drawings, markings, symbols, or graffiti were left at the scene of the incident.

Organized hate groups or their members were involved. A hate group has claimed responsibility for the crime, or symbols of organized hate groups were left at the crime scene.

The victim previously had received bias-motivated harassing mail or phone calls. Several bias motivated incidents have occurred in the same area.

The victim's or witness's perception of the incident may affect the outcome. Victims or witnesses believe that the incident was motivated by bias.

The location of the incident indicates bias motivation.

- The victim was in or near a place commonly associated with or frequented by individuals of a particular racial identity, religion, ethnic/national origin, disability, sexual orientation, or gender.
- The incident occurred at or near a place of worship, a religious cemetery, the home of a family that is a minority within a particular neighborhood, or a gay bar.

Can a Hate Crime Be Committed With Nothing More Than Words?. The use of bigoted and prejudiced language does not in itself violate hate crime laws. This type of behavior is frequently classified as a bias incident. However, hate crime laws apply when words threaten violence. Similarly, hate crime laws apply when bias-motivated graffiti damages or destroys property.

Does Bias Have To Be the Only Motivation To Charge Someone With a Hate Crime?. In general, no, although the answer may depend on how courts in a particular jurisdiction or state have interpreted hate crime laws. It is not uncommon for people to commit crimes for more than one reason. Many hate crimes are successfully prosecuted even when motivations in addition to bias are present.

Is Domestic Violence or Sexual Assault Against a Woman Considered a Hate Crime?. Domestic violence or sexual assault can be prosecuted as a hate crime if gender is included in applicable hate crime laws and if evidence can be obtained demonstrating that the assault was motivated, in whole or in part, by bias against the victim because of her gender.

Do Hate Crime Laws Protect White People?. Yes. Hate crime laws are colorblind. Racially motivated crimes targeting white people, although far less common than hate crimes targeting people of color, occur and the perpetrators are prosecuted. Many of the hate crimes motivated by bias against a victim's religion, nationality, gender, or sexual orientation are directed at white people.

Do Victims Frequently Fabricate Hate Crimes?. As with any crime, fabricated complaints about hate crimes do occur, but very rarely. In fact, police have found that victims often are reluctant to report hate crimes or even acknowledge that what appears to others to be a hate crime is motivated by bias. The fear and isolation that hate crime victims feel lead to underreporting more often than to fabrication.

Why Should These Laws Protect Homosexuals?.   Hate crime laws prohibit violence, threats, or property damage motivated by bias. Hate crime laws have always applied to people who choose to be in a targeted group, such as those who choose to convert to a different religion. The resolution of the debate over whether gays and lesbians are genetically predisposed or choose their sexual orientation is not relevant under the law. No person should be subject to violence, threats, or property damage because of his or her status, whether it be race, ethnicity, nationality, religion, gender, physical or mental disability, or sexual orientation.

Do Hate Crime Laws Confer Special Rights on Certain Groups?.   Hate crime laws protect every person in this country. Anyone could be a victim of a hate crime because of his or her race, nationality, ethnicity, physical or mental disability, sexual orientation, gender, or religion. Some people have been victimized by hate crimes due to a perpetrator's mistaken belief that the victim is of a particular race, nationality, ethnicity, or sexual orientation. Hate crimes do not confer special rights on anyone. Rather, they protect the rights of individuals to conduct their everyday activities—to live in their homes, do their jobs, receive an education— without being subjected to violence because of who they are or what they believe.

The Growing Problem of Hate on the Web

Published in September 2003 by Partners Against Hate, an umbrella organization consisting of the Anti-Defamation League (ADL), the Leadership Conference on Civil Rights Education Fund (LCCREF), and the Center for the Prevention of Hate Violence (CPHV), this report was jointly funded by the U.S. Department of Justice, Office of Juvenile Justice and Delinquency Prevention (OJJDP), and the U.S. Department of Education, Safe and Drug-Free Schools Program. The document is abridged and represents the views of the authors and does not necessarily represent the official positions of the above-mentioned government agencies or civil rights organizations. The report discusses the problem of harassment and racial incitement on email and the proliferation of extremist websites that advocate violence against racial, religious, and other minorities. The authors advocate the use of specific federal and state criminal statutes to deter violent speech that is

unprotected by the First Amendment. The full report can be found at:
http://www.partnersagainsthate.org/publications/investigating_hc.pdf

Investigating Hate Crimes on the Internet

Introduction

All Americans have a stake in effective response to hate crimes. These crimes demand priority attention because of their special impact. Bias crimes are designed to intimidate the victim and members of the victim's community, leaving them feeling isolated, vulnerable, and unprotected by the law. Failure to address this unique type of crime could cause an isolated incident to explode into widespread community tension. The damage done by hate crimes, therefore, cannot be measured solely in terms of physical injury or dollars and cents. By making members of targeted communities fearful, angry, and suspicious of other groups—and of the power structure that is supposed to protect them—hate crimes can damage the fabric of our society and fragment communities. The Internet has rapidly transformed the way people worldwide communicate messages and ideas, do business, and live their lives. The ability to send information instantaneously at any time for relatively little or no cost is truly revolutionary. As the Internet's important and significant benefits expand, however, the possibilities to use this medium for unlawful activity grow as well. Unfortunately, the Internet has become a new frontier in spreading hate. The Internet is an especially inviting host for the virus of hate. Whereas hate mongers once had to stand on street corners and hand out their message of bigotry on mimeographed leaflets, now these extremists have seized new technologies to promote their causes at sites on the World Wide Web and in chat rooms. The Internet has allowed extremists expanded access to a potential audience of millions—including impressionable youth. It has also facilitated communication among like-minded bigots across borders and oceans and enhances their ability to promote and recruit for their causes anonymously and cheaply. In a criminal context, e-mail messages containing threats can be sent behind a cloak of anonymity or false identity. Persons can be chosen to receive messages without their consent or knowledge. Although hate speech is offensive and hurtful, the First Amendment usually protects such expression. Beyond spreading hate, however, there is a growing, disturbing trend to use the Internet to intimidate and harass individuals on the basis of their race, religion, sexual orientation, or national origin. When speech contains a direct, credible threat against an identifiable individual, organization, or institution, it crosses the line to criminal conduct. **Hate speech containing criminal threats is not protected by the First Amendment.**

Criminal cases concerning hate speech on the Internet have, to date, been few in number. The Internet is vast and perpetrators of online hate crimes hide behind anonymous screen names, electronically garbled addresses, and Web sites that can be relocated and abandoned overnight. Despite these special challenges, law enforcement authorities can learn much from the first few successful prosecutions outlined in this Technical Assistance Brief.

United States v. Machado

In September 1996, a 21-year-old expelled college student who lived in Southern California sent a threatening e-mail message to 60 Asian students at the University of California Irvine ("UC Irvine"). The message expressed a hatred for Asians and stated that UC Irvine would be a much more popular school without Asian students. The message further blamed Asians for all crimes that occurred on campus, and concluded with a clear threat to hunt down and kill all Asians on campus if they did not leave the university: "I personally will make it my life career [sic] to find and kill everyone one [sic] of you personally. OK?????? That's how determined I am . . .." The message was signed "Asian Hater." The sender did not sign his name to the message, and the message was sent from an e-mail account that hid his identity. Ultimately, however, in voluntary interviews with UC Irvine police, Richard Machado admitted that he sent the threatening message. He was charged with violating the Federal Civil Rights laws, which [prohibit] (among other things) interference by force or threat of force based on race or national origin with a person's attendance at a public university.

Machado's first trial ended in a hung jury. A second trial in 1998 resulted in Machado's conviction, and he was sentenced to one year in prison.

The urgent national need for both a tough law enforcement response to hate crimes, and education and programming, to confront violent bigotry has only increased over the past year. In the aftermath of the September 11, 2001, terrorism, the nation has witnessed a disturbing increase in attacks against American citizens and others who appear to be of Muslim, Middle Eastern, and South Asian descent. Perhaps acting out of anger at the terrorists involved in the September 11, 2001 attacks, the perpetrators of these crimes are irrationally lashing out at innocent people because of their personal characteristics—their race, religion, or ethnicity. Law enforcement officials have investigated hundreds of incidents reported from coast to coast—places of worship, neighborhood centers, grocery stores, gas stations, restaurants, and homes—including vandalism, intimidation, assaults, and several murders. This Brief provides essential information about the growing problem of hate crimes on the Internet and tips for investigation and prosecution of hate crimes on the Internet. First, the Brief defines hate crimes, summarizes the principal Federal and State hate crime laws, and describes a number of reported cases. Second, the Brief examines key legal elements involved in the investigation of hate crimes on the Internet. Finally, the Brief focuses on three issues that can arise in hate crime investigations, including First Amendment protections for hate Web sites, the jurisdictional aspects of prosecution of threats on the Internet, and potential problems encountered in the collection and preservation of electronic evidence.

II. Addressing Bias-Motivated Crimes: A Law Enforcement Priority

Hate Crimes and Bias Incidents.   The Federal government defines a **hate crime** as "a crime in which the defendant selects a victim, or in the case of a property crime, the property that is the object of the crime, because of the actual or perceived race, color, religion, national origin, ethnicity, gender, disability, or sexual orientation of any person." 28 U.S.C. § 994, *as amended.* Like hate crime penalty enhancement statutes that now exist in 45 states and the District of Columbia, this law increases sentences for bias-motivated federal crimes. With respect to the Internet, a hate crime is almost always a threat.

A **bias incident** is an act that is motivated by bias or prejudice that does not involve criminal conduct. For example, the distribution of hate literature is a bias incident. The definition of what constitutes a hate crime varies from state to state and under Federal law. Hate crime offenders may be prosecuted under Federal or state criminal and civil rights laws. Participants in bias incidents cannot be prosecuted criminally, but state law may provide a civil remedy.

Federal Laws—Federal Criminal Civil Rights Statutes.   State and local law enforcement authorities play the primary role in the prosecution of bias-motivated violence. Current Federal law contains significant gaps and limitations, reaching only certain bias-motivated violence, which is intended to interfere with the victim's federal rights or participation in a federally protected activity. The Federal government does play a critical role in supplementing state and local prosecutions in appropriate circumstances.

42 U.S.C. Section 3631, the criminal portion of the Fair Housing Act of 1968, prohibits housing-related violence on the basis of race, color, religion, sex, handicap, familial status, or national origin. The violence usually prosecuted under this section includes cross-burnings, fire bombings, arsons, gunshots, rock throwing, and vandalism. The statute reaches all persons involved in any housing-related activity—sellers, buyers, landlords, tenants, and real estate agents.

18 U.S.C. Section 245 is the primary criminal civil rights statute for racial violence cases that do not involve housing. As enacted in 1968, Section 245 prohibits the use of force or threats of force against individuals because of their race, color, religion, or national origin, and because those individuals are engaged in certain specified activities. Section 245 protects against race-based interference in the right to enroll in a public school or college; the right to participate in and enjoy any benefit, service, or program administered by a state; employment by any private employer or state or local agency; travel in or use of a facility of interstate commerce; and enjoyment of goods or services of any place of public accommodation.

18 U.S.C. Section 247 criminalizes attacks on religious property and obstructions of persons who are enjoying the free exercise of their religious beliefs. This statute, originally enacted in 1988 and amended by the Church Arson Prevention Act of 1996, covers racially-motivated church burnings and bombings, as well as acts of desecration motivated by religious animus when the defendant has traveled in interstate commerce or has used a facility or instrumentality of interstate commerce.

18 U.S.C. Section 241 broadly prohibits a conspiracy to injure or threaten "any person" in the free exercise or enjoyment of any right or privilege secured to him by the Constitution or laws of the United States.

28 U.S.C. § 994, the Hate Crimes Sentencing Act, enhances the penalties only for bias-motivated federal crimes that occur in National Parks and on other federally owned property. Under the Act, a hate crime is "a crime in which the defendant selects a victim, or in the case of a property crime, the property that is the object of the crime, because of the actual or perceived race, color, religion, national origin, ethnicity, gender, disability, or sexual orientation of any person." 28 U.S.C. § 994, *as amended* (2000).

In addition, the **1990 Hate Crime Statistics Act** requires the U.S. Department of Justice to collect data on crimes motivated by bias or prejudice based on race, religion, sexual orientation, ethnicity, or disability from law enforcement agencies across the country, and to publish an annual report of these statistics. 28 U.S.C. § 534, *as amended*. These annual reports can increase the effectiveness of law enforcement agencies by providing information necessary to determine patterns of hate crimes, to anticipate changes in the incidence of hate crimes, and to foster better police-community relations on a local level [Editor's Note: D. Rosenberg and M. Lieberman, 1999 *Hate Crimes Laws*, New York: Anti-Defamation League]

State Laws. Almost every state has a law that punishes some bias-motivated crimes. Forty-five states and the District of Columbia have hate crime penalty enhancement laws that more severely punish crimes intentionally directed at individuals or institutions because of their personal characteristics, such as race, religion, national origin, sexual orientation, gender, or disability. All the states include race, religion, and ethnicity or national origin as protected characteristics; about half the states include gender, sexual orientation, or disability. A few states have hate crime laws that cover political or age bias. Hate crime laws typically fall into three categories. First, a small number of states have laws in which the hate violence stands alone as a separate crime. Second, as previously mentioned, 45 states and the District of Columbia provide stiffer sentences for an offender whose criminal activity is intentionally directed at an individual or institution because of the victim's personal characteristics. Finally, approximately 20 states have civil hate crime laws that authorize the State Attorney General to obtain injunctions against perpetrators to prohibit repeat behavior and to seek the imposition of civil fines. The civil rather than criminal approach is adopted for a variety of reasons, including quicker enforcement, a lower burden of proof (preponderance of the evidence versus beyond a reasonable doubt), and avoidance of overcrowded state court criminal dockets. Many of the state hate crime laws and national hate crime statistics can be found at the Anti-Defamation League's Web site, www.adl.org, and the Partners Against Hate Web site at www.partnersagainsthate.org/hate_response_database/.

Reported Cases: Hate Crimes on the Internet. As previously mentioned, the small number of reported Internet hate crime cases is instructive. Like the Machado case described at the outset, the majority of these cases result from e-mail messages containing threats. Some of these reported Internet hate crime cases are listed below.

State v. Belanger. In 1997, Casey Belanger was a 19-year-old freshm[a]n student at the University of Maine at Orono. He posted his resume, which included a statement that he "dislike[d] fags," on the university's computer network. In response, another student posted a message attacking Belanger's resume and asking whom Belanger thought he was. This subsequent message was sent to student groups organized on the university's Internet system for Religion, Gay/Lesbian/ Bisexual, Politics, and Debate.

Later that same day, Belanger posted a message to all of these same groups, which stated [expletives deleted]:

> I hope that you die screaming in hell . . .you'd [sic] better watch your . . .back you little . . .I'm [sic] gonna shoot you in the back of the . . .head . . .die screaming [name of student],

burn in eternal . . .hell I hate gay/lesbian/bisexuals, so . . .what . . ..

The State Attorney General brought an action against Belanger under the Maine Civil Hate Crime Act seeking an injunction to require Belanger to cease from threatening any person because of the person's sexual orientation, race, color, religion, ancestry, sex, national origin, or physical or mental disability. The Court issued a permanent injunction against Belanger.

Commonwealth of Pennsylvania v. *ALPHA HQ.* In 1998, a white supremacist in Pennsylvania named Ryan Wilson was charged by the Commonwealth's Attorney General with threats, harassment, and ethnic intimidation in connection with a Web site that Wilson owned and operated for his racist organization, ALPHA. Among other images, the Web site depicted a bomb destroying the office of Bonnie Jouhari, a fair housing specialist who regularly organized anti-hate activities. Next to her picture, the ALPHA Web site stated, "Traitors like this should beware, for in our day, they will be hung from the neck from the nearest tree or lamp post." Wilson did not contest the State's action under Pennsylvania's Civil Hate Crimes Act; the site was removed from the Internet, and the Court issued an injunction against Wilson and his organizations barring them from displaying certain messages on the Internet.

United States v. *Kingman Quon.* A college student, Kingman Quon, sent e-mail messages to 42 Hispanic faculty members at California State University at Los Angeles, 25 Hispanic students at the Massachusetts Institute of Technology, and numerous other Hispanic persons employed at various institutions and businesses across the nation. Quon's racially derogatory messages discussed his hatred of Latinos, accused them of being "too stupid" to have been accepted at the university or have obtained employment without the help of affirmative action programs, and concluded that he intended to "come down and kill" them. In 1999, the U.S. Department of Justice charged Quon with interfering with the students' Federal rights in violation of Federal Civil Rights laws. Quon plead guilty and received a two-year prison sentence.

Reasons for Likely Increase in Internet Hate Crimes. Although there are relatively few reported cases, local police and high school and college administrators indicate that the use of the Internet to send bias-motivated messages and threats is increasing. Internet use has increased exponentially in recent years. Approximately 533 million people now use the Internet to search for information, to create material to share with large audiences, and to communicate with others throughout the world for little or no cost. Users in the United States are estimated at approximately 149 million (Information Please, 2001). Web sites, chat rooms, and e-mail messages have become a reliable method of communication for much of the population. These mo[d]es of communications, however, typically permit a user to remain anonymous or adopt a false identity, providing an opportunity for that person to express freely his or her most bigoted views.

Widespread Internet use combines nearly limitless reach of communication with apparent lack of accountability. For the bias-motivated user, this combination is tantalizing, as the user can both send a threatening message and, theoretically, remain unknown to the recipient. As revealed in recent litigation concerning illicit use of the Internet, however, some users have wrongly assumed that their apparent anonymity would shield them from prosecution.

III. Investigating Hate Crimes on the Internet

Investigating hate crimes on the Internet can *appear* to be unusually complicated because of the involvement of electronically sent messages. While the investigation of Internet hate crimes occasionally involves complicated legal and investigatory issues such as those described in the **Additional Issues** section later in this Brief, the far greater number of investigations are the same or similar to routine investigations of threats by telephone or mail.

The fact that messages were sent through the Internet does not affect the basic legal analysis of whether the message itself constitutes a threat and whether the threat was motivated by bias or prejudice. Additionally, the determination of who sent the threat must be guided by the same investigative strategies that law enforcement officers use in cases of telephone or mail threats.

Determining Whether a Message Constitutes a Threat. The definition of criminal threat will vary from state to state. Under most State laws, the crime of threatening requires proof that an individual has sent a message that causes another to have a reasonable fear of imminent bodily injury. This definition does not vary whether the threat was made in person or by telephone, mail, facsimile or e-mail. In some states, prosecutors must also prove that the perpetrator must have the ability to carry out the threat.

The definition of harassment also varies from state to state. In general, for speech to be harassing it must be targeted at specific individuals and it must be persistent, pernicious, and inflict great emotional or physical harm. The starting point for analysis in Internet hate crimes investigations is the message itself. Law enforcement officers must determine whether the message—on its face—threatens imminent bodily injury to the target of the threat. This determination becomes more difficult if the language of the message is vague with respect to the threat or with regard to the intended recipient.

A second critical step in determining whether a message constitutes a threat is the interview with the target of the threat. It is difficult both legally and practically to bring a criminal charge of threatening to a message that, while it may appear to a law enforcement officer to threaten imminent bodily injury, is perceived by the recipient or target as being innocuous. In short, if the target of a possibly threatening message does not believe that he or she is being placed in imminent danger of bodily injury and is not "scared" by the message, then prosecution will be extraordinarily difficult.

Most police officers have had experience investigating threats. The investigative strategies and tactics for determining whether an Internet communication is a threat does not vary in any significant respect from investigations into either mail or telephone threats.

Bias Motivation: The Importance of Bias Crime Indicators. Establishing that a threatening message also constitutes a hate crime requires the investigator to determine that the message was intentionally directed at an individual or institution because of the victim's personal characteristics. Since bias or prejudice can explain the reason for this criminal conduct, determining whether the message itself was motivated by bias is at the heart of investigating potential hate crimes. Investigators will need to closely examine the applicable hate crime statute to determine which bias motivations are included in the statute. See **Addressing Bias-Motivated Crimes: A Law Enforcement Priority, Hate Crimes and Bias Incidents** section.

Identifying bias crime indicators and confirming bias motivation are essential building blocks for investigating and, ultimately, successfully prosecuting Internet hate crimes. Bias indicators are objective facts; circumstances or patterns attending a criminal act that, standing alone or in conjunction with other facts or circumstances, suggest that the offender's actions were motivated in whole or in part by bias. The factors and sub-factors listed in the **Appendix** are the most significant bias indicators, but it is critical to recognize that the existence of one or more bias crime indicators does not in and of itself establish that the act investigated was in fact motivated by bias. Rather, law enforcement officers must assess all relevant bias indicators and then make a reasoned judgment based upon experience as to whether the conduct in question was motivated by bias or prejudice.

Examining the Message Itself. In Internet threat cases (as in any investigation of a potential bias-motivated threat), the most important evidence usually is the message itself. Most hate crime investigations of threats originate because the content of the message clearly indicates a bias motivation. This fact was true of the e-mail messages in the *Machado* and *Belanger* cases and of the Web site at issue in *Commonwealth of Pennsylvania* v. *ALPHA HQ.*

Interviewing the Recipient of the Message. Even if the message appears to be bias-motivated, investigators must interview the recipient to determine whether there were any other motivations for sending the message other than the bias apparent in the context of the message itself. It is, obviously, important to interview friends, family members, roommates, and coworkers to obtain information. A further inquiry into the recipient's background may be necessary.

Identifying the Sender. Frequently, the most difficult investigative issue in an Internet threat or harassment case is the identification of the sender. Most e-mail threats are anonymous. While there may be complexities involved in trying to identify who sent an e-mail message, many of the same investigative tools that police officers use to determine who sent an anonymous letter or placed an anonymous telephone call are equally applicable to anonymous messages over the Internet. Most (but certainly not all) threats are sent by people who know each other, and the recipient of the threat often has some idea (perhaps a very clear one, perhaps an educated guess) as to who is responsible. Again, interviews with the victim and with friends, roommates, family members, neighbors, and coworkers is a critical first step to obtain information necessary to identify the sender of the message.

Collection and Preservation of Evidence. Because communications sent over the Internet can be easily destroyed, deleted, or modified, law enforcement officials must know how best to gather, preserve, and authenticate electronic evidence. While several of the issues that can arise for law enforcement agencies in the collection and preservation of evidence for the successful prosecution of an Internet hate crime are common to any criminal investigation, a few have different application[s] and considerations.

For instance, the need for probable cause to conduct a search exists in any investigation, but an investigator of an Internet hate crime must consider whether probable cause exists separately to seize from a computer the hardware, software, and other stored data. Assuming probable cause exists to obtain a warrant, investigators must be careful to ensure that the material searched is within the scope of the warrant, a somewhat more difficult task when searching evidence on a computer than when searching most crime scenes.[1] While use of the Internet introduces some novel investigative and prosecutorial concerns, investigators and prosecutors for the most part already are armed with the skills needed to pursue these cases and should not be deterred by the Internet connection. Indeed, it is essential that Internet hate crimes cases be rigorously investigated and prosecuted, so that the apparent anonymity that spurs the hate-motivated actor is not coupled with a lack of accountability.

---

[1] An extremely useful source for the practical aspects of searches and seizures in this area is *Best Practices for Seizing Electronic Evidence* (a joint project of the International Association of Chief's [sic] of Police and the U.S. Secret Service).

IV. Additional Issues

Hate Web Sites. For relatively modest fees or free of charge, most Internet Service Providers willingly "host" any and all Web pages regardless of content and provide nearly unlimited use of the hardware and communications lines for creation of a Web site. As would be expected, Web sites that contain bias or prejudice based on race, religion, ethnicity, gender, disability, and sexual orientation have taken full advantage of the low-cost opportunity to spread their messages 24 hours a day to millions of people at an instant (Kessler, 1999).

As previously mentioned, generally even the most reprehensible and bigoted Web sites receive First Amendment free speech protection, so long as the sites cannot be interpreted to satisfy the narrow exceptions for threats or harassing speech directed at specific individuals or identifiable groups. One Federal case that sought to establish a line over which hate Web sites could not step is *Planned Parenthood of the Columbia/ Willamette, Inc. v. American Coalition of Life Activists*, 23 F. Supp. 2d 1182 (D. Or. 1999), *inj. granted*, 41 F. Supp. 2d 1130 (D. Or. 1999), *vacated and remanded*, 244 F.3d 1007 (9th Cir. 2001), *reh'g en banc granted*, 268 F.3d 908 (9th Cir. 2001), *aff'd in part, vacated in part and remanded*, 290 F. 3d. 1058 (9th Cir. 2002), *cert. den*, 123 S. Ct. 2637 (2003). In this case, an anti-abortion group created a Web site [that] included the names, photographs, home addresses, license plate numbers, and the names of spouses and children of doctors who allegedly performed abortions. Headlined "Visualize Abortionists on Trial" and depicting blood dripping from aborted fetus parts, the site called for these doctors to be brought to justice for crimes against humanity. The names of doctors who had been wounded by anti-abortion protesters were listed in gray. Doctors who had been killed by anti-abortionists were shown with a line through their names. The anti-abortion group also printed posters with the word "Guilty" at the top, a comparison of abortions to Nazi war crimes and a list of names of physicians who provide abortion services. Three physicians named on the poster and the Web site were subsequently murdered.

Several doctors and abortion clinics sued the antiabortion groups alleging that they had been the specific targets of threats to kill, assault or cause bodily harm. The jury agreed, finding that the Web site constituted a threat to the plaintiff physicians. Rejecting defendants' free speech claims, the jury ordered the Web site owners and operators to pay plaintiffs more than $100 million in damages. Consistent with the jury's verdict, the judge subsequently determined that the plaintiffs reasonably felt threatened by the materials, and issued a permanent injunction to prevent the defendants from providing additional information to the Web site.

This verdict and injunction were reversed on appeal in March 2001 by a unanimous three-judge panel of the U.S. Court of Appeals for the Ninth Circuit. Contrary to the lower court rulings, the Court of Appeals held that the defendants' Web site was a lawful expression of views protected by the First Amendment. The Court of Appeals concluded that "[u]nless [defendants] threatened that its members would themselves assault the doctors, the First Amendment protects its speech." 244 F.3d 1007, 1015 (9th Cir. 2001). In October 2001, the Court of Appeals decided to rehear the case before all members of the Court, and it held that the Web site constituted a true "threat of force" and was not protected by the First Amendment. 290 F.3d 1058, 1063 (9th Cir. 2002). The 9th Circuit's decision is an important development because it establishes that Web sites do not always have First Amendment protection.

However, as a general matter, the First Amendment protection for hate Web sites remains an extremely high bar to hurdle. At least for now, law enforcement agencies should seek careful direction from the U.S. Attorneys in their districts, State Attorneys General, or local District Attorneys before pursuing investigations of complaints against offensive or hate Web sites.

Jurisdiction. Perpetrators of Internet hate crimes are not hampered by the existence of national or international boundaries, because information can be easily transmitted worldwide through communications and data networks. Even though connections may be of short duration, most computers are physically located in identifiable places. Of course, computers can be accessed remotely, regardless of the location of the persons who post, send, view, or receive information online.

As a result, it is at least possible that a perpetrator of a threat or harassing speech need not be at the actual scene of the crime (or within 5,000 miles, for that matter) to prey on his or her victims. Just as telephones have been used to create distance between offenders and victims, a computer server from which a threat or harassing speech is sent can be located in California and the recipients scattered throughout

New England. Likewise, evidence of an Internet hate crime can be stored at a remote location, either for the purpose of concealing the crime from law enforcement or simply because of the design of the network used. To be sure, the Internet increases the ability of law enforcement officials and others to detect and gather evidence from a distance. Long-distance detection and collection of evidence, however, can require that the investigation and prosecution of the crime extend beyond the borders of any single jurisdiction. The traditional investigative tools available—interviews, physical or electronic surveillance, and subpoenas for the production of documents or for testimony—may not always be adequate to compel information from a wrongdoer who is located in a place far away from the victim. The challenge to law enforcement, then, is to identify that location, and to determine which laws apply to the investigation and incidents at issue.

For example, if a threat or harassing speech is communicated to a resident of State A by an offender in State B, and State A issues a subpoena for investigators to search records of the State B offender, no formal procedural mechanism currently exists for the service and enforcement of that subpoena. Although the prosecutors in State A might obtain assistance from the State B authorities, this assistance is a matter of professional courtesy rather than legal process. There is no guarantee that prosecutors in one state have the authority to issue a subpoena in another state, or that the subpoena will be properly served or adequately enforced, which could mean the end of the State investigation (National Cybercrime Training Partnership, 2000).

Virtually identical problems are presented with the interstate enforcement and execution of search warrants and judicial electronic surveillance orders. And beyond these and other problems law enforcement agencies encounter with interstate investigations, international investigations of Internet hate crimes pose even greater challenges (National Cybercrime Training Partnership, 2000). Because of these complex issues, some prosecutors believe that Federal authorities may be better suited to conduct investigations involving Internet messages that cross state or national lines.

These problematic issues, however, are unlikely to arise in many Internet hate crimes cases in which messages are sent from within the same community in which the victim lives. Traditional investigative techniques typically will prove adequate in investigation of localized hate crimes on the Internet.

V. Conclusion

Hate crimes perpetrated over the World Wide Web pose special challenges for investigators and prosecutors. Those who send threatening e-mail communications through the Internet may convey these messages anonymously across state lines to victims in another part of the country. Prosecutors face the daunting task of identifying the perpetrator, collecting and preserving evidence, and establishing jurisdiction over the criminal act. It is essential that law enforcement authorities be equipped to address these challenges in order to hold perpetrators of these crimes fully accountable.

VI. Appendix: Bias Crime Indicators

Identifying bias crime indicators and confirming bias motivation are the essential building blocks for responding to the needs of victims and the community and successfully prosecuting hate crimes. Bias crime indicators are objective facts, circumstances, or patterns attending a criminal act that, standing alone or in conjunction with other facts or circumstances, suggest that the offender's actions were motivated, in whole or in part, by bias. The following factors may indicate bias motivation:

1. **Racial, Ethnic, Gender, and Cultural Differences Between Perpetrator and Victim**
   a. Racial identity, religion, ethnicity/national origin, disability, or sexual orientation of the victim differs from that of the offender.
   b. Victim is a member of a group overwhelmingly outnumbered by members of another group in the area where the incident occurred.
   c. Victim was engaged in activities promoting his or her group.
   d. Incident coincided with a holiday or date of particular significance to the victim's group.
   e. Victim, although not a member of the targeted group, is a member of an advocacy group that supports the targeted group or was in the company of a member of the targeted group.
   f. Long-established animosity exists between the victim's group and the offender's group.
2. **Comments, Written Statements, and Gestures**
   a. Bias-related comments, written statements, or gestures were made by the offender.
   b. Bias-related e-mails or Web sites were made by the offender.
3. **Drawings, Markings, Symbols, and Graffiti**
   a. Bias-related drawings, markings, symbols, or graffiti were left at the scene of the incident.
4. **Involvement of Organized Hate Group or Its Members**

a. Objects or items that represent the work of an organized hate group were left at the crime scene.

b. There were indications that a hate group was involved. For example, a hate group claimed responsibility for the crime or was active in the neighborhood at the time of the crime.

5. **Previous Existence of Bias Crimes/Incidents.**

a. Victim was visiting a location where bias crimes had been committed against members of the victim's group.

b. Several incidents occurred in the same area, and victims were members of the same group.

c. Victim had received harassing mail or phone calls previously or had been subjected to verbal abuse based on his or her affiliation with a targeted group.

6. **Victim/Witness Perception**

a. Victims or witnesses perceive that the incident was motivated by bias.

7. **Motive(s) of Suspect**

a. Offender was involved in a similar incident or is a member of, or associates with members of an organized hate group.

b. Victim was in the company of, or married to, a member of a targeted group.

c. Offender has a history of committing crimes with a similar modus operandi, and there have been multiple victims with the same racial identity, religion, ethnic/national origin, disability, sexual orientation, or gender.

8. **Location of Incident**

a. Victim was in or near an area or place commonly associated with or frequented by individuals of a particular racial identity, religion, ethnic/national origin, disability, sexual orientation, or gender.

b. The incident occurred at or near a place of worship, a religious cemetery, the home of a minority family living in a predominantly white neighborhood, or a gay bar.

9. **Lack of Other Motives**

a. No clear economic or other motive for the incident exists.

6

Directory of Organizations

This chapter includes descriptions of selected human and civil rights organizations that both monitor hate crime incidents and extremist and violent hate groups and try to foster interethnic and interreligious harmony. The descriptions are mostly derived from the publications and/or Internet sites of the organizations. For more detailed and comprehensive information about some of these organizations, please consult chapter 2 of *Confronting Right-Wing Extremism and Terrorism in the USA*, by George Michael (Routledge, 2003).

American Islamic Congress (AIC)
1770 Massachusetts Avenue, #623
Cambridge, MA 02140
617-621-1511
Internet: http://www.aicongress.org/

Organized by concerned Muslims in New Haven, Connecticut, following the September 11, 2001, terrorist attacks, the AIC is dedicated to building interfaith and interethnic understanding. Charging that many American Muslims were silent in the face of Muslim extremism, the organization aims to foster respect and tolerance between Muslims and non-Muslims. AIC members live throughout the United States and in largely Muslim countries throughout the world, including Egypt, Malaysia, Nigeria, Kuwait, and Morocco. The organization has been featured on major television and radio programs, and articles by and about the group have been published in the *Toronto Globe and Mail*, the *Boston Globe*, and the *Wall Street Journal*.

163

The AIC compiled *Responding to Hate Speech: A Citizen's Guide,* a handbook to help Muslims respond to incidents of intolerance directed against or provoked by Muslims. The AIC also produced the *Teachers' Guide on Islam and September 11,* for parents and teachers in the United States who want to learn about the richness and diversity of Muslim peoples and Islamic civilization. In addition, the organization produces guides for foreign Muslim parents and educators to help them better understand the United States. To strengthen interfaith understanding, the AIC has been involved in the Children of Abraham Peace Project, which helps organize and suggests guidelines for interfaith dialogues between Muslims and non-Muslims throughout the United States.

Finally, the group organized a memorial vigil for Daniel Pearl, the *Wall Street Journal* reporter who was murdered by terrorists, and an interfaith tour with an imam, a minister, and a rabbi.

American Jewish Committee (AJC)
P.O. Box 705
New York, NY 10150
212-751-4000
Fax: 212-891-1492
Internet: http://www.ajc.org/

Founded in 1906 in response to anti-Jewish pogroms in Russia and other parts of Europe, the AJC is a membership organization with chapters nationwide. Its programs are guided by the values of Jewish teachings and the principles of American democracy. Committed to working in partnership with the diverse racial, ethnic, and religious groups in the United States, the AJC promotes intergroup relations and combats anti-Jewish hatred and other forms of racism and bigotry. On Capitol Hill and in statehouses across the country, the AJC supports legislation mandating severe penalties for hate crimes and for the collection of reliable statistics about these incidents. In its earlier years, the AJC pioneered the "quarantine" or "dynamic silence" approach to counter notorious anti-Jewish and racist rabble-rousers. This tactic aimed to minimize the publicity for these speakers. Instead of confronting these bigots in counterdemonstrations, Jewish and civil rights advocates stayed away from these racist rallies and thus the news media had no story to cover and the event went unreported. Although this approach was successful for many years, author George Michael points out that the Internet and talk show programs have now limited the effectiveness of this strategy. In recent years, in fact, the AJC has actively exposed extremist groups and publicized the violent activities of the militia movement even before the 1995 bombing in Oklahoma City. The AJC publishes the *American Jewish Year Book,* an authoritative reference work that covers many aspects of Jewish life, including anti-Jewish activities and extremist groups around the world. The organization has regional offices in major U.S. cities and overseas bureaus in Jerusalem, Berlin, Brussels, Geneva, and Warsaw.

Anti-Defamation League (ADL)
823 United Nations Plaza
New York, NY 10017
212-885-7700
Internet: http://www.adl.org/

In 1913, Sigmund Livingston, a Chicago attorney, persuaded B'nai B'rith, the oldest Jewish communal organization in the country whose Hebrew name means "Children of the Covenant," to establish a defense agency to combat growing anti-Jewish hatred in the United States. Only two years later, a mob in Georgia lynched Leo Frank, a Jewish factory supervisor in Atlanta who was falsely accused of murdering a thirteen-year-old female employee. This notorious lynching was spurred on by much anti-Jewish agitation and sparked great fear among American Jews. The ADL is the preeminent U.S. organization that combats anti-Semitism, all forms of bigotry, and discrimination and helps promote harmonious relations among diverse religious, ethnic, and racial groups. The ADL's mission is to "stop the defamation of the Jewish people and to secure justice and fair treatment to all citizens alike." National headquarters are in New York City, and there are many regional and local offices throughout the United States. The ADL also has offices in countries abroad, including Israel and Russia.

The League has led state and national efforts to deter and combat hate-motivated crimes. In 1981, it developed model hate crime statutes that have subsequently been adopted by most state governments and many municipalities throughout the United States. The League has also been at the forefront to develop sentencing options for youths who commit bias crimes. The ADL provides training on issues related to hate crimes to agents of the Federal Bureau of Investigation as well as to state and local law enforcement agencies. The organization publishes an extensive number of materials on human relations, diversity, and intergroup relations (see chapter 8). *Audits of Anti-Semitic Incidents* is the most comprehensive nongovernmental annual report documenting anti-Jewish attacks on individuals and property. It also contains a survey of anti-Jewish and racist hate groups. LEARN (Law Enforcement Agency Research Network) provides a wide variety of materials for police and other law enforcement officials.

Center for Democratic Renewal (CDR)
P.O. Box 50469
Atlanta, GA 30302
404-221-0025
Fax: 404-221-0045
Internet: http://www.thecdr.org

Founded in 1979 by Rev. C. T. Vivian and Anne Braden as the National Anti-Klan Network, the multiracial CDR advocates a "democratic, diverse and just society, free of racism and bigotry." The organization formally changed its name in 1985 to reflect its broadened agenda: to serve as a clearinghouse for constructive responses to hate groups and hate-motivated violence, as well as to advocate reproductive rights and support for immigrants, among other issues. The CDR has allied itself with other human rights and antiviolence groups to achieve mutual goals. During the 1980s, the CDR worked with farm organizations, churches, and Jewish groups to combat anti-Jewish propaganda aimed at American farmers. The CDR also claims that its report on hate crimes in Georgia convinced the Georgia state legislature to enact its first law against bias-motivated crimes. *When Hate Groups Come to Town: A Manual of Effective Community Response* has been widely distributed to community and human rights groups throughout the United States.

Center for the Prevention of Hate Violence (CPHV)
96 Falmouth Street
Box 9300
Portland, Maine 04104-9300
207-780-4756
Fax: 207-228-8550
Internet: http://www.cphv.usm.maine.edu/about.htm

In July 1999 the University of Maine System approved the creation of the CPHV at the University of Southern Maine. The CPHV has two objectives: to develop and implement hate crime prevention curricula and programs and to develop and encourage increased research, writing, teaching, and dialogue on the history, causes, and prevention of hate violence. The center has published several reports, educational manuals, and guides to educate teachers, students, and the public about hate crimes.

Gonzaga University Institute for Action Against Hate
AD Box 43
502 East Boone Avenue
Spokane, WA 99258-0043
509 -323-3665
Internet: http://guweb2.gonzaga.edu/againsthate/

Founded in 1997 in response to some racist incidents on the Gonzaga University campus, the institute is an academic organization devoted to combating hate through research, education, and advocacy. The institute publishes reports, a newsletter, and a new academic journal, *The Journal of Hate Studies*. In March 2004 the institute sponsored an international conference to promote the establishment of an academic field for hate studies that attracted more than 100 scholars and researchers.

National Asian Pacific American Legal Consortium (NAPALC)
1140 Connecticut Avenue NW
Washington, DC 20036
202-296-2300
Internet: http://www.napalc.org/

Founded in Washington, D.C., in 1993, NAPALC is a nonprofit, nonpartisan organization whose mission is to advance and protect the legal and civil rights of the nation's Asian Pacific Americans through litigation, advocacy, public education, and public policy development. Its priorities include anti-Asian violence prevention and education. The consortium is affiliated with two civil rights legal organizations: the Asian Law Caucus (San Francisco) and the Asian Pacific American Legal Center of Southern California (Los Angeles). In their work to address and prevent anti-Asian violence, NAPALC and its affiliates monitor and document hate-motivated violence and educate their community and law enforcement officials about the problem of violent bigotry. The consortium also advocates the passage of strict hate crime laws and defends the constitutionality of hate crime statutes before state and federal courts. The consortium publishes the *NAPALC Audit of Violence Against Asian Pacific Americans*, the only nationwide nongovernmental compilation and analysis of anti-Asian violence in the United States.

National Gay and Lesbian Task Force (NGLTF)
1325 Massachusetts Avenue NW
Suite 600
Washington, DC 20005
202-393-5177
Fax: 202-393-2241
Internet: http://www.ngltf.org/

The NGLTF is the leading civil rights organization for lesbian, gay, bisexual, and transgender rights. Founded in New York in 1973, the organization combats antigay violence and job discrimination and lobbies for gay rights legislation. In 1984 the NGLTF published the first national study focusing exclusively on antigay violence. Two years earlier the task force created an antiviolence project to promote an official response to violence and harassment perpetrated against individuals because of their sexual orientation. The NGLTF's publications include *Hate Crimes Map*, a unique source indicating the extent of hate crime laws covering sexual orientation in all fifty states; press releases; and other materials concerning local and federal hate crimes legislation.

New York City Gay and Lesbian Anti-Violence Project (AVP)
240 West 35th Street, Suite 200
New York, NY 10001
212-714-1184
Hotline: 212-714-1141 (24 hours)
Internet: http://www.avp.org/

Founded in New York City in 1980, this pioneering organization was organized in response to anti-gay neighborhood violence and the lack of response from the local police. Currently, the AVP serves lesbian, gay, transgender, bisexual, and HIV-positive victims of violence, and others affected by violence, by providing free and confidential services.

Although this organization primarily focuses on antigay violence in New York City, the AVP serves as a national clearinghouse for statistics and information on hate crimes motivated by sexual orientation throughout the United States. A member of the National Coalition of Anti-Violence Programs—a network of more than twenty community organizations dealing with violence both within and directed at the gay community—the AVP distributes an annual hate crimes report through its Web site.

Political Research Associates (PRA)
1310 Broadway, Suite 201
Somerville, MA 02144-1731
617-666-5300
Fax: 617-666-6622
Internet: http://www.publiceye.org/index.html

Founded in 1981 in Chicago as Midwest Research, the organization relocated to the Boston area under its current name in 1987. PRA is an independent nonprofit research center that examines the U.S. political right. The organization collects and analyzes information on antidemocratic, authoritarian, and racist right-wing movements and publishes educational resources that explain their ideologies, tactics, agendas, and financing. PRA has its own library and an extensive publications list, including information packets, topical reports, monographs, and books. Senior analyst Chip Berlet has written, edited, and coauthored many PRA publications. *Public Eye* is the organization's newsletter.

Prejudice Institute
2743 Maryland Avenue
Baltimore, MD 21218
410-243-6987
http://www.prejudiceinstitute.org

Founded in 1984 as the National Institute against Prejudice and Violence, this nonmembership organization studies the problems of prejudice, discrimination, conflict, and violence. The organization also conducts research on the causes and prevalence of prejudice and violence and their effects on victims and society. Publications include *Prejudice and Ethnoviolence on Campus; Community Response to Bias Crimes and Incidents; The Ecology of Anti-Gay Violence; Harassment—What to Do If It Happens to You; The Lawyer's Role in Combating Bias-Motivated Violence; Reporting Ethnoviolence;* and *Traumatic Effects of Ethnoviolence.*

Simon Wiesenthal Center
1399 South Roxbury Drive
Los Angeles, CA 90035
310-553-9036; toll-free number in the U.S.: 1-800-900-9036
Internet: http://www.wiesenthal.com/

Founded in 1977, the Simon Wiesenthal Center is an international institute for Holocaust remembrance and the defense of human rights for Jewish people and other groups. Headquartered in Los Angeles, the center's mandate combines social action, public outreach, scholarship, education, and media projects. The organization also maintains offices in New York, Toronto, Miami, Jerusalem, Paris, and Buenos Aires. The Wiesenthal Center monitors the activities of hate groups, publicizes the existence of violent hate Web sites, assists in the prosecution of Nazi war criminals, and has offered monetary rewards for information leading to the prosecution of hate crime perpetrators. The Task Force against Hate and Terrorism, established in 1991, helps combat Holocaust denial and educates students and teachers about anti-Jewish and other forms of bigotry. Located in New York and Los Angeles, the Museum of Tolerance is a hands-on experiential museum that focuses on two themes in its exhibits: racism and prejudice in the United States and the history of the Holocaust. A third location is planned for Jerusalem. The

Wiesenthal Center publishes *Response*, a quarterly newsletter sent to 400,000 members.

Southern Poverty Law Center (SPLC)
400 Washington Avenue
Montgomery, AL 36104
334-956-8200
Internet: http://www.splcenter.org/

Founded in 1971 by Morris Dees and Joe Levin, two southern lawyers, the SPLC monitors hate activity across the United States, promotes tolerance education, and litigates against violent racist groups. Located in Montgomery, Alabama, the center's Civil Rights Memorial commemorates forty individuals who died during the civil rights era. Since 1979, the SPLC has helped victims of racist violence sue for monetary damages by bringing lawsuits against white supremacist organizations. As the result of a 1990 civil suit in response to the killing of Mulugeta Seraw, an Ethiopian student in Oregon, SPLC attorneys won $12.5 million in damages from Tom Metzger and his racist organization, White Aryan Resistance. In September 2000, an Idaho jury awarded a $6.3 million judgment against the racist group Aryan Nations for assaulting a Native American woman and her son near their compound. The SPLC sued the organization on the victims' behalf and effectively bankrupted the largest neo-Nazi organization in the United States. The SPLC's publications include *Intelligence Report*, an award-winning quarterly magazine providing extensive coverage of racist and violent hate groups and individuals, and *Teaching Tolerance*, a semiannual journal aimed at educators to promote positive intergroup relations.

Stephen Roth Institute for the Study of
Contemporary Anti-Semitism and Racism
Wiener Library
Tel Aviv University
P.O. Box 39040
Ramat Aviv
Tel Aviv, 69978
Israel
Tel: 972-3-6408779
http://www.tau.ac.il/Anti-Semitism/institute.html

This center began operating as the Project for the Study of Anti-Semitism in the fall of 1991 at Tel Aviv University in Israel. Housed in the Wiener Library—one of the world's largest collections of anti-Jewish, Nazi, and extremist literature—the project monitors manifestations of anti-Semitism around the world and operates a computerized database on contemporary anti-Jewish and other hate groups. The database provides statistics for the institute's annual report, the most recent edition of which is *Anti-Semitism Worldwide 2003–2004*. Other publications include *The Jews Cannot Defeat Me: The Anti-Jewish Campaign of Louis Farrakhan and the Nation of Islam* (November 1995).

7

Print Resources

S ince the publication of the first edition of this book, the literature on hate crimes has burgeoned, making it difficult to
compile a comprehensive listing even for materials published since 1999. Since many books on this topic often provide
important and, occasionally, unique historical and analytical information not easily accessible elsewhere, this list includes many
previously listed titles in addition to the many recent new books.
Almost all the magazine and journal citations, however, cover
material published from 1999 through January 2005. The following list is necessarily selective and will provide the student and
researcher with annotated citations to significant and diverse
publications on the topic.

Books

Allport, Gordon. *The Nature of Prejudice.* Menlo Park, CA:
Addison-Wesley, 1979 (originally published in 1954).

A pioneering work by a Harvard psychologist on the social
and psychological nature of bigotry.

Barkun, Michael. *Religion and the Racist Right: The Origins of
the Christian Identity Movement.* Chapel Hill: University of
North Carolina Press, 1994.

A survey and analysis of the Christian Identity movement,
a racist and anti-Jewish ideology whose adherents claim is a
religion.

Bell, Jeannine. *Policing Hatred: Law Enforcement, Civil Rights and Hate Crime.* New York: New York University Press, 2002.

This ethnographic study analyzes the way law enforcement officers enforce hate crime laws and discusses the societal impacts of their efforts.

Bellant, Russ. *Old Nazis, the New Right and the Republican Party.* Boston: South End, 1991.

A disturbing investigation of the heretofore unknown ties of former Nazis who immigrated to this country after World War II and established ties to mainstream political groups.

Blee, Kathleen. *Inside Organized Racism: Women in the Hate Movement.* Berkeley: University of California Press, 2002.

Author of an earlier work on women in the Ku Klux Klan (see below), University of Pittsburgh sociology professor Kathleen Blee provides unique insight on women involved in contemporary violently racist movements. After interviewing a few dozen participants over a two-year period, she learned that the common stereotype of these women—poor, uneducated, raised in abusive families, and mainly recruited by boyfriends or husbands—was not usually true.

———. *Women of the Klan: Racism and Gender in the 1920s.* Berkeley: University of California Press, 1991.

This historical volume examines the involvement of women in the most notorious racist organization in the United States. The author interviewed many former members living in the Midwest and learned that some of these women were involved with women's suffrage and other progressive movements.

Chanes, Jerome A. *Antisemitism: A Reference Handbook.* Santa Barbara, CA: ABC-CLIO, 2004.

This volume surveys the historical, political and sociological manifestations of anti-Jewish prejudice and violence in more than fifty countries. The work includes an extensive introductory essay, a chronology of significant events, movements and legislation, print and nonprint surveys of the topic, and a list of organizations combating this age-old hatred. Chanes, a U.S. Jewish communal leader, also discusses governmental, judicial and other efforts to counteract anti-Semitism.

Cleary, Edward J. *Beyond the Burning Cross: The First Amendment and the Landmark R.A.V. Case.* New York: Random House, 1994.

This work offers an extensive discussion of the legal ramifications of the Supreme Court case involving a hate crime in St. Paul, Minnesota, in 1992.

Coates, James. *Armed and Dangerous: The Rise of the Survivalist Right.* New York: Hill and Wang, 1995.

An investigative reporter for the *Chicago Tribune*, Coates has written an informative survey of the main organizations and individuals on the violent wing of the extreme political right in the United States. A preface to this edition updates events since its initial publication in 1987. Especially noteworthy is the bibliographic notes section, which provides access to a wide variety of relevant newspaper and magazine articles and books published in the 1980s.

Comstock, Gary David. *Violence against Lesbians and Gay Men.* New York: Columbia University Press, 1991.

This study provides statistical data on the extent of antigay violence nationwide and offers a theoretical framework to examine its origins. The book includes a chapter on police violence and empirical data on perpetrators. Also contains extensive footnotes and a bibliography.

Dees, Morris, and Steve Fiffer. *Hate on Trial: The Case against America's Most Dangerous Neo-Nazi.* New York: Villard Books, 1993.

The story of the lawsuit brought by a founder of the Southern Poverty Law Center against Tom Metzger, a neo-Nazi, who instigated the murder of an Ethiopian student in Portland, Oregon. Metzger and his skinhead group were required to pay a multimillion-dollar settlement to the family of the murdered African immigrant.

———. *A Lawyer's Journey: The Morris Dees Story.* Chicago: American Bar Association, 2001.

Originally published in 1991 as *A Season for Justice.* This volume brings Dees's autobiography up to date as of 2001 and includes new material on Dees's most recent legal victory over the Aryan Nations in Idaho.

Dobratz, Betty A., and Stephanie L. Shanks-Meile. *White Power, White Pride: The White Separatist Movement in the United States.* New York: Twayne, 1997.

This work examines the white separatist movement through extensive interviews with more than one hundred active participants. The authors attended rallies and other gatherings to chronicle the history and strategies of the movement.

Dyer, Joel. *Harvest of Rage: Why the Oklahoma City Bombing Is Only the Beginning.* Boulder, CO: Westview Press, 1997.

Dyer surveys the rise of violent antigovernment and extremist hate groups to better understand the attitudes that resulted in the horrific bombing of the federal building in Oklahoma City in 1995 which killed 168 people.

Ezekiel, Raphael S. *The Racist Mind: Portraits of American Neo-Nazis and Klansmen.* New York: Vintage, 1995.

A senior research scientist at the Harvard School of Public Health, Ezekiel spent four years conducting extensive interviews with members of a neo-Nazi group and leaders of racist organizations in order to understand the origin of their views.

Ferrell, Claudine L. *Nightmare and Dream: Anti-Lynching in Congress, 1917–1922.* New York: Garland, 1986.

Originally a doctoral dissertation, this work surveys legislative initiatives in Congress to end the wave of southern lynchings during the early part of the twentieth century.

Flint, Colin, ed. *Spaces of Hate: Geographies of Discrimination and Intolerance in the U.S.A.* New York: Routledge, 2004.

This anthology provides a geographic perspective of hate-motivated activity. The authors are primarily social science professors who adapt postmodern concepts and jargon—critical race, postcolonial, and whiteness theories—to analyze hate crimes and other types of bigotry.

Foster, Arnold. *Square One.* New York: Donald I. Fine, 1988.

A memoir by the former general counsel of the Anti-Defamation League describes his lifelong battle against anti-Semitism and his concern for the welfare and rights of the Jewish people.

Gaylin, Willard. *Hatred: The Psychological Descent into Violence.* New York: Public Affairs, 2003.

Gaylin, a psychoanalyst and author of more than a dozen works, debunks the widespread "therapeutic trivialization of morality." In this brilliant and thought-provoking critique, he condemns societal attitudes that attempt to excuse the murderous actions of terrorists and bigots because of their alleged grievances or family background.

Gerstenfeld, Phyllis B., and Diana R. Grant. *Crimes of Hate: Selected Readings.* Thousand Oaks, CA: Sage Publications, 2004.

This anthology includes essays from a variety of academic fields, including criminology, sociology, psychology, and political science.

———. *Hate Crimes: Causes, Controls and Controversies.* Thousand Oaks, CA: Sage Publications, 2004.

Designed as a college textbook with exercises and discussion questions, this work is a companion volume to *Crimes of Hate: Selected Readings* (see above) that provides an overview of the history and effectiveness of hate crime legislation, the activities of violent hate groups, and the international dimensions of the problem. Well-organized and well-designed, this volume serves as an excellent primer.

Greene, Melissa Fay. *The Temple Bombing.* Reading, MA: Addison-Wesley, 1996.

Engaging and well written, this work chronicles the bombing of the oldest synagogue in Atlanta on October 12, 1958. The author did an enormous amount of research to recount the worst anti-Jewish incident in southern history since the lynching of Leo Frank in 1915.

Hall, Patricia Wong, and Victor M. Hwang. *Anti-Asian Violence in North America: Asian-American and Asian Canadian Reflections on Hate, Healing and Resistance.* Walnut Creek: CA: AltaMira Press, 2001.

This anthology discusses a variety of problems affecting North Americans of Asian ancestry, including civil rights, ethnic identity, and, especially, hate crimes, economic scapegoating, and Internet racism. An introductory essay briefly surveys the history of anti-Asian violence in the United States and Canada and includes a directory of organizations (such as Asian, Jewish, and antiracist) that combat racial bigotry and intolerance.

Hamm, Mark S. *American Skinheads: The Criminology and Control of Hate Crime.* Westport, CT: Praeger, 1993.
This volume examines the social and psychological dimensions of the skinhead movement and, through interviews with some members, analyzes its development. According to the author, "Not all acts of terrorism can be considered hate crimes, and hate crimes are not necessarily terrorism unless such prejudiced violence has a political or social underpinning."

————. *Hate Crime: International Perspectives on Causes and Control.* Highland Heights, KY: Academy of Criminal Justice Sciences, Northern Kentucky University; and Cincinnati, OH: Anderson, 1994.

————. *In Bad Company: America's Terrorist Underground.* Boston: Northeastern University Press, 2002.
Hamm, a professor of criminology at Indiana State University, provides an exhaustive survey of the Aryan Republic Army, a little-known paramilitary radical right-wing gang associated with Oklahoma City bomber Timothy McVeigh.

Hate Crimes: A Bibliography. Compiled by Joan Nordquist. Santa Cruz, CA: Reference and Research Services, 2002.
An unannotated bibliography arranged by topic. Among the fifteen chapters in this useful reference source are "The Victim: Psychological Aspects," "Gender and Hate Crimes," and "Hate Crimes in the Schools and Colleges."

Hate Groups: Opposing Viewpoints. Compiled by Mary E. Williams, book ed. Farmington Hills, MI: Greenhaven, 2004.
This anthology primarily consists of previously published articles from magazines, books, newspaper articles, and columns; a list of organizations; and a bibliography.

Hentoff, Nat. *Free Speech for Me—But not for Thee: How the American Left and Right Relentlessly Censor Each Other.*
New York: HarperCollins, 1992. Hentoff, a prolific writer on

civil liberties, presents an absolutist interpretation of the First Amendment to the U.S. Constitution.

Herek, Gregory M., and Kevin T. Berrill. *Hate Crimes: Confronting Violence against Lesbians and Gay Men.* Newbury Park, CA: Sage Publications, 1992.

The first major monograph on antigay violence in the United States, this anthology includes an overview of the topic, essays on perpetrators and victims, and suggestions for public policy responses. Data and analysis from the first national study conducted by the National Gay and Lesbian Task Force in 1984 are presented.

Jacobs, James B., and Kimberly Potter. *Hate Crimes: Criminal Law and Identity Politics.* New York: Oxford University Press, 1998.

Jacobs, a New York University law professor and preeminent critic of hate crimes legislation, along with his coauthor, argue that these laws are both subjective and unnecessary and also infringe on basic First Amendment rights. An important critical contribution to the hate crimes debate.

Jenness, Valerie, and Kendal Broad. *Hate Crimes: New Social Movements and the Politics of Violence.* New York: Aldine de Gruyter, 1997.

This work examines why bias-motivated violence has recently become a serious issue and the reason some minority constituencies have been categorized as victims while others have gone relatively unnoticed. A sociopolitical analysis, the book also discusses the response to violence against gays and women.

Jenness, Valerie, Kendal Broad, and Ryken Grattet. *Making Hate a Crime: From Social Movement Concept to Law Enforcement.* New York: Russell Sage Foundation, 2001.

The authors analyze, from a sociological perspective, the symbolic importance of hate crime laws but also raise questions about their effectiveness in combating hate-motivated violence.

Johnson, Sandra E. *Standing on the Ground: A Triumph over Hate Crime in the Deep South.* New York: St. Martin's Press, 2002.

A poignant journalistic account of a 1995 racist arson attack on the St. John Baptist Church in Dixiana, South Carolina, and the valiant work of two women—Barbara Simmons, an African American, and Ammie Murray, a white—to rebuild the church.

Kelly, Robert J., ed. *Bias Crime: American Law Enforcement and Legal Responses.* Chicago: Office of International Criminal Justice, University of Illinois at Chicago, 1993.

This anthology covers various methods used by police and other law enforcement officials to prosecute violent hate crimes. Although much of the material covers the mid- to late 1980s, it still provides a useful overview for government attorneys, prosecutors, and other public officials.

King, Joyce. *Hate Crime: The Story of a Dragging in Jasper, Texas.* New York: Knopf, 2003.

Written by a Dallas-based broadcast journalist, this volume recounts the savage racist murder of James Byrd Jr., an African American, on June 7, 1998. The author describes the background of the three white murderers, who met while in a Texas prison. (See also Temple-Raston, below.)

Kotlowitz, Alex. *The Other Side of the River: A Story of Two Towns, a Death, and America's Dilemma.* New York: Nan A. Talese/Doubleday, 1998.

When the Coast Guard pulled the body of Eric McGinnis, a black teenager, out of southwestern Michigan's St. Joseph's River in May 1991, the mostly white residents of St. Joseph assumed the drowning was accidental. But African Americans in Benton Harbor, a mostly black town on the other side of the river, believed that whites chased him into the water for dating a white girl and that the crime was covered up by the white-dominated St. Joseph police force. Written by the author of the award-winning book *There Are No Children Here,* this work deals brilliantly with how differing perceptions of events are filtered through one's racial background.

Kressel, Neil J. *Mass Hate: The Global Rise of Genocide and Terror.* New York: Westview Press, 2002.

Written by a psychology professor and licensed psychologist, this work is a revised and updated edition of his earlier 1996 volume. Kressel surveys the horrors of mass slaughter and genocide throughout the twentieth century and the alarming rise of Islamic terrorism.

Lamy, Philip. *Millennium Rage.* New York: Plenum Press, 1996. This work discusses the growth of extreme right-wing groups and militias as the year 2000 approached. The author, a professor at Castleton State College in Vermont, examines the growth of this movement and its influence.

Langer, Elinor. *A Hundred Little Hitlers: The Death of a Black Man, the Trial of a White Racist and the Rise of the Neo-Nazi Movement in America.* New York: Henry Holt, 2003.
    A thoroughly researched study of the skinhead murder of an Ethiopian immigrant, Mulugeta Seraw, in Portland, Oregon, on November 13, 1988. The author interviewed the murderers and discusses the successful Southern Poverty Law Center lawsuit against their organization, White Aryan Resistance.

Lawrence, Frederick M. *Punishing Hate: Bias Crimes under American Law.* Cambridge, MA: Harvard University Press, 1999.
    Lawrence, a Boston University law school professor, examines the legal basis for hate crime statutes and strongly advocates the enactment of these laws. Some legislators and civil rights advocates have praised this volume as a landmark contribution in support of these criminal laws.

Levin, Jack, and Jack McDevitt. *Hate Crimes Revisited.* Boulder, CO: Westview Press, 2002.
    This volume updates the authors' earlier 1993 volume, with special emphasis on the impact of the 9/11 Arab terrorist attack.

MacLean, Nancy. *Behind the Mask of Chivalry: The Making of the Second Ku Klux Klan.* New York: Oxford University Press, 1994.
    This work discusses the rebirth of the KKK, its attitude toward white women, blacks, Catholics, Jews, and immigrants, and how it foments terror through lynching and other violent crimes.

Martinez, Thomas, with John Guinther. *Brotherhood of Murder.* New York: McGraw-Hill, 1988.
    A first-person account by a former member of the neo-Nazi group The Order. After Martinez revealed the organization's activities to federal law enforcement agencies, his ex-comrades threatened his life.

Metress, Christopher, ed. *The Lynching of Emmett Till: A Documentary Narrative.* Charlottesville, VA: University of Virginia, 2002.

Containing more than one hundred documents, this work includes news accounts, memoirs and literary works about the murder of fourteen-year-old Emmett Till on August 28, 1955. (See also Whitfield, below.)

Michael, George. *Confronting Right-Wing Extremism and Terrorism in the U.S.A.* New York: Routledge, 2003.

An expansion of a doctoral dissertation, this work surveys the rise of the far right since 1990. It includes interviews with some of the far right's leaders and also with former government officials and human rights activists.

Neiwart, David A. *Death on the Fourth of July: The Story of a Killing, a Trial, and Hate Crime in America.* New York: Palgrave Macmillan, 2004.

On July 4, 2000, a group of drunken white males—who dressed like skinheads—yelled racial epithets at some Asian Americans shopping at a convenience store in Ocean Shores, Washington. A violent fight erupted and one of the white men was fatally stabbed. Written by a freelance journalist, this work reports the details of the murder and examines the broader social and legal issues surrounding hate crimes.

Newton, Michael and Judy, eds. *Ku Klux Klan: An Encyclopedia.* New York: Garland, 1991.

Probably the only event worth commemorating on the 125th anniversary of the "world's oldest, most persistent terrorist organization" is the publication of this useful reference source. Meticulous and diligent researchers, the Newtons have compiled an essential guide for students and researchers.

————. *Racial and Religious Violence in America: A Chronology.* New York: Garland, 1991.

An outstanding reference source, this work provides a unique chronology of many bias-motivated violent incidents throughout U.S. history.

Perry, Barbara. *Hate and Bias Crime: A Reader.* New York: Routledge, 2003.

This anthology examines hate groups and hate crimes from a wide range of academic disciplines, including sociology, criminology and criminal justice, psychology and social psychology, political science and law.

————. *In the Name of Hate: Understanding Hate Crimes.* New York: Routledge, 2001.

The author, a professor of criminology at Northern Arizona University, uses a theoretical framework called "structured action theory" to analyze hate crimes. Her analysis contends that hate crime is an "instrument that defends the gendered and racialized social ordering of American culture."

Quarles, Chester L. *Ku Klux Klan and Related American Racialist and Antisemitic Organizations: A History and Analysis.* Jefferson, NC: McFarland, 1999.

Quarles, a professor of political science at the University of Mississippi, describes the membership, ideology, and philosophy of this notorious hate group, including its formerly secret oaths.

Ridgeway, James. *Blood in the Face: The Ku Klux Klan, Aryan Nations, Nazi Skinheads, and the Rise of a New White Culture.* New York: Thunder's Mouth Press, 1995.

In this updated second edition, a *Village Voice* journalist surveys the rise of violent racist groups throughout the country. The book is well illustrated with photographs and artwork; especially noteworthy is a chart showing the interrelationships among the various groups and individuals. The author has filmed a documentary in conjunction with this work.

Robins, Robert S., and Jerrold M. Post. *Political Paranoia: The Psychopolitics of Hatred.* New Haven: Yale University Press, 1997.

Written by a political scientist and psychiatrist, this work surveys the phenomenon of the paranoid personality and how it generates various political and social movements. Hitler, Stalin, Christian Identity, and the Nation of Islam are some of the topics discussed in this wide-ranging work.

Sargent, Lyman Tower, ed. *Extremism in America: A Reader.* New York: New York University Press, 1995.

This unique anthology contains the actual texts of the hard-to-locate publications, articles, and tracts issued from both ends of the political spectrum—the far left and the far right. The work is conveniently organized by topic, including race, gender, economics, and education.

Sims, Patsy. *The Klan.* Lexington: University Press of Kentucky, 1996.
A survey of the history and recent activities of this notorious organization based on interviews with current members.

Smith, Brent L. *Terrorism in America: Pipe Bombs and Pipe Dreams.* New York: State University of New York Press, 1994.
The author, a professor of criminal justice and sociology at the University of Alabama, provides empirical data and analysis of left-wing and right-wing terrorist groups in the United States.

Stanton, Bill. *Klanwatch: Bringing the Ku Klux Klan to Justice.* New York: Grove Weidenfeld, 1991.
The former director of the Southern Poverty Law Center's Klanwatch project chronicles the history of the organization's "multi-pronged anti-Klan program," which included filing lawsuits, publishing educational materials, and monitoring the activities of the KKK. Engagingly written, the book contains several photographs.

Swigonski, Mary E., et al. *From Hate Crimes to Human Rights: A Tribute to Matthew Shepard.* Binghamton, NY: Harrington Park Press, 2001.
Originally published as an issue of the *Journal of Gay and Lesbian Social Service* (vol. 3, no.1/2, 2001), this separately published monograph covers a wide variety of gay- and lesbian-related topics, including hate crimes.

Temple-Raston, Dina. *A Death in Texas: A Story of Race, Murder, and a Small Town's Struggle for Redemption.* New York: Henry Holt, 2003.
Similar to the Joyce King book (see above), this work describes the brutal lynching of James Byrd Jr., an African American, by three white racists, on June 7, 1998. The author interviewed law enforcement and townspeople in the small Texas town of Jasper, where this internationally reported crime occurred.

Tunnell, Kenneth D. *Political Crime in Contemporary America: A Critical Approach.* New York: Garland Publishing, 1993.

This volume contains a chapter by Wayman C. Mullins, editor of the *Journal of Police and Criminal Psychology*, entitled "Hate Crime and the Far Right."

Vollers, Maryanne. *Ghosts of Mississippi: The Murder of Medgar Evers, the Trials of Byron De La Beckwith, and the Haunting of the New South.* Boston: Little Brown, 1995.

Vollers provides background to the murder conviction of a white supremacist in the 1963 murder of Medgar Evers, leader of the National Association for the Advancement of Colored People (NAACP). After two mistrials, Beckwith was convicted in 1992.

Wade, Wyn Craig. *The Fiery Cross: The Ku Klux Klan in America.* New York: Simon and Schuster, 1987.

A journalistic history, this work traces the activities and influence of the KKK throughout U.S. history.

Walker, Samuel. *Hate Speech: The History of an American Controversy.* Lincoln: University of Nebraska Press, 1994.

The author, a professor of criminal justice at the University of Nebraska at Omaha, surveys the history of hate speech from the 1920s to the present and the varying views of organizations about suppressing such speech, from the American Civil Liberties Union to the American Jewish Committee and the National Association for the Advancement of Colored People (NAACP).

Wang, Lu-In. *Hate Crimes Law.* Deerfield, IL: Clark Boardman Callaghan, 1994– (with annual updates).

A comprehensive reference source on the federal and state statutes enacted to address bias-motivated hate crimes. An outstanding and essential work for law students, law enforcement officials, scholars, and researchers.

Whitfield, Stephen J. *A Death in the Delta: The Story of Emmett Till.* New York: Free Press, 1988.

A meritorious work that deserves wider recognition. The book recounts the story of a black teenager who was murdered in Money, Mississippi, in 1955 for allegedly whistling at a white female. Many historians view this incident as the beginning of the modern civil rights movement. (See also Metress.)

Articles

Abrams, Kathryn. **"Fighting Fire with Fire: Rethinking the Role of Disgust in Hate Crimes."** *California Law Review* 90, no. 5 (October 2002): 1423–1465.

Abrams analyzes the community-based responses to hate crimes in the United States and the role of disgust as a response to hate crimes.

"Accused Killer of Three Is Linked to Racist Writing." *New York Times;* March 3, 2000, A12.

A black man accused of killing three people and wounding two in a shooting rampage in Wilkinsburg, Pennsylvania, had antiwhite writings in his apartment and singled out whites during the attack.

Alter, Jonathan. **"A Question of Anti-Semitism."** *Newsweek,* October 7, 2002, 45.

Alter, a *Newsweek* editor, analyzes how anti-Israel campus politics, along with other such political activities throughout the world, may help encourage the dangerous perceptions of some Palestinian Arabs who want to destroy the state of Israel.

"Although Scapegoated, Muslims, Sikhs and Arabs Are Patriotic, Integrated—and Growing." *Time,* October 1, 2001, 72–75.

This essay discusses the scapegoating of some non-Christian Americans following the 9/11 terrorist attacks.

Anderson, James F., et al. **"Preventing Hate Crime and Profiling Hate Crime Offenders."** *Western Journal of Black Studies* (Fall 2002): 140–149.

Proposes methods for preventing hate crimes and profiling hate crime offenders in the United States and suggests educational campaigns in cultural diversity awareness and racial tolerance.

"Anti-Semitism: An Enduring Virus." *The Economist,* November 22, 2003, 44.

This editorial analyzes the rise of anti-Jewish incidents and observes that many Jews in Israel and throughout the world feel that this alarming phenomenon is not incited by the conflict with

Palestinian Arabs. Instead, the conflict is used as a "convenient excuse for the anti-Semites."

"Black, Jewish Congress Members Condemn Rash of Hate Crimes." *Jet,* August 16, 1999, 4.

This article looks at a petition denouncing an outbreak of hate crimes, including the firebombing of three synagogues in California, that was signed by fifty-five black and Jewish members of Congress.

Bragg, Rick. **"In One Last Trial, Alabama Faces Old Wound."** *New York Times,* May 12, 2002, A1.

Bragg discusses the pending murder trial of Bobby Frank Cherry for his role in the bombing death of four girls at the Sixteenth Street Baptist Church in Birmingham, Alabama, in 1963.

Clemetson, Lynette. **"The New Victims of Hate."** *Newsweek,* November 6, 2000, 61.

Clemetson discusses the increase in violent attacks against Asian-Americans and their reluctance to report these crimes.

———. **"A Slaying in 1982 Maintains Its Grip on Asian-Americans."** *New York Times,* June 18, 2002, A1.

This front page article focuses on the commemoration of the June 19, 1982, killing of Chinese American Vincent Chin in Detroit, Michigan, and the crime's profound impact on Asian American politics and identity.

Clines, Francis X. **"Slaying of a Gay Black Spurs Call for Justice."** *New York Times,* July 13, 2000, A16.

Clines covers the demonstrations held in Fairmont, West Virginia—a state with no hate crime law—following the murder of Arthur Warren, an African American gay man.

Cloud, John. **"Is Hate on the Rise?"** *Time,* July 19, 1999, 33.

Although many hate groups have not achieved great financial or political power, some experts believe hate-motivated violence is on the rise, in part because these groups are using powerful new tools like the Internet to attract new followers. Rabbi Abraham Cooper of the Simon Wiesenthal Center notes that many racist organizers know they will never have a mass movement, but with the help of the Internet, they will be able to recruit people who are ready to violently act out their beliefs.

Dao, James. **"Indictment Makes Start at Lifting a 40-Year-Old Cloud over a Mississippi County."** *New York Times,* January 8, 2005, A11.

After a Mississippi prosecutor gathered new criminal evidence, Edgar Ray Killen, a former leader of the local Ku Klux Klan chapter, is charged with the murder of three civil rights workers, Andrew Goodman, Michael H. Schwerner and James E. Chaney, in Philadelphia, Mississippi in 1964. Killen was originally charged with federal civil rights violations in 1967 but the jury was deadlocked and he was released from prison.

Decter, Midge. **"Crimes du Jour: Hate Crime Laws."** *National Review,* September 13, 1999, 22–24.

A well-known conservative author claims that many people who once advocated leniency toward certain crimes on grounds of the mental or emotional state of the offender now support stern laws against hate crimes.

Dees, Morris. S. **"Hate Crimes Address, September 22, 1999."** *Vital Speeches of the Day,* February 1, 2000, 247–252.

In an address to Eureka College in Eureka, Illinois, the director of the Southern Poverty Law Center discusses cases of discrimination that have involved the Ku Klux Klan and skinheads.

Dinnerstein, Leonard. **"Is There a New Anti-Semitism in the United States?"** *Society,* January/February 2004, 53–58.

Professor Dinnerstein, who has written widely about the history of anti-Jewish attitudes and incidents in the United States analyzes the current political climate for American Jews.

Egan, Timothy. **"A Racist Attack, a Town Plagued."** *New York Times,* October 15, 2000, 24.

Egan explores issues of racial hatred in relation to manslaughter charges facing Asian American Min Duc Hong for the death of Christopher Kinison in Ocean Shores, Washington, on July 4, 2000.

Elder, Larry. **"When the Bad Guy Is Black."** *Human Events,* March 31, 2000, 13.

Elder criticizes the double standard of mass media regarding hate crimes in the United States in the case of Ronald Taylor, an African American who deliberately shot and killed whites.

Feder, Don. **"Hate-Crime Laws Penalize Ideas in Name of Tolerance."** *Human Events*, September 3, 1999, 10.
A conservative columnist questions the legal basis for enforcement of hate crimes legislation.

———. **"Hate Crimes' Laws Would Criminalize Thought."** *Human Events*, August 26, 2002, 18.
This essay questions the philosophical basis of hate crime laws.

Firestone, David. **"Trial in Gay Killing Opens; Conspiracy of Hate Is Cited."** *New York Times*, August 4, 1999, A8.
Firestone looks at Charles Monroe Butler Jr., who admitted to conspiring to kill Billy Jack Gaither, a gay man, and rejected a plea agreement for the murder case.

Fries, Jacob H. **"Complaints of Anti-Arab Bias Crimes Dip, but Concerns Linger."** *New York Times*, December 22, 2001, B8.
Fries reports on the decrease in the number of hate crimes committed against Arab Americans and Muslims in the United States as of December 2001, three months after the terrorist attacks in September of that year.

Goodstein, Laurie, and Gustav Niebuhr. **"Attacks and Harassment of Arab-Americans Increase."** *New York Times*, September 14, 2001, A14.
Goodstein and Niebuhr report that although President Bush condemned attacks against Muslim and Arab Americans, harassment and violent attacks continued to take place in several parts of the United States.

Goodstein, Laurie, and Tamar Lewin. **"Victims of Mistaken Identity, Sikhs Pay a Price for Turbans."** *New York Times*, September 19, 2001, A1.
Goodstein and Lewin look at the murder of Balbir Singh Sodhi, a turban-wearing Sikh who was murdered in Mesa, Arizona, and his co-religionists, who experienced harassment and physical attacks throughout the United States.

Gootman, Elissa. **"Hate Motives Are Argued in Beating of Mexicans."** *New York Times,* August 3, 2001, B5.

Gootman discusses an attack on Mexican immigrant day laborers in Suffolk County, New York.

"Guilty Plea Is Entered for Anti-Semitic Acts." *New York Times,* March 18, 2001, 19.

An article about Alex James Curtis, a twenty-five-year-old publisher of a white supremacist Internet newsletter, who pleaded guilty to civil rights violations for threatening Rep. Bob Filner (D-CA), a Jewish congressman, and other officials and vandalizing two synagogues. Under the plea agreement, he would serve no more than three years in prison.

Hammer, Joshua. **"The 'Gay Panic' Defense."** *Newsweek,* November 8, 1999, 40–42.

Hammer reports on the start of the Laramie, Wyoming, murder trial of Aaron McKinney in the October 1998 death of Matthew Shepard, to which accomplice Russell Henderson had previously pleaded guilty.

Hardi, Joel. **"P.R. 101: Don't Joke About Hate Crimes."** *Chronicle of Higher Education,* May 26, 2000, A12.

Article on a comment made by the University of Iowa's vice president for university relations, Ann Rhodes, which was interpreted as biased.

Harris, Hamil R. **"Ex-Klansman Found Guilty of 1963 Church Bombing."** *The New Crisis,* July–August 2001, 7–9.

This article examines the criminal case against Thomas E. Blanton, found guilty nearly forty years later of a 1963 church bombing in Alabama that claimed the lives of four African American children.

"Hate Crimes Up against Muslims." *New York Times,* November 26, 2002, A16. A report on the findings of the Federal Bureau of Investigation on the increase in 2001 of hate crimes in the United States against Muslims and people who are or appear to be of Middle Eastern descent.

"Hatred Unexplained." *The Economist,* July 10, 1999, 2.

This article discusses the three-day, two-state shooting spree that began on July 2, 1999, by twenty-one-year-old university student and member of the World Church of the Creator Benjamin Smith, who killed an African American and a Korean and injured nine Jews, blacks, and Asians.

Herek, Gregory M., et al. **"Victim Experiences in Hate Crimes Based on Sexual Orientation."** *Journal of Social Issues,* June 2002, 319–340.

Using interview data from a sample of 450 lesbian, gay, and bisexual adults, this article discusses the varieties of victim experiences. An important factor on deciding whether to report antigay crimes was the fear that the perpetrator would not be punished.

Horowitz, Craig. **"The Return of Anti-Semitism."** *New York,* December 15, 2003, 28–33.

The author discusses the alarming increase in anti-Jewish incidents and hostile rhetoric around the world.

Husselbee, L. Paul, and Larry Elliott. **"Looking beyond Hate: How National and Regional Newspapers Framed Hate Crimes in Jasper, Texas, and Laramie, Wyoming."** *Journalism & Mass Communication Quarterly,* Winter 2002, 833–853.

The article examines two infamous and nationally reported hate crimes directed against an African American and a gay student.

Hutchinson, Earl Ofari. **"The Price of Black Silence on Certain Hate Crimes."** *Christian Science Monitor,* March 8, 2000, 9.

Hutchinson discusses the racially motivated shootings in Pennsylvania of five white men by one black man. The author claims that black leaders and organizations should have quickly condemned the shootings.

Janofsky, Michael. **"Gay Man's Death Led to Epiphany for Wyoming Officer."** *New York Times,* September 30, 2000, A9.

A profile of David S. O'Malley, commander of the investigations unit of the Laramie, Wyoming, police department, who discusses how the murder of Matthew Shepard led to his campaign for national hate crimes legislation.

———. **"Parents of Gay Obtain Mercy for His Killer."** *New York Times,* November 5, 1999, A1.

A front page article about the parents of murdered gay Wyoming student Matthew Shepard, who requested that Aaron McKinney be spared the death sentence.

Jenness, Valerie. **"Managing Differences and Making Legislation: Social Movements and the Racialization, Sexualization, and Gendering of Federal Hate Crime Law in the U.S., 1985–1998."** *Social Problems,* November 1999, 548–571.

A sociological analysis of the emergence and evolution of federal hate crime laws, including the Hate Crimes Statistics Act, the Violence against Women Act, and the Hate Crimes Sentencing Enhancement Act.

Kim, Richard. **"The Truth about Hate Crimes Laws."** *Nation,* July 12, 1999, 20.

The author believes that national lesbian and gay organizations are expending too much effort trying to pass hate crime laws. Instead, he advocates local community organizing and forming coalitions with other minority advocacy groups.

Lappin, Shalom. **"Israel and the New Anti-Semitism."** *Dissent,* Spring 2003, 18–24.

A prolific analyst notes that although much of the criticism directed against Israel since September 2000 is legitimate, the growing antagonism stems in part from strong hostility to the existence of a Jewish state and also a widespread European attitude that Israel is no longer a nation of victims.

Lee, Felicia R. **"ABC News Revisits Student's Killing and Angers Some Gays."** *New York Times,* November 26, 2004, A33.

The ABC news program *20/20* claims in an investigative report that the widely-publicized murder of Matthew Shepard, a Wyoming gay student, was not a hate crime but a botched robbery committed by men high on drugs.

Lee, Stephen. **"U.S. Intervention in the Middle East, the 'War on Terror' and Domestic Hate Crimes: An Amerasia Journal Chronology."** *Amerasia Journal* 27/28, no. 3/1 (2001/2002): 295–319.

Lee presents a chronology of domestic hate crimes since the terrorist attack on September 11, 2001, and the U.S. war against the Taliban-ruled Afghanistan.

Leo, John. **"Faking the Hate."** *U.S. News & World Report,* June 5, 2000, 22.

This essay discusses fraudulent reports of race and gender crimes on college campuses in the United States, including alleged hate crimes at the University of Massachusetts and other institutions that were revealed to be hoaxes.

———. **"Not Fit to Print?"** *U.S. News & World Report,* April 16, 2001, 14.

Jesse Dirkhising, a thirteen-year-old Arkansas boy, was drugged, tied to a bed, raped, tortured, and suffocated in September 1999 by two gay men. The columnist claims this story received far less media attention than the Matthew Shepard murder.

McNeil, Donald G. **"France Vows Harsh Action after More Synagogues Burn"** *New York Times,* April 2, 2002, A3.

Article about the alarming increase of anti-Jewish violence in France. Among other incidents, a gunman fired at a kosher butcher shop, vandals set fire to a Strasbourg synagogue, and hooded men crashed a car into a Lyon synagogue.

McPhail, Beverly A. **"Gender-Bias Hate Crimes."** *Trauma, Violence & Abuse,* April 2002, 125–144.

The author, a doctoral student at the University of Texas School of Social Work, surveys the history of the initial exclusion, then inclusion, of gender in the hate crime laws and also discusses its implications for social work research, practice, and policy.

———. **"Hating Hate: Policy Implications of Hate Crime Legislation."** *Social Service Review,* December 2000, 635–653.

McPhail believes it is important for social workers to be actively involved in the debate about hate crime laws.

Milloy, Ross E. **"Texas Senate Passes Hate Crimes Bill that Bush's Allies Killed."** *New York Times,* May 8, 2001, A16.

Texas legislators passed the James Byrd Jr. Hate Crimes Act with provisions to include crimes against gays and lesbians.

"More Insulted and Attacked after Sept. 11." *New York Times,* March 11, 2002, A12.

A report on the increasing number of attacks on South Asian immigrants in the United States after the September 11, 2001, tragedy, based on information from a survey by the National Asian Pacific American Legal Consortium.

Murphy, Dean E. **"Survey Finds an Increase in Anti-Semitic Incidents."** *New York Times,* March 21, 2001, B2.

A survey by the Anti-Defamation League shows that anti-Jewish incidents in New York City rose by about 49 percent in 2000, an increase the group said might be a spillover from the conflict in the Middle East.

————. **"Three Are Charged in Death of Man Who Dressed Like a Woman."** *New York Times,* October 19, 2002, A11.

Reports on the hate crime charges filed against several men for the death of Eddie Araujo, a transgendered man, in Newark, California.

Newman, Maria. **"Victims of Hate Crime Calls High Court Ruling a 'Slap in the Face.'"** *New York Times;* June 27, 2000, B5. Newman discusses the effect of the U.S. Supreme Court's decision to reverse a New Jersey lower court decision on a hate crimes case.

Niebuhr, Gustav. **"Abhorring Terror at an Ohio Mosque."** *New York Times,* September 22, 2001, A11.

Niebuhr examines a story of forgiveness by the worshippers at a Parma, Ohio, mosque. After a perpetrator deliberately crashed his car into the mosque, the imam and the congregants forgave him for his violent attack.

Nieves, Evelyn. **"Slain Arab-American May Have Been Hate-Crime Victim."** *New York Times,* October 6, 2001, A8.

Nieves looks at the case of Abdo Ali Ahmed, a Yemeni Muslim who was murdered in his Reedley, California, grocery store. No money was stolen during the crime.

Noelle, Monique. **"The Ripple Effect of the Matthew Shepard Murder: Impact on the Assumptive Worlds of Members of the Targeted Group."** *American Behavioral Scientist,* September 2002, 27–51.

This research article investigates the psychological impact of the Shepard murder, a widely publicized antigay hate crime in 1998, on nonvictims who are also gay.

Nolan III, James J., et al. **"The Hate Crime Statistics Act of 1990: Developing a Method for Measuring the Occurrence of Hate Violence."** *American Behavioral Scientist*, September 2002, 136–154.

A report on the Hate Crime Statistics Act of 1990, which helped establish the mechanisms for identifying and collecting data on the occurrence of hate crimes in this country.

Poussaint, Alvin F. **"They Hate. They Kill. Are They Insane?"** *New York Times*, August 26, 1999, A17.

Harvard Medical School psychiatrist Poussaint urges the American Psychiatric Association to designate extreme racism as a mental health problem and advocates that clinicians use guidelines for recognizing delusional racism.

Pruzan, Adam. **"What Is a Hate Crime? Media Bias in Coverage."** *The American Enterprise*, January/February 2000, 10.

The author compares and contrasts the coverage in the *New York Times* of a gun attack at the North Valley Jewish Community Center in Los Angeles, California, and of the murder of seven people at a Baptist church in Fort Worth, Texas.

Rabinowitz, Dorothy. **"The Hate-Crimes Bandwagon."** *Wall Street Journal*, June 27, 2000, A30.

A distinguished columnist and reporter raises questions about the politicization of hate crimes legislation.

"Report Calls for Better Prevention for Hate Crimes." *National Catholic Reporter*, November 29, 2002, 9.

This article discusses a Human Rights Watch report issued on November 14, 2002, which called for better prevention of hate crimes.

Rose, Suzanna M., and Mindy B. Mechanic. **"Psychological Distress, Crime Features, and Help-Seeking Behaviors Related to Homophobic Bias Incidents."** *American Behavioral Scientist*, September 2002, 14–27.

A psychological study of victims of antigay hate incidents.

Rutenberg, Jim. **"Against Hate Crimes."** *New York Times*, January 10, 2001, E10.

Rutenberg covers the decision by MTV to preempt all of its regular programming for seventeen and a half hours—with no commercial interruptions—as it scrolls the names of victims of hate crimes and recounts the stories behind the crimes.

Saulny, Susan. **"Man Who Killed Two outside Gay Bar Remains Mentally Ill, a Jury Finds."** *New York Times,* June 14, 2001, B8.

Saulny reports a ruling by a New York State Supreme Court jury that Ronald K. Crumpley, who shot and killed two people and wounded six others outside a Greenwich Village gay bar in 1980, was still mentally ill.

Sherry, Mark. **"Hate Crimes against Disabled People."** *Social Alternatives;* October 2000, 23–30.

A rare article examining underreported hate crimes directed against the disabled. The author claims these incidents often go unrecognized because the crime is often referred to as "abuse" or "neglect"and such "euphemisms deny the validity" of its magnitude.

Sterngold, James. **"Supremacist Who Killed Postal Worker Avoids Death Sentence."** The *New York Times,* January 24, 2001, A13.

The author looks at Buford O. Furrow, who sprayed automatic gunfire in a Los Angeles Jewish community center filled with children in 1999, then confessed to murdering a Filipino letter carrier. Furrow planned to plead guilty to sixteen felony counts in return for a sentence that would allow him to avoid the death penalty.

"Student Accused of Sending Hate E-Mails." *New York Times;* October 3, 1999, 50.

A report on a Bridgewater-Raritan High School student in New Jersey who was charged with sending 108 racially charged e-mail hate messages.

Sullivan, Andrew. **"What's So Bad about Hate?"** *New York Times Magazine,* September 26, 1999, 50.

Sullivan, the former editor of the *New Republic* and a widely respected author, analyzes the complex legal and philosophical issues of hate speech and hate crime.

Tatchell, Peter. **"Why Can Blacks Bash Gays?"** *New Statesman,* October 14, 2002, 14–15.

This British magazine discusses the homophobic lyrics found in the song "Chi Chi Man," performed by the Jamaican music group TOK and hate crimes and violence against gay people.

Tavernise, Sabrina. **"Bomb Attack Shows that Russia Hasn't Rooted Out Anti-Semitism."** *New York Times,* June 1, 2002, p. A1.

Tavernise notes that despite the efforts of President Vladimir Putin to eradicate anti-Jewish attitudes resulting in frequent violence directed at Russian Jews, it is still present at the local level and among ordinary Russians.

————. **"Russian Parliament Passes a Hate-Crime Bill Backed by Putin."** *New York Times,* June 28, 2002, pA9.

Tavernise reports on a Kremlin-backed bill that was passed by the lower house of the Russian Parliament to fight hate crimes and attacks by fascist groups.

Thomas, Jo. **"New Face of Terror Crimes: 'Lone Wolf' Weaned on Hate."** *New York Times,* August 16, 1999, A1.

Thomas reports that, after examining recent hate crimes—including bombings, shootings, and robberies—federal and state investigators have determined that no evidence exists of an organized coordination among violent right-wing groups and individuals against racial and religious minorities.

Tsesis, Alexander. **"Contextualizing Bias Crimes: A Social and Theoretical Perspectives."** *Law & Social Inquiry;* Winter 2003, 315–340.

An analysis of the arguments supporting hate crimes legislation and a review of *Punishing Hate: Bias Crimes under American Law,* by Frederick M. Lawrence.

"Two Attacked at Mosque." *New York Times,* March 18, 2001, 19.

A report of two Muslim men who were injured, one critically, when they were attacked outside a Sparks, Nevada, mosque in what the police called a possible hate crime. An Associated Press story published in the March 21, 2001 issue of the *Las Vegas Review-Journal* notes that police investigators later claimed it was a "robbery-motivated assault," not a hate crime.

"United States: Suspect in Murder of Lesbian Hikers Apprehended after Six Years." *Off Our Backs*, May/June2002, 7.

This issue of *Off Our Backs* reports on the apprehension of Darrel David Rice for the murder of lesbian hikers and also discusses hate crimes directed against lesbians.

Watts, Meredith W. **"Aggressive Youth Cultures and Hate Crime: Skinheads and Xenophobic Youth in Germany."** *American Behavioral Scientist*, December 2001, 600–616.

Watts notes that bias crime in Germany increased dramatically after unification in 1990 and remained at a relatively high level for the rest of the decade. Hatred of foreigners and other targeted groups not only seems linked to violent elements of youth culture but appears to be stimulated by local and international right-wing and fascist networks.

Wisse, Ruth R. **"On Ignoring Anti-Semitism."** *Commentary*, October 2002, 26–33.

Harvard professor Ruth Wisse warns about the dangers of ignoring anti-Jewish attitudes and violence and the tragic historical consequences.

Wistrich, Robert S. **"The Old-New Anti-Semitism."** *National Interest*, Summer 2003, 59–70. A distinguished historian and academic adviser to the British television documentary *The Longest Hatred*, Wistrich analyzes the current resurgence of anti-Jewish hatred throughout the world.

Reports

The U.S. government, state and municipal entities, and many private organizations publish reports and documents on hate crimes, hate groups, and the growth of bigotry throughout the country. The following selections include some important publications issued in recent years. Although the U.S. government publications should be available in most libraries designated as government depositories, the nongovernmental watchdog organizations must be contacted to obtain their materials. For easier access, U.S. Congressional hearings and reports include the Superintendent of Documents number.

U.S. Government Documents and Reports

U.S. Congress, House Committee on the Judiciary, 108th Congress, 1st Session (Superintendent of Documents no. Y1.1/8: 108-249). *Condemning Bigotry and Violence against Arab-Americans, Muslim-Americans, South Asian-Americans, and Sikh-Americans: Report, September 3, 2003.*

This report provides background about the discriminatory backlash crimes in the wake of the September 11, 2001, terrorist attacks and contains the text of a congressional resolution deploring the harassment and violence committed against the above-mentioned groups and urging law enforcement authorities to vigorously prosecute these crimes.

U.S. Congress, House Committee on the Judiciary, 106th Congress, 1st session (Superintendent of Documents no. Y4.J89/1: 106/47). *Hate Crimes Violence: (Hearing) August 4, 1999.*

This hearing considered the passage of the Hate Crimes Prevention Act of 1999 to expand federal jurisdiction over bias-motivated crimes. The witnesses included Frederick M. Lawrence, professor of Law at Boston University; Reuben Greenberg, chief of police of Charleston, South Carolina; an assault victim; and the mother of a murdered victim.

U.S. Congress, House Committee on the Judiciary, 105th Congress, 1st session (Superintendent of Documents no.: Y4.J89/1:105/4). *Implementation of the Church Arson Prevention Act of 1996: Hearing, March 19, 1997.*

This hearing examined how federal agencies implemented this act, including the provisions that clarified and expanded the jurisdiction of U.S. federal law enforcement over offenses involving religious property destruction. Witnesses included Patricia C. Glenn, national coordinator of the Church Burning Response Team of the U.S. Department of Justice; Harold McDougall, an official with the National Association for the Advancement of Colored People (NAACP); and Elder T. Myers, a pastor in a South Carolina church. The report of the hearing also includes the Center for Democratic Renewal's document issued in March 1997, "Fourth Wave: A Continuing Conspiracy to Burn Black Churches."

U.S. Congress, House Committee on the Judiciary, 100th Congress, 2nd session (Superintendent of Documents no.: Y4.J89/1:100/144). *Racially Motivated Violence: Hearings, May 11 and July 12, 1988.*

This hearing considered legislation to establish the Commission on Racially Motivated Violence. The hearing also examined the prevalence of and responses to acts of violence against members of minority groups and surveyed the history of racial prejudice in the United States and the increase of racial tensions in colleges and universities. Witnesses included Rev. C. T. Vivian, chairman of the Center for Democratic Renewal; Benjamin L. Hooks, executive director of the National Association of the Advancement of Colored People; Douglas Seymour, an undercover police agent who infiltrated the Ku Klux Klan in California; and Reginald Wilson, director of the Office of Minority Concerns, American Council on Education.

U.S. Congress, House Committee on the Judiciary, Subcommittee on Civil and Constitutional Rights, 100th Congress, 1st session (Superintendent of Documents no.: Y4.J89/1:100/116). *Anti-Asian Violence: Oversight Hearing, November 10, 1987.*

This hearing examined the causes of and possible responses to recent violent acts committed against Asians and Asian Americans. Witnesses included Rep. Norman Y. Mineta (D-CA); Rep. Robert T. Matsui (D-CA); Floyd D. Shinomura of the Japanese American Citizens League; James C. Tso, president of the Organization of Chinese Americans; and Arthur Soong, president of the Asian American Legal Defense and Education Fund. The report includes a compilation of articles from 1983 to 1987 on violence against Asian immigrants and Asian Americans in Massachusetts and a February 1987 report issued by the Los Angeles County Commission on Human Relations on ethnic- and religious-motivated violence in that region.

U.S. Congress, House Committee on the Judiciary, Subcommittee on Civil and Constitutional Rights, 103rd Congress, 1st session (Superintendent of Documents no.: Y4.J 89/1:103/51). *Crimes of Violence Motivated by Gender: Hearing, November 16, 1993.*

The hearing examined proposed legislation that would make crimes of violence motivated by gender actionable under civil rights and hate crimes laws.

U.S. Congress, House Committee on the Judiciary, Subcommittee on Crime and Criminal Justice, 102nd Congress, 2nd session (Superintendent of Documents no.: Y4.J 89/1:102/80). *Bias Crimes: Hearing, May 11, 1992.*

This hearing focused on crimes motivated by prejudice against the racial, ethnic, religious, or sexual orientation of the victim. The witnesses discussed the Hate Crimes Sentencing Act of 1992, which directs the U.S. Sentencing Commission to revise sentencing guidelines to increase penalties for hate crimes. Witnesses included Rabbi Melvin Burg, whose Los Angeles synagogue was vandalized; Charles J. Hynes, district attorney of Kings County, Brooklyn, New York; and Gary Stoops of the Federal Bureau of Investigation. Other witnesses represented Asian American, Jewish, and gay and women's rights organizations. The hearing report includes the article "Sticks and Stones Can Put You in Jail, but Can Words Increase Your Sentence? Constitutional and Policy Dilemmas for Ethnic Intimidation Laws," by Professor Susan Gellman, published in the *UCLA Law Review,* December 1991 (see *Anti-Gay Violence: Hearings, October 9, 1986* entry).

U.S. Congress, House Committee on the Judiciary, Subcommittee on Crime and Criminal Justice, 102nd Congress, 2nd session (Superintendent of Documents no.: Y4:J89/1:102/64). *Hate Crimes Sentencing Enhancement Act of 1992: Hearing, July 29, 1992.*

This hearing examined the use of penalty enhancement for hate crimes and the implications on the constitutionality of hate crime laws following the June 1992 Supreme Court decision *R. A. V. v. City of St. Paul,* which struck down a Minnesota hate crime statute. The following witnesses offered varied views on the constitutionality of the proposed legislation: Laurence H. Tribe, a professor at Harvard University Law School; Floyd Abrams, a prominent constitutional law attorney; Robert S. Peck, legislative counsel of the American Civil Liberties Union; and Susan Gellman, assistant public defender, Ohio Public Defender Commission.

U.S. Congress, House Committee on the Judiciary, Subcommittee on Criminal Justice, 99th Congress, 2nd session (Superintendent of Documents no.: Y4.J89/1:99/132). *Anti-Gay Violence: Hearing, October 9, 1986.*

This hearing examined the problem of violence against gay men and lesbians. The report includes descriptions of violent acts, the nature and extent of the violence, and surveys of cultural and social prejudicial attitudes toward gay people. Rep. Barney Frank (D-MA) presented a statement and participated in interviewing witnesses, who included Kevin Berrill, director of the Violence Project of the National Gay and Lesbian Task Force; Dr. Gregory M. Herek, a psychology professor; and Robert J. Johnston, chief of the New York City Police Department. In addition, some gay victims of violence told of their own experiences.

U.S. Congress, House Committee on the Judiciary, Subcommittee on Criminal Justice, 99th Congress, 1st session (Superintendent of Documents no.: Y4.J89/1:99/134). *Crimes against Religious Practices and Property: Hearings, May 16 and June 19, 1985.*
These hearings considered a bill to establish federal penalties for damaging any religious building or cemetery or intimidating any person in the exercise of religious beliefs. Witnesses included Victoria Toensing, deputy assistant attorney general, who objected to the proposed legislation and advocated state, not federal, prosecution of such crimes. Richard Foltin, associate legal director of the American Jewish Committee, testified in support of the legislation.

U.S. Congress, House Committee on the Judiciary, Subcommittee on Criminal Justice, 99th Congress, 2nd session (Superintendent of Documents no.: Y4.J89/1:99/135). *Ethnically Motivated Violence against Arab-Americans: Hearing, July 16, 1986.*
This hearing examined reports of harassment and violence directed against Arab Americans in the United States. Witnesses included Oliver B. Revell III, the executive assistant director of the FBI; David Sadd, executive director of the National Association of Arab Americans; and David M. Gordis, executive vice president of the American Jewish Committee. The report included testimony of Rep. Mary Oakar (D-OH) and Rep. Nick Joe Rahall (D-WV).

U.S. Congress, House Committee on the Judiciary, Subcommittee on Criminal Justice, 99th Congress, 1st session (Superintendent of Documents no.: Y4.J89/1:99/137). *Hate Crime Statistics Act: Hearing, March 21, 1985.*
The first congressional hearing held to discuss passage of a law requiring the U.S. Justice Department to collect and publish statistics on crimes motivated by racial, ethnic, or religious preju-

dice. Witnesses in support of this legislation included Elaine Jones of the Legal, Defense, and Education Fund of the National Association for the Advancement of Colored People (NAACP); Jerome Bakst of the Anti-Defamation League of B'nai B'rith; and Rep. Mario Biaggi (D-NY). Opponents of the legislation discussed the anticipated difficulties of determining the motivation for certain crimes and the problems of incorporating these statistics into the Uniform Crime Reporting program administered by the U.S. Department of Justice. These witnesses included William M. Baker, assistant director of the Office of Congressional and Public Affairs of the FBI, and Steven R. Schlesinger, director of the Bureau of Justice Statistics. Other witnesses included Rep. Norman Y. Mineta (D-CA) and Rep. Barbara B. Kennelly (D-CT), who testified on crimes of violence against members of ethnic, racial, and religious minorities.

U.S. Congress, House Committee on National Security, 104th Congress, 2nd session (Superintendent of Documents no.: Y4.Se2/1 A:995-96). *Extremist Activity in the Military: Hearing, June 25, 1996.*

This hearing examined the participation of current or former U.S. Army personnel in antigovernment hate groups and militia organizations. It also studied the murder of an African American couple in Fayetteville, North Carolina, by soldiers of the 82nd Airborne Division based at Fort Bragg, who were affiliated with white supremacist groups.

U.S. Congress, Senate Committee on the Judiciary, 104th Congress, 2nd session (Superintendent of Documents no.: Y4.J 89/2:S.hrg.104-851). *Church Burnings: Hearing, June 27, 1996, on the Federal Response to Recent Incidents of Church Burnings in Predominantly Black Churches across the South.*

This hearing surveyed the rash of arson against black churches and acts of violence against other houses of worship. It also examined the federal investigation and prosecution of the perpetrators and the financial support given to assist in rebuilding the burned buildings.

U.S. Congress, Senate Committee on the Judiciary, 106th Congress, 1st session (Superintendent of Documents no.: Y4.J89/2: 106-517). *Combating Hate Crimes: Promoting a Responsive and Responsible Role for the Federal Government, May 11, 1999.*

This hearing discussed the passage of the Hate Crimes Prevention Act of 1999 to expand federal jurisdiction of bias-motivated crimes related to interstate commerce. The witnesses offered different opinions on the constitutionality and desirability of this proposed legislation.

U.S. Congress, Senate Committee on the Judiciary, 104th Congress, 2nd session (Superintendent of Documents no. Y4.J89/2:S.hrg 104-842). *Combating Violence against Women: Hearing, May 15, 1996.*

This hearing examined the implementation of the Violence against Women Act (VAWA) of 1994, providing protection for women against violent crime. Witnesses included Sen. Kay Bailey Hutchinson (R-TX); U.S. Attorney General Janet Reno; Kathryn J. Rogers, executive director of the National Organization for Women (NOW) Legal Defense and Education Fund; and Denise Brown, director of the Nicole Brown Simpson Charitable Foundation.

U.S. Congress, Senate Committee on the Judiciary, 106th Congress, 1st session (Superintendent of Documents no.: Y4.J89/2: 106-803). *Hate Crime on the Internet, September 14, 1999.*

This hearing explored the issues related to the use of the Internet to promote prejudice and bias-motivated crimes. The witnesses included Rabbi Abraham Cooper, the associate director of the Simon Wiesenthal Center; Howard Berkowitz, the national chairman of the Anti-Defamation League; and Joseph T. Roy, an official of the Southern Poverty Law Center.

U.S. Congress, Senate Committee on the Judiciary, 100th Congress, 2nd session (Superintendent of Documents no.: Y4.J89/2:S.hrg.100-1069). *Hate Crime Statistics Act of 1988: Hearing, June 21, 1988.*

This hearing considered the proposed legislation to require the U.S. Department of Justice to collect and publish statistics on crimes motivated by racial, ethnic, or religious prejudice. The witnesses endorsing the legislation included Alan M. Schwartz, director of the Research and Evaluation Department of the Anti-Defamation League of B'nai B'rith; Patricia Clark, director of the Klanwatch project of the Southern Poverty Law Center; Joan C. Weiss, executive director of the National Institute against Prejudice and Violence; William Yoshino, midwestern region director of the Japanese American Citizens League; and Kevin Berrill, director of the Anti-Violence Project of the National Gay and Lesbian Task Force.

U.S. Congress, Senate Committee on the Judiciary, 105th Congress, 2nd session (Superintendent of Documents no.: Y4.J89/2: 105-904). *Hate Crimes Prevention Act of 1998: Hearing July 8, 1998.*
This hearing discussed proposed legislation to expand the federal jurisdiction to allow the prosecution of crimes motivated by prejudice against a victim's sexual orientation, gender, or disability and to eliminate the stipulation that victims must be engaged in a federally protected activity in order to have federal prosecution.

U.S. Congress, Senate Committee on the Judiciary, 103rd Congress, 2nd session (Superintendent of Documents no.: Y4. J 89/2: S.hrg. 103-1078). *Hate Crimes Statistics Act: Hearing, June 28, 1994.*
This hearing reviewed the implementation of the Hate Crime Statistics Act of 1990, requiring that the FBI collect and publish statistics on crimes motivated by racial, ethnic, or religious prejudice. The report also examined educational efforts of private organizations to promote tolerance and to prevent hate crimes. One witness was Steven Spielberg, the acclaimed motion picture director and producer, who discussed his perspectives on the making of the award-winning movie *Schindler's List* and its educational value. Other witnesses included Robert Machleder, chairman of the New York Regional Board of the Anti-Defamation League; Sara Bullard, education director of the Southern Poverty Law Center; and Deedee Corradini, mayor of Salt Lake City, Utah, representing the U.S. Conference of Mayors.

U.S. Congress, Senate Committee on the Judiciary, 104th Congress, 2nd session (Superintendent of Documents no.: Y4.J89/2: S.hrg. 104-845). *Reauthorization of the Hate Crime Statistics Act: Hearing, March 19, 1996.*
This hearing considered amending the Hate Crime Statistics Act of 1990 to permanently reauthorize the FBI programs to collect and publish statistics on crimes motivated by race, ethnicity, sexual orientation, disability, or religious prejudice. The witnesses included Charles W. Archer, assistant director of the FBI's Criminal Justice Information Services Division; Emanuel Cleaver II, mayor of Kansas City, Missouri, who represented the

U.S. Conference of Mayors; Stephen Arent, vice chairman of the National Civil Rights Committee of the Anti-Defamation League; and Karen M. Lawson, executive director of the Leadership Conference Education Fund. The report includes the FBI document "Summary Reporting System: National Incident-Based Reporting System; Hate Crime Data Collection Guidelines" and the 1994 Covington and Burlington law firm report "D.C. Bias-Related Crime Act: An Unused Weapon Against Violent Crime," prepared for the National Asian Pacific American Bar Association.

U.S. Congress, Senate Committee on the Judiciary, 102nd Congress, 1st session (Superintendent of Documents no. Y4.J89/2:S.hrg. 102–369). *Violence against Women: Victims of the System; Hearing, April 9, 1991.*
This hearing considered the Violence against Women Act of 1991, in particular to amend various acts to revise and expand protections against rape and other violent crime. The witnesses included Bonnie J. Campbell, attorney general of Iowa; Roland W. Burris, attorney general of Illinois; and Cass R. Sunstein, a professor at the University of Chicago Law School. The subsequent document includes a committee staff report entitled "Violence against Women: The Increase of Rape in America, 1990," with tables and graphs.

U.S. Congress, Senate Committee on the Judiciary, Subcommittee on the Constitution, 102nd Congress, 2nd session (Superintendent of Documents no.: Y4.J89/2: S.hrg. 102-1131). *Hate Crimes Statistics Act: Hearing, August 5, 1992.*
This hearing reviewed the implementation of the Hate Crime Statistics Act of 1990 by the FBI, state crime reporting agencies, and local law enforcement agencies under the direction of the U.S. Department of Justice. Witnesses included G. Norman Christensen, assistant director of the Criminal Justice Information Services Division of the FBI; Jack McDevitt, coauthor of *Hate Crimes;* and Elsie L. Scott, deputy commissioner of training for the New York City Police Department, representing the National Organization of Black Law Enforcement Executives. Also called to speak were Harold Gershowitz, chairman of the Chicago Regional Board of the Anti-Defamation League; and Elizabeth R. Ouyang, staff attorney for the Asian American

Legal Defense and Education Fund, who expressed concern about the possible underreporting of hate crimes against Asian Americans. This report also included the FBI document "Hate Crime Data Collection Guidelines: Uniform Crime Reporting" and the 1991 annual report issued by the Massachusetts Executive Office of Public Safety, entitled "Hate Crime/Hate Incidents in Massachusetts."

U.S. Department of Justice, Bureau of Justice Assistance. *A Policymaker's Guide to Hate Crimes,* 1997.
   This report surveys the scope and nature of hate crimes and the response to the problem by federal, state, and local government agencies.

U.S. Department of Justice, Federal Bureau of Investigation. *Hate Crime Statistics.* An annual report mandated by the Hate Crime Statistics Act of 1990.
   The FBI is the major U.S. government agency collecting, tabulating, and publishing official data on the extent of hate crimes nationwide.

U.S. Department of Justice, Federal Bureau of Investigation. *Training Guide for Hate Crime Data Collection: Uniform Crime Reporting,* 1997.
   Aimed at local law enforcement officials, this manual provides specific guidelines about the collecting and reporting of hate crime statistics.

Weekly Compilation of Presidential Documents, **Remarks at the Dedication of Mount Zion A.M.E. Church in Greeleyville, South Carolina,** June 17, 1996: 1038–1042.
   The text of remarks by President Bill Clinton in which he promises to prosecute those responsible for the church burnings and to assist communities in rebuilding their houses of worship.

Weekly Compilation of Presidential Documents, **Statement on the Attack on Jewish Students in Brooklyn, New York, March 2, 1994,** March 7, 1994: 418.
   The text of a statement in which President Bill Clinton condemns the shooting incident directed against Hasidic Jewish students riding across the Brooklyn Bridge.

Weekly Compilation of Presidential Documents, **Statement on Hate Crimes Legislation,** October 18, 1999: 2024–2025.

The text of a statement given by President Bill Clinton on October 13, 1999, which deals with the hate crimes legislation.

Weekly Compilation of Presidential Documents, **Letter to the Speaker of the House of Representatives on the Proposed "Hate Crimes Prevention Act,"** July 17, 2000: 1627.

The text of a letter given by President Bill Clinton on July 12, 2000, which deals with the proposed Hate Crimes Prevention Act.

Weekly Compilation of Presidential Documents, **Statement on Senate Action on Hate Crimes Legislation,** June 26, 2000: 1416–1418.

The text of a statement given by President Bill Clinton on June 20, 2000.

Weekly Compilation of Presidential Documents, **Remarks on Proposed Hate Crimes Legislation,** May 1, 2000: 920–923.

The text of remarks given by President Bill Clinton on April 25, 2000.

State Reports

California. California Department of Justice, Division of Criminal Justice Information Services. *Hate Crime in California,* 1994–present. http://caag.state.ca.us/cjsc/publications/ hate-crimes/pub.htm.

An annual report regarding crimes motivated by the victim's race, ethnicity, national origin, religion, gender, sexual orientation, or physical or mental disability as reported by law enforcement agencies. Only law enforcement agencies can identify and submit reports of hate crimes to the U.S. Department of Justice.

California Attorney General's Civil Rights Commission on Hate Crimes. *Reporting Hate Crime,* 2001.

A group composed of ethnic and civil rights leaders examines the problems in accurately obtaining and recording hate crime incidents.

The Ralph and Bane Civil Rights Acts: A Manual for Attorneys.
Sacramento, CA: Department of Fair Employment and Housing
and the Fair Employment and Housing Commission, 1991.

A manual for attorneys representing victims of hate violence
in civil proceedings.

Illinois. O'Malley, Jack. *A Prosecutor's Guide to Hate Crime.*
Chicago: Cook County State's Attorney's Office, 1994.

Compiled by legal experts, including the ADL Greater
Chicago Regional Office, the U.S. Department of Justice, and the
Illinois Criminal Justice Information Authority, this handbook
provides Illinois prosecutors with a comprehensive approach to
understanding hate crimes.

Kentucky. Kentucky Criminal Justice Council. *Hate Crime and
Hate Incidents in the Commonwealth of Kentucky,* March 2002.
http://www.kcjc.state.ky.us/documents/ 2002hatecrimereport.pdf.

Modeled after a similar publication in West Virginia, this report contains official statistics from Kentucky law enforcement
officials as well as anecdotal material provided by state human
rights organizations.

Massachusetts. Harshbarger, Scott. *A Special Report Regarding
the Constitutionality of Massachusetts Civil and Criminal Civil
Rights Laws.* Boston: Commonwealth of Massachusetts, Office of
the Attorney General, 1993.

In response to the 1992 U.S. Supreme Court decision, *R.A.V. v.
City of St. Paul,* declaring this hate crime statute unconstitutional,
the Office of the Attorney General of Massachusetts conducted a
legal review of all similar laws in the commonwealth. This report
concluded that all the pertinent Massachusetts civil and criminal
rights statutes were constitutional.

Massachusetts Governor's Task Force on Hate Crimes. *Hate
Crimes in Massachusetts: Annual Report* (formerly entitled
"Hate Crimes/Hate Incidents in Massachusetts"). Boston: Gover-
nor's Task Force on Hate Crimes, 1993–.

Organization Reports

Nongovernmental organizations and associations have published many major and important studies on hate crimes and extremist organizations. Since the last edition of this book, many of these publications are available electronically on various organizations' Web sites. The following list includes print titles of some of these documents. See Chapter 6 for additional information on these organizations and other publications.

Anti-Defamation League (ADL). The cost of the following publications vary and can be obtained from ADL Materials Library, P.O. Box 1084, 190 Route 17M, Harriman, NY 10926; telephone: 1-800-343-5540; e-mail: catalog@adl.org

Confronting Anti-Semitism: A Practical Guide, by Leonard Zakim. Written by the respected late New England regional director of the ADL, this book provides educators, Christian clergy, rabbis, and many others with useful information to combat anti-Jewish hatred.

Poisoning the Web: Hatred Online, An ADL Report on Internet Bigotry and Violence. This report documents how racists easily, inexpensively, and sometimes anonymously communicate on the Internet.

Skinhead International: A Worldwide Survey of Neo-Nazi Skinheads. This report examines how Nazi skinheads propagate their ideology, using music, publications, and computer bulletin boards.

International Association of Chiefs of Police (IACP). The IACP has produced the following publications that are available in print. For further information, contact the organization at 515 North Washington Street, Alexandria, VA 22314; phone: 703-836-6767.

Hate Crime in America: Summit Recommendations, 1998. In partnership with the Office of Justice Programs at the U.S. Department of Justice, the IACP convened a two-day national summit in Alexandria, Virginia, where police, civil rights officials, and governmental prosecutors discussed ways of preventing and prosecuting hate crimes.

Responding to Hate Crimes: A Police Officer's Guide to Investigation and Prevention, 2003. This IACP guide is aimed to enhance the ability of police departments to combat hate crimes and intolerance in communities throughout the United States.

8

Nonprint Resources

In recent years, a growing amount of material on hate crimes has been appearing in nonprint format, including videos, films, television, and the Internet. This chapter includes information on some of the more accessible and useful nonprint sources. Please note that the availability and cost of the videos and films are subject to change.

Anti-Gay Hate Crimes
Media Type: VHS
Running Time: 50 minutes
Release Date: 1999
Cost: $24.95
Distributor: A&E Home Video
                 P.O. Box 2284
                 South Burlington, VT 05407
                 1-888-423-1212

Although the brutal murder of gay student Matthew Shepard understandably received national attention, this documentary examines other vicious but lesser-known antigay hate crimes. In addition, the show surveys the activities of the most vocal groups opposed to the so-called homosexual agenda.

Assault on Gay America:
The Life and Death of Billy Jack Gaither
Media Type: VHS
Running Time: 60 minutes

Release Date: 2000
Cost: $19.98
Distributor: PBS Video
P.O. Box 609
Melbourne, FL 32902-0609
1-800-531-4727

In February 1999, in Sylacauga, Alabama, Billy Jack Gaither was murdered by a white supremacist who later testified that he killed the thirty-year-old computer programmer because he was "queer." This film explores the roots of homophobia in the United States and examines how these beliefs and fears contribute to the recent rise in violence against gays and lesbians.

Beyond Hate
Media Type: VHS
Running Time: 91 minutes
Release Date: 1997
Cost: $159.95
Distributor: Films for the Humanities and Sciences
P.O. Box 2053
Princeton, NJ 08543-2053
1-800-257-5126

In these two programs, Bill Moyers examines the origins and dimensions of hate through the eyes of world leaders, human rights activists, Arabs and Israelis, high school students, youth gangs, and U.S. white supremacist groups.

The Brandon Teena Story
Running Time: 88 minutes
Release Date: 1998
Distributor: Available from several distributors

A true story about transgendered teen Brandon Teena and the hostile reaction he received in a Nebraska town. Teena arrived in rural Falls City, Nebraska, in 1993, where he found new friends. Three weeks later, he was raped and beaten by these friends, who had discovered that Brandon was actually a woman. The film was named best documentary at the 1998 Berlin Film Festival and the 1998 Vancouver Film Festival.

Brotherhood of Hate
Media Type: VHS
Running Time: 52 minutes
Release Date: 2000
Cost: sale: $390; rental: $75
Distributor: First Run/Icarus
                          32 Court Street
                          Brooklyn, NY 11201
                          718-488-8900

This film documents one family's legacy of hate, showing how it was handed down from one generation to the next. It is the story of eight brothers raised to be white supremacist warriors.

Hate across America
Media Type: VHS
Running Time: 50 minutes
Release Date: 1996
Cost: $24.95
Distributor: A&E Home Video
                          P.O. Box 2284
                          South Burlington, VT 05407
                          1-888-423-1212

This film surveys the history of violent hate crimes, from the murder of three civil rights workers in Mississippi in 1964 to the present day.

Hate Crime
Media Type: VHS
Running Time: 58 minutes
Release Date: 1999
Cost: $129.95
Distributor: Films for the Humanities and Sciences
                          P.O. Box 2053

Princeton, NJ 08543-2053
1-800-257-5126

This film highlights two communities that are having some success in solving the problem of hate crimes. Following the burning of African American churches in South Carolina, law enforcement officials arrested members of the Ku Klux Klan (KKK). One
of the black churches filed a lawsuit against the KKK and won a
$38 million judgment against the Klan from a racially mixed jury.
The second case features a high school class on tolerance, developed by teacher Joe Moros, that has changed the social climate at
San Clemente High School in California, where tensions among
whites, Hispanics, blacks, and Asian Americans led to brutal violence and killing in the 1990s.

Hate Groups USA
Media Type: VHS
Running Time: 48 minutes
Release Date: 1999
Cost: $149.95
Distributor: Films for the Humanities and Sciences
P.O. Box 2053
Princeton, NJ 08543-2053
1-800-257-5126

Originally a BBC broadcast entitled *The Heart of Darkness,* this
documentary contains interviews with some leading racist leaders as well as government officials and civil rights leaders who
try to combat their hateful activities.

Hate.com: Extremists on the Internet
Media Type: VHS
Running Time: 42 minutes
Release Date: 2000
Cost: $129.95
Distributor: Films for the Humanities and Sciences
P.O. Box 2053
Princeton, NJ 08543-2053
1-800-257-5126

This documentary discusses the use of the Internet to spread messages of hate and violence and contains segments on the leaders of racist movements, including Don Black, founder of Stormfront; Matt Hale, founder of the World Church of the Creator; Richard Butler, founder of Aryan Nations and Christian Identity; and Dr. William Pierce, founder of the National Alliance and author of *The Turner Diaries*. The film also profiles so-called lone wolves—individuals apparently without organizational support who perpetrated violent hate crimes—including Timothy McVeigh, Benjamin Smith, the lynchers of James Byrd Jr., and others.

Journey to a Hate-Free Millennium:
Stories of Compassion and Hope
Media Type: DVD
Running Time: 78 minutes
Release Date: 2000
Cost: $24.95
Distributor: New Light Media
                   100 South Sunrise Way #276
                   Palm Springs, CA 92262
                   1-760-322-4455

This film discusses some infamous hate crimes in the United States. Victims as well as students, teachers, celebrities, and others affected by these incidents are interviewed.

The Matthew Shepard Story: Death in the High Desert
Media Type: VHS
Running Time: 46 minutes
Release Date: 2001
Cost: $29.95
Distributor: A&E Home Video
                   P.O. Box 2284
                   South Burlington, VT 05407
                   1-888-423-1212

This film discusses the events surrounding the murder of Matthew Shepard (1976–1998), who was murdered in Laramie,

Wyoming, because he was gay. The video includes profiles of the murderers and excerpts from their confessions. It also explores the impact on the community and the legal issues concerning a fair trial for the accused murderers.

Responding to Hate Crimes:
A Roll Call Training Video for Police Officers
Media Type: VHS
Running Time: 20 minutes
Release Date: 2000
Cost: Contact Bureau of Justice Assistance
Distributor: Bureau of Justice Assistance
                       810 Seventh Street NW
                       Fourth Floor
                       Washington, DC 20531
                       202-616-6500

This video explains the differences between a hate incident and a hate crime and how law enforcement officials should address community concerns.

South
Media Type: VHS
Running Time: 70 minutes
Release Date: 1999
Cost: sale: $440; rental: $100
Distributor: First Run/Icarus
                       32 Court Street
                       21st Floor
                       Brooklyn, NY 11201
                       718-488-8900
                       http://www.frif.com

Director Chantal Akerman changed the focus of this film, originally intended as a documentary on the American South, to examine the gruesome lynching of James Byrd Jr., an African American, in Jasper, Texas.

Two Towns of Jasper
Media Type: VHS
Running Time: 90 minutes
Release Date: 2003
Cost: $49.98
Distributor: PBS Video
P.O. Box 609
Melbourne, FL 32902-0609
1-800-531-4727

This video examines the different reactions in the white and black communities to the lynching of James Byrd Jr., an African American, by three white men in Jasper, Texas.

Understanding Hate Crimes
Media Type: VHS
Running Time: 47 minutes
Release Date: 2000
Cost: $79.95
Distributor: Cambridge Educational
2572 Brunswick Avenue
Lawrenceville, NJ 08648-4128
1-800-468-4227

A dramatization of the impact on a community after a junior high school student is abducted and beaten to death for being gay. While fellow students prepare a memorial service for the boy they hardly knew, they begin to question the forces that led to the murder. Comments from a variety of professionals are interspersed throughout.

Antibias Videos

The Anti-Defamation League (ADL) is one of the largest producers and distributors of human relations materials, including videos, books, teachers' discussion guides, and classroom program activities. To obtain the ADL material, contact:

ADL Materials Library
P.O. Box 1084
190 Route 17M
Harriman, NY 10926
1-800-343-5540
Fax: 845-774-2945
E-mail: catalog@adl.org
http://www.adl.org/catalog

Breaking through Stereotypes
Media Type: VHS
Running Time: 15 minutes
Release: 1994
Cost: $75 (includes teacher's discussion guide)

Produced by and for teenagers, this documentary explores how stereotypes influence human interactions and relationships. Hollywood films depicting Hispanic, Asian, African American, Italian, and Jewish stereotypes are discussed.

Crimes of Hate
Media Type: VHS
Running Time: 27 minutes
Release Date: 1990
Cost: $69.95 (includes teacher's discussion guide)

This video provides an overview of hate crimes in three segments: racism, anti-Semitism, and gay bashing.

Distorted Image: Stereotype and
Caricature in America, 1850–1922
Media Type: VHS
Running Time: 28 minutes
Release Date: 1973

This documentary provides a historical overview of the stereotyping of minority groups in the United States through archival caricatures from popular magazines of the time.

Hate Comes Home
Media Type: CD-ROM
Release Date: 2003
Cost: $89.95

This interactive CD-ROM offers high school students the opportunity to decide whether they will attempt to confront bigotry and intolerance. Four students of different ethnic and racial backgrounds are faced with various aspects of prejudice, and the viewer is asked to make decisions about the appropriate way to respond.

Hate Crimes: A Training Film for Police Officers
Media Type: VHS
Running Time: 17 minutes
Release Date: 1989
Cost: $89.95 (includes teacher's discussion guide)

This video and discussion guide for law enforcement agencies is designed to train individual police officers in how to properly investigate hate crimes and assist individual victims and their community. Produced in cooperation with the New Jersey Department of Law and Public Safety, this video is useful for law enforcement officials throughout the United States.

Not in Our Town
Media Type: VHS
Running Time: 27 minutes
Release Date: 1995
Cost: $99   (includes teacher's discussion guide)

This dramatic video documents events in Billings, Montana, after white supremacists victimized Jewish, Native American, and African American residents. To display solidarity with their Jewish neighbors, residents displayed pictures of a menorah during Hanukkah. The video shows how a community can unite and battle hatred and violent bigotry.

Skinheads USA: The Pathology of Hate
Media Type: VHS/DVD
Running Time: 54 minutes

Release Date: 1996
Cost: VHS: $129.95; DVD: $154.95

This HBO presentation investigates the growth of white supremacy groups in the United States, providing an inside look at a neo-Nazi organization, its operations, and its personalities.

Other Topics
The ADL produces a large number of videos on the subjects of diversity and ethnicity, covering groups such as African Americans, Hispanic Americans, Jewish Americans and Native Americans, among other minorities. In addition, the ADL is a major source for materials on the Holocaust and interfaith relations. Request the complete catalog, *Anti-Defamation League Material Resources Catalog for Classroom and Community,* at the Web site or mailing address listed above.

Internet and the World Wide Web

American Islamic Congress (AIC)
http://www.aicongress.org

The AIC is an organization dedicated to building interfaith and interethnic understanding. Growing out of the ashes of September 11, 2001, this group represents many American-born and immigrant Muslims who want to confront Islamic extremism and project a better image of Islam to the American public. The Web site includes newspaper and magazine articles and projects devoted to building tolerance and fostering a respect for human rights and social justice. These include a teacher's guide on Islam and September 11, a guide to Muslim interfaith dialogue, a citizen's guide to responding to hate speech, and information on the Children of Abraham Peace Project.

American Jewish Committee (AJC)
http://www.ajc.org/

This Web site contains information on the programs and activities of the AJC, a century-old organization with local offices throughout the United States, Europe, and Israel. The pages include material on interreligious and interethnic activities, Jewish identity, human rights, the Holocaust, Israel, and combating anti-Semitism and extremism. The founding mission of the AJC is the protection of Jewish rights from extremist and anti-Jewish attack, and the site provides much useful material promoting a multicultural and multiethnic society. The site also contains information on Hands across the Campus, a program that promotes tolerance and combats prejudice in secondary schools throughout the country. This site is an important resource to learn about the malignant growth of anti-Jewish hate and other forms of prejudice and to find programs to combat intolerance.

Anti-Defamation League (ADL)
http://www.adl.org/

The Web site of the largest organization in the world combating anti-Jewish hatred and prejudice against minority groups is an outstanding source of information for students, researchers, and the concerned layperson. (The "Search" link expedites viewing of the site.) The full text or summaries of some ADL print publications appear on this site, including *Hate Crimes Laws, Extremism in America, A Parent's Guide to Hate on the Internet,* and *Hate Hurts: How Children Learn and Unlearn Prejudice.* In addition, the site contains ADL Model Crime Penalty Enhancement Laws. Other pages contain:

- *Audit of Anti-Semitic Incidents,* the authoritative and most comprehensive annual report listing anti-Jewish acts during the past year
- Information on how to report anti-Jewish incidents
- Information on the WORLD OF DIFFERENCE Institute, a program that strengthens pluralism and advances diversity education in the United States
- *101 Ways to Combat Prejudice,* a brochure offering advice on combating bigotry in the classroom, the workplace, the community, and houses of worship
- The *Anti-Defamation League Material Resources Catalog for the Classroom and Community,* which contains summaries of the publications, audio-visual programs, posters,

magazines, and other materials produced or distributed by the ADL

- Hate Symbols Database, a visual glossary of extremist hate symbols, logos, and tattoos
- *Discussing Hate and Violence with your Children* is a Web page on the ADL site offering guidelines for parents on educating their children about the dangers of prejudice.
- *Racist Video Games,* a Web page on the ADL site, contains a report on neo-Nazi and racist computer games created by different hate groups
- *ADL on the Frontline,* current and back issues of the national newsletter of the Anti-Defamation League
- Anti-Defamation League Hate Filter® is a free software product designed to protect children by blocking access to World Wide Web sites of individuals or groups that, in the judgment of the Anti-Defamation League, advocate hatred, bigotry, and violence toward Jews and other groups on the basis of their religion, race, ethnicity, sexual orientation, or other immutable characteristics

Center for Democratic Renewal (CDR)
http://www.thecdr.org/

This Web site includes the history and mission of the CDR, an organization that monitors white supremacist and other hate-motivated groups. It also contains material on anti-immigrant vigilantism; the "Far Right and Public Policy," brief summaries of news stories on court cases and legislation involving extreme right-wing and violent extremist groups; and a survey of extremist meetings and events monitored by the CDR staff. The site includes a descriptive list of some of the CDR's print publications, including, "Near the Cross: A Ten Year Chronology of Cross Burning."

Coalition against Hate Crimes
http://www.againsthate.pdx.edu/news.htm

Organized by the American Jewish Committee in 1997, this umbrella group consists of many civil rights, Jewish, gay, and other minority organizations in Oregon and Washington. The Web site reports on hate crimes in the Pacific Northwest and the activities of the groups combating them.

Federal Bureau of Investigation (FBI)
http://www.fbi.gov/ucr/ucr.htm

This Web site contains a link to *Hate Crime Statistics*, the official U.S. government data on bias-motivated criminal incidents, with breakdowns by race, religion, sexual orientation, and ethnicity/national origin. As of January 1, 1997, disability bias crimes have been included. The offense categories included in the collection of hate crime data are murder and nonnegligent manslaughter, forcible rape, robbery, aggravated assault, burglary, larceny, motor vehicle theft, arson, simple assault, intimidation, and destruction/damage/vandalism to property. In addition, the site also has links to *Hate Crime Data Collection Guidelines* and the *Training Guide for Hate Crime Data Collection Guidelines*. These Web sites help instruct law enforcement officials throughout the United States on the collection and analysis of hate crimes statistics, as mandated by the Hate Crimes Statistics Act of 1990.

Gonzaga University Institute for Action against Hate
http://guweb2.gonzaga.edu/againsthate/

Founded in 1997, the Institute for Action against Hate, based at Gonzaga University in Spokane, Washington, engages in a multidisciplinary approach to studying the causes of hate as well as potential strategies for combating hate and hate crimes on campuses and in communities throughout the nation. The Web site offers full-text access to some issues of the *Journal of Hate Studies*, a unique university-based academic journal. In addition, the site provides access to newsletters, conference information, pertinent bibliographies, and resources.

Leadership Conference on Civil Rights (LCCR)
http://www.civilrights.org/issues/hate/

This site is sponsored by the Leadership Conference on Civil Rights (LCCR) and the Leadership Conference on Civil Rights

Education Fund (LCCREF), the nation's oldest, largest, and most diverse coalition of civil rights organizations (numbering more than 180 groups). The Web site contains the full text of the 1997 report *Cause for Concern: Hate Crimes in America* and provides useful links to the FBI annual hate crimes report, current hate crimes legislation, Anti-Defamation League press releases, the Southern Poverty Law Center site, and many other sources.

**National Asian Pacific American
Legal Consortium (NAPALC)**
http://www.napalc.org/

This Web site contains a wide range of political and civil rights material about the Asian American community, including census data and information on immigrant rights, language access, and voting rights. The site also provides unique information on the extent of anti-Asian violence and links to full-text copies of NAPALC's reports since 1996. The annual *Audit of Violence against Asian Pacific Americans* is the only comprehensive, nationwide, nongovernmental compilation covering anti-Asian violence in the United States.

National Gay and Lesbian Task Force (NGLTF)
http://www.ngltf.org/

The NGLTF Web site includes a map of state hate crime laws in the United States, noting those states with statutes punishing crimes specifically directed at individuals because of their sexual orientation. In addition, the site provides access to legislative lobbying materials, press releases, publications, and other documents.

**New York City Gay and Lesbian
Anti-Violence Project (AVP)**
http://www.avp.org/

Although this organization deals mostly with crime victims in the New York area, the Web site has a national focus and provides useful information on reporting hate crimes and offering links to articles on antigay violence. The site provides access to the full-text annual reports (from 1998 to the present) of the National Coalition of Anti-Violence Programs (NCAVP), which provide the most extensive documentation of antigay violence throughout the United States. These annual reports attempt to rectify the underreporting of these incidents to law enforcement agencies. In addition, the site includes addresses and phone numbers of antigay violence programs throughout the United States and links to other gay-related organizations.

Partners against Hate
http://www.partnersagainsthate.org/

A collaboration of the Anti-Defamation League, the Leadership Conference on Civil Rights Education Fund, and the Center for the Prevention of Hate Violence, Partners against Hate features on-line and off-line resources and support in the fight against youth-initiated hate violence. Partners against Hate was created to help prevent, deter, and reduce juvenile hate-related behavior. The Web site provides numerous links to useful manuals, newsletters, programs, laws, and statistics.

Political Research Associates (PRA)
http://www.publiceye.org/

This Web site contains an extensive range of information, including documentation and analysis of right-wing conspiracy theories; material from racist, anti-Jewish, and antigay publications; a list of PRA publications; topical reports; bibliographies and reading lists; and some current and back issues of *Public Eye*, PRA's quarterly newsletter.

Simon Wiesenthal Center
http://www.wiesenthal.com/

This Web site provides information on the activities of the Simon Wiesenthal Center, an international institute for Holocaust remembrance and the defense of human rights for the Jewish people and other groups. The pages include a calendar of events and membership information; current issues of *Response*, the organization's journal; and information on the Museum of Tolerance. The link to the Task Force against Hate offers access to general information about the task force's conferences, police training workshops, and publications. The *Digital Hate and Terrorism* CD-ROM is issued annually and is designed to assist law enforcement officers, public officials, educators, parents, and the media to understand better the nature and proliferation of extremist Web sites. Earlier versions of *Digital Terrorism and Hate* have been presented before the U.S. Congress, the United Nations, and the European Union.

Southern Poverty Law Center (SPLC)
http://www.splcenter.org

This site contains information on the activities of the SPLC, a major hate-monitoring organization. The site provides access to *Intelligence Report*, the quarterly newsletter that profiles extremist groups and monitors domestic terrorism; press releases; news articles; and numerous links to other pertinent literature on hate-motivated violence and hate groups and classroom resources. *Hatewatch* provides updated news articles and stories about prejudice, hate speech, and hate crimes. Hate Groups Map is a unique source providing geographical information. The site also offers an on-line hate crime training course for law enforcement officials.

Stephen Roth Institute for the Study of Contemporary Anti-Semitism and Racism
http://www.tau.ac.il/Anti-Semitism/

The Stephen Roth Institute at Tel Aviv University began operating as the Project for the Study of Anti-Semitism in the fall of 1991. It is housed in the Wiener Library, which contains one of the largest collections of anti-Jewish, Nazi, and extremist literature in the world. This Web site contains an "Anti-Semitism and Racism Update," which offers timely news articles.

The Database of the Stephen Roth Institute monitors contemporary manifestations of anti-Semitism and racism around the world as well as extremist hate groups (right-wing, left-wing, and Islamist). Unlike most databases, it is a catalog not only of documents but also of event descriptions (abstracted in English), based on one or more foreign or English-language sources. The site also features *Anti-Semitism Worldwide*, an annual report that surveys and analyzes anti-Jewish activities by country.

**Vidal Sassoon International Center
for the Study of Anti-Semitism**
http://sicsa.huji.ac.il/

Established in 1982 and located at the Hebrew University of Jerusalem, this interdisciplinary research center is dedicated to an independent, nonpolitical approach to understanding the phenomenon of anti-Semitism and engages in research on anti-Jewish hatred throughout the ages. Its Web site was started in 1994, and the home page guides the user to both summary and full-text materials, including the *Analysis of Current Trends in Anti-Semitism* and other research reports on anti-Jewish activities in various countries throughout the world. Especially useful is the collection of links to other academic and historical Web sites on anti-Jewish attitudes and violence. The site also contains annual reports and back issues of the center's newsletter. Video recordings of international conferences sponsored by the center, featuring distinguished scholars and authors, can also be accessed from the home page.

Users may also access the Felix Posen Bibliographic Project on Anti-Semitism, an outstanding online database of works published throughout the world about anti-Jewish hatred, including books, dissertations, and articles from periodicals and anthologies.

Index

231

About the Author

Donald Altschiller is a librarian at Boston University. He has edited eight reference books and his articles have been published in the the *Boston Globe*, the *Baltimore Sun*, and the *Los Angeles Times*. A reviewer of reference books for several library journals, he also has contributed essays to almost a dozen encyclopedias, including *The Historical Encyclopedia of World Slavery* and the *Encyclopedia of the American Civil War*, both published by ABC-CLIO.